Praise for The Clinician's G
and Treatment of Pers

Dr. Fox has effectively pulled together modern thinking, current research and historical perspective into an efficient approach for addressing personality disorders. He does this in a way that is straightforward and presents this distinctive collection of material in a manner that is a pleasure to read. One of the great features of this work is that it attends to therapist's ethical challenges and self-care needs specific to working with this often difficult population. Dr. Fox's *Clinician's Guide to the Diagnosis and Treatment of Personality Disorders* appears to be setting a standard for applied clinical reference in the age of the DSM-5®.

—Russell Wood, Ph.D.

Dr. Fox has given clinicians a strong, straightforward grasp of personality disorders in his book *The Clinician's Guide to The Diagnosis and Treatment of Personality Disorders*. He also gathered all of the treatment modalities currently available that promotes movement for the client from their inflexible and pervasive patterns to develop skills that generate success. Whether you are a professional or supervisor looking for ways to support your practice or a general reader on a path of self-help, you can benefit from this clear, informative guide to understanding personality disorders.

—Lillian Solis-Smith, Ph.D., LPC, LMFT

Daniel Fox has compiled, integrated, and analyzed a vast amount of information regarding the developing conceptualization of personality disorders. More than a targeted workbook, this text allows the practitioner to gain an in-depth understanding regarding the history of personality disorders, as well as the state of current research, diagnosis, and treatment for personality disorders as a whole and individually. In addition, the diagnosis and treatment recommendations are clear, well-founded in the literature, and provide an excellent framework for working with this difficult population. Moreover, this text provides information and tools which will prove useful in transitioning from the DSM-IV-TR® to the DSM-5®. It is well-written, practical, and useful for practitioners across the career spectrum."

—Ashley Christiansen, Ph.D.

An exceptionally well thought-out and artful conceptualization of working with personality disordered clients. A great source material for the novice and seasoned clinician who is seeking practical knowledge and tools in treating personality disorders.

—Kevin Jacques Siffert, Ph.D.

The Clinician's Guide to the Diagnosis and Treatment of Personality Disorders

by

Daniel J. Fox, Ph.D.

PESI Publishing and Media
www.pesipublishing.com

This book is dedicated to my three heartbeats:
My wife Lydia and my two children Alexandra and Sebastian.

Table of Contents

About the Author

Daniel J. Fox, PhD, has been treating and specializing in the treatment and assessment of individuals with personality disorders for the last 12 years in the state and federal prison system, universities, and in private practice. Dr. Fox's specialty area is in ethics and ethical conflicts and how they arise when working with individuals with various personality disorders and other mental health issues.

He is currently a staff psychologist at the Federal Detention Center in Houston, Texas. Dr. Fox has a private practice that specializes in working with difficult clients, and he continues to teach and provide supervision to master's and doctoral students of University of Houston and Sam Houston State University in Texas.

Personality Disorders

Personality has been studied for centuries, starting with Plato who wrote that the soul is the foundation of personality. Psychology and psychiatry adopted this notion to better explain individual differences and anticipated reactions within various situations. The work of Theophrastus, a student of Plato then Aristotle, identified 30 brief sketches of "average people" with undesirable traits, which we would now come to call personality disorders. In 1952, the first *Diagnostic and Statistical Manual* (APA, 1952) was published and identified five broad categories and subcategories of aberrant personality. In the following edition, DSM-II (APA, 1968) identified nine "personality disorders and certain non-psychotic mental disorders" listed below:

Paranoid Personality

Cyclothymic Personality

Schizoid Personality

Explosive Personality

Obsessive Compulsive Personality

Hysterical Personality

Asthenic Personality

Antisocial Personality

Inadequate Personality

It was not until the DSM-III (APA, 1980) that personality disorders were broken down into clusters of personality traits that were "inflexible and maladaptive and cause either significant functional impairment or subjective distress" (p. 305). This view of personality disorders was maintained throughout subsequent editions of the DSM and continues into the current edition, DSM-5 (APA, 2013).

An alternative approach to conceptualize personality disorders is a hybrid dimensional-categorical model, and only six personality disorders remain: antisocial, avoidant, borderline, narcissistic, obsessive-compulsive, and schizotypal. The diagnosis of personality disorder not otherwise specified will be replaced with personality disorder trait specified (PDTS). This alternative model is located in Section III of the DSM-5 (APA, 2013) to encourage further study.

Personality disorder not otherwise specified was removed from the DSM-5 (APA, 2013) and replaced with other specified personality disorder and unspecified personality disorder. The biggest difference between these two diagnoses is that the clinician can *choose* to "communicate the specific reason that the presentation does not meet criteria for any specific personality disorder" (p. 684). This would be logged as 'other specified personality disorder, passive-aggressive traits.'

WHAT THE CLINICIAN NEEDS TO KNOW ABOUT PERSONALITY DISORDER TREATMENT

This guide is designed with the clinician in mind: the person who screens, assesses, and works with the client who fascinates and challenges on a session-by-session basis. There are extensive research studies presented in this guide that illustrate empirical findings and a solid basis for the conceptualization, diagnosis, and treatment of personality disorders, and ultimately for the betterment of the client and the clinician.

Oscar Wilde said: "I knew that I had come face to face with someone whose mere personality was so fascinating that, if I allowed it to do so, it would absorb my whole nature, my whole soul, my very art itself" (Wilde, 1980, p. 15). This statement personifies working with the personality-disordered client. If allowed, the personality-disordered client will consume your practice and potentially your life. Below are several key points to remember in working with personality disorders.

Ethical Risks of Working with Personality Disordered Clients

There is a paucity of research on personality disorders and ethics, though it can be reasonably determined that those with personality dysfunction are more likely to bring ethical complaints against their therapists. Reciprocally, clinicians who possess personality disordered traits or disorders are at greater risk of committing ethical violations as well as being filed against.

There are several ethical aspects that must be addressed when working with individuals with personality disorders (PD). These were delineated by Magnavita and colleagues (2010). They address the importance of competence when working with PD individuals: Though no specific competency guidelines exist, considering the potential risk for harm to self or others, ethical consideration is critical. An eclectic approach and appropriate balance of confidentiality, boundaries, and competence when working with PDs must be continually assessed. The central aspect of providing treatment to PDs is the awareness and management of boundaries and the utilization of a flexible approach.

Transference/Countertransference Issues and Personality Disorders

Transference and counter transference reactions should be expected when working with personality disordered individuals. Benjamin (1996) identifies transference issues when working with each personality disorder:

TRANSFERENCE REACTIONS IN PERSONALITY DISORDERS	
Personality Disorder	**Transference Reaction**
Paranoid personality disorder	Attempt to control treatment, slow to trust therapist, "hypersensitive" to therapist's criticism, as well as being critical of therapist, and continual tendency to withdraw.
Schizoid personality disorder	No data is provided.
Schizotypal personality disorder	See therapist as attacking or humiliating, tendency to keep distant to feel safe, may be vulnerable to dismissing self-interest for participation in negative relationships.
Borderline personality disorder	Overt efforts to derive nurturing and caring from therapist, resistance to getting well leading to abandonment so client demands more from therapist until burnout. Therapist feels a loss of control due to personal and professional violations, therapist questions effectiveness and confidence due to continual cycle of "unfair rule of interpersonal play [engagement/interaction]."
Narcissistic personality disorder	Demand for support and admiration, wish to control treatment, intense anger at therapist's failure to meet client needs, high likelihood of withdrawing from treatment when it becomes difficult.
Histrionic personality disorder	"Demanding dependency" through attractive dress and coquettish behavior. In same-sex therapeutic relationships, challenge and belittlement are likely.
Antisocial personality disorder	Intensive resistance to collaboration, subterfuge by client, unlikely to "break through" to true self.
Dependent personality disorder	Extensive compliance with little to no therapeutic movement, high likelihood of developing co-dependent relationship between therapist and client.
Obsessive-Compulsive personality disorder	Tendency to defer to therapist and be a "perfect" client, resistance to "loosening-up." Likely to use work as a means to avoid treatment sessions, attempt to control sessions, high likelihood of rage expression due to unattained control.

Personality Disorder	Transference Reaction
Avoidant personality disorder	Tendency to not share in treatment, "hold things in," attempt to provide what therapist wants to hear, hypersensitive, easily injured, attempts to gain nurturance, feels degraded, premature termination due to feeling slighted or hurt.

These transference and counter transference issues must be addressed in treatment, and the therapist needs to be knowledgeable about their expression. If not, therapy will not progress and the therapist puts himself or herself at risk for burnout, ethical violations, or worse.

Therapist Burnout and Personality Disorders

There is a myth that all personality disorders are untreatable, and that the therapist is doomed to be figuratively beaten, chastised, and branded a loser by the client and the therapeutic community. I have countless students who shudder at the idea of working with the personality disordered client, simply because they are reacting to hyperbole. However, without guidance and structure on how to treat these disorders, burnout is highly likely.

It has been found that working with individuals with personality disorders and the subsequent issues that arise can significantly lead to burnout in mental health professionals (Burnard, et al., 2000; Loughrey, et al., 1997; Melchior, et al., 1997). Burnout can be defined as an increase in the intensity and frequency of client contact which can eventually generalize to adversely impact client-related, work-related, and social and personal aspects of one's environment to the point of loss of personal and professional efficacy.

The typical pattern of therapist burnout begins with compassion fatigue, which is preoccupation with absorbing the trauma and emotional stressors of others. Its symptoms are related to burnout, but onset is quicker with a better chance of recovery. Burnout is more insidious and includes feeling ineffective, callous, negative, emotionally absent, and "stuck." It is up to the therapist to maintain appropriate boundaries and conform to the code of ethics, especially when working with personality disordered clients, which increases the chance of committing an ethical violation due to compassion fatigue or burnout.

Five tips for avoiding burnout when working with personality disordered clients:

(1) Know the person you are working with. Having knowledge about the personality disorder and its likely manifest content can provide the therapist with valuable information, allow for the implementation of effective strategies, and define parameters for treatment that significantly decrease therapist burnout and enhance therapeutic efficacy.

(2) Utilize a solid support network. I am fortunate to have several other psychologists I can consult with on cases and issues that arise. These psychologists have their own specialties, and we all operate from different therapeutic modalities, but we talk about our cases and any transference/countertransference reactions. In addition, I also run some particularly intense client issues (anonymously, of course) by someone who is not in the field, but a longtime friend.

By doing this, I get grounded in how the greater society may perceive these issues. Mental health practitioners are highly likely to lose sight of the issues we contend with by constantly being immersed in them.

(3) Develop your own barometer. A particularly clever and skilled narcissistic and antisocial personality disordered client I was working with in a prison persuaded me to provide him with pictures from a recent trip I had taken. Fortunately, I never did this, as while I was walking out of the secured unit I stopped and thought to myself, "Did I really just agree to show my pictures to my client/inmate?" I immediately spoke with my advisor about the issue (I was a doctoral student at the time) and addressed it with the client during the following session. He cleverly turned it around and said he only did it to prove that I was ethical and to validate his wanting to continue to work with me. I emerged from this experience unscathed, but I also developed a habit of processing each session and the interaction that took place. My internal barometer is very keen and sensitive to manipulation and issues that arise in session that "just don't feel right." Always self-appraise after each session.

(4) Limit clients. This is taboo to most therapists as lifestyle and living expenses are typically contingent upon how many clients you can see. However, as you see more than eight clients per day (I know someone who sees 13 per day), your efficacy decreases and the probability of ethical issues rises significantly. When you include personality disordered clients in that mix and the intensity that the typical session entails, you are ineffective and cannot maintain appropriate limits and effective treatment for too long.

(5) Utilize one of these quick tips for six weeks to decrease compassion fatigue or burnout:

- Limit caffeine intake to 8oz. per day.
- Allow yourself to make errors—they are good for you.
- Eat well and avoid alcohol as it has been shown to increase cortisol—the primary stress hormone.
- Have hobbies and interests outside of mental health—yes, you do have the time.
- Set realistic and definable personal and professional goals—these are different and should be.
- Reduce long working hours.
- Exercise—you can work out, run, etc. for 30 minutes and gain the same benefit as a longer and more intensive workout; and treat yourself—I like to reward myself with Godiva chocolate cheesecake about 4 times per year on particular days that things went well.

Making a Personality Disorder Diagnosis

In graduate school we all learned about making an accurate diagnosis, but as time goes on, we forget to assess the five critical factors that need to be present to make certain the diagnosis is accurate.

Is the behavior Ego-Syntonic?

(ego-syntonic behavior is behavior that is in harmony with the ego; for example, the client sees nothing wrong with screaming as loudly as possible in a crowded restaurant to get his or her needs met)

Is behavior pervasive?

(the client's behavior occurs within occupational, social, and intimate settings and relationships)

Does the client use an internal or external locus of control?

(Clients with personality disorders typically utilize an external locus of control; for example, he or she was fired because the boss was jealous, not because he or she acted out in the workplace. He or she deflects personal responsibility)

Is the client's behavior episodic or enduring?

(Does the client behave in a particular manner across all settings or is it specific to the workplace? The personality disordered individual will display the behavior continuously, not in response to a specific environment or situation)

Inflexibility

(The personality disordered client is not likely to adjust behaviors, views, or responses across contexts and will exhibit his or her behavior patterns no matter what the external stimulus may be; this includes your waiting room)

Factors Critical to Accurate Diagnosis

It is my hope that this guide serves you well, expands your knowledge of personality disorders, and increases your therapeutic efficacy.

Paranoid Personality Disorder

Paranoid personality disorder (PPD) is a complex set of behaviors and assessments of environments, and those within them, that leans toward persecutions and an inherent mistrust of others, including family, friends, and acquaintances. In 1905, Emil Kraepelin wrote of a personality that was constantly vigilant to find complaint but functioned within a distorted view of the world, with additional characteristics to include vanity, self-absorption, sensitivity to criticism, irritability, litigiousness, stubbornness, and anger with the world. In 1921, he enlarged his description of these individuals to include intense distrustfulness, feelings of being unjustly treated and subjected to hostility on a routine basis, and called it paranoid personality (Akhtar, 1990). Kraepelin further noted the inherent conflict within these individuals: though they stubbornly hold onto their unusual beliefs, they often accept every rumor and scandalous report as truth, especially those that are negative in connotation.

Kraepelin (1921) went on to note that those individuals he saw with paranoid personality tended to develop paranoid psychosis. Kraepelin was followed by Bleuler (1924) who identified a "contentious psychopathy" or "paranoid constitution" which displayed a triad of features: suspiciousness, grandiosity and feelings of persecution.

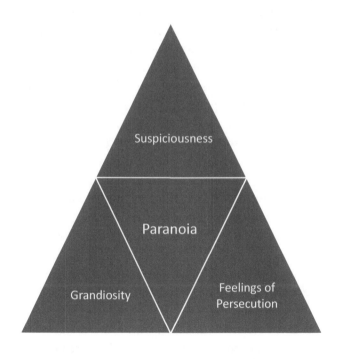

The Triad of Paranoid Features

Bleuler found that individuals who fit into this disorder pattern and displayed these symptoms did not form a genuine delusion.

In 1918, Ernst Kretschmer in 1918 published *Ideas of Reference in Oversensitive Personalities, a Contribution to the Theory of Paranoid* that examined paranoia from the standpoint of the body, environment, and personality. He went on to classify these individuals as experiencing feelings of shyness and inadequacy associated with a sense of entitlement. He further reported that these individuals tend to attribute their failures to the conspiracies of others, but internally fear their own inadequacy. Lastly, he noted that these individuals also tend to experience perpetual tension between feelings of importance and a perception of the environment as unappreciative and humiliating.

In 1950, Schneider termed individuals who stressed their intensity and rigidity in confrontations with others as "fanatic psychopaths." These can be broken down into two categories: the combative type, which is insistent and argumentative, and the eccentric type which is passive, secretive, and suspicious of others.

Paranoid personality disorder has been listed in the *Diagnostic and Statistical Manual of Mental Disorders* since the manual's inception in 1952 (APA, 1952). In DSM-I, PPD was called paranoid personality, which fell under personality pattern disturbance and was identified as a characterization of many traits of schizoid personality (likely seen as the PPD individual's tendency to keep to himself/herself), in addition to an "exquisite sensitivity to interpersonal relations" (APA, 1952, p. 36) and a tendency to be suspicious through utilizing a "projection mechanism" exercised through suspiciousness, envy, extreme jealousy, and stubbornness.

In 1968, the DSM-II addressed the issue of paranoid personality and expanded its definition:

> This behavioral pattern is characterized by hypersensitivity, rigidity, unwarranted suspicion, jealousy, envy, excessive self-importance, and a tendency to blame others and ascribe evil motives to them. These characteristics often interfere with the patient's ability to maintain satisfactory interpersonal relations. Of course, the presence of suspicion of itself does not justify this diagnosis, since the suspicion may be warranted in some instances (p. 42).

The DSM-II first mentions socioeconomic dysfunction brought about by the disorder and adds the disqualifying information that simple paranoia is not enough to warrant the paranoid personality diagnosis.

Polatin (1975) made further distinctions and insights into paranoid personality by providing a list of traits and possible presentation styles. He noted that the paranoid personality tends to be rigid, suspicious, watchful, self-centered, selfish, inwardly hypersensitive but emotionally inhibited. It is not until the DSM-III in 1980 that "diagnosis had, at best, a minor role in dynamic psychiatry. In 1980, at one stroke, the diagnostically based DSM-III radically transformed the nature of mental illness" (Mayes & Horwitz, 2005, p. 250) by adding diagnostic criteria for particular disorders.

To meet the criteria for paranoid personality in the DSM-III, individuals were required to meet three criteria for suspiciousness, two for restricted affect, and two for hypersensitivity

(APA, 1980). In 1987, the less restrictive DSM-III-R (APA, 1987) required any combination of four of seven criteria to meet the diagnosis of PPD. The DSM-IV had only minor changes to reduce overlap among various disorders (APA, 1994). There were no changes to PPD in the DSM-IV-TR (APA, 2000) or the DSM-5 (APA, 2013).

Paranoid personality disorder has been hypothesized to lie within the schizophrenia spectrum and to be a product of a common genetic predisposition. Behavioral models have suggested that suspiciousness and mistrust are learned, leading to social withdrawal, testing of others, and ruminative distrust. It is the chronic nature of the paranoid personality's suspiciousness and mistrust that impedes positive social interaction and growth and leads to some degree of disorder within each aspect of their lives.

ETIOLOGY

There is very limited information on the etiology of PPD. Very early in the history of this disorder, psychoanalytic theory proposed that it is housed in the defense mechanism of projection. Freud (1963) discussed a case of Schreber's in which paranoia evolved from repressed urges. Throughout a series of defensive transmutations, the thought "I love him" was denounced and transformed through reaction formation into "I don't love him, I hate him." This more acceptable conscious idea was then further transformed into "it's not that I hate him, he hates me!" As this thought is closest to the individual's consciousness, he or she could modify the idea by using rationalization to become "I hate him because of his hatred for me." It was through this case that Freud accounted for the range of persecutory, erotic, and jealous delusions as the mutation of foundational unacceptable libidinal drives.

Several studies link the use of projection with paranoid and other severe personality disorders (Drake & Valliant, 1985; Koenigsberg et al., 2001; Lingiardi et al., 1999). Bond and Perry (2004) found that working with clients to improve maladaptive defenses, such as projection, has been found to predict the outcome of psychotherapy using psychodynamic theory above other outcome variables.

Cameron (1963) has postulated that hostile, unloving, possibly abusive environments, lacking the components necessary for the development of basic trust are strongly correlated with the development of the paranoid personality.

Benjamin (1996) notes that the future PPD individual likely grew up in a home that was sadistic, degrading, and controlling and is "usually an abused child himself or herself" (p. 314). The parent(s) behave in a harsh and cruel manner so as to fulfill their perceptions of appropriate parental behavior. Parental hostility is likely to be visited upon the child (later to be the PPD individual) as an emotional reaction of anger linked to perceived insult, mistreatment, or malice on the part of the child. In infancy, the PPD individual was likely handled in a rough manner even when little or no stress was present in the environment. Crying was usually dealt with by beating or other physical consequences. The PPD individual's parents tended to view crying far beyond the stimulus and response paradigm most people understand. The PPD parent saw crying as an accusation of poor parenting and a command for action.

As the PPD child grows and encounters typical childhood experiences, such as falling, the PPD parent would attack or hit the child as opposed to comforting or soothing him or her.

If the child engaged in a fight with other children, the PPD individual's parent would assume the child was the one who started it. As the child aged and would cry, the parent would view the behavior as a manipulation to get results. The child might be hit or "scolded into silence by being told, 'You are too sensitive'" (p. 315). The PPD individual learns not to cry as he or she develops and further internalizes the imperative of not needing anything from anyone else, not asking for assistance even if the request is genuine, not trusting others, avoiding intimacy, having learned that independence and self-protection are the safest route. As an adult, the PPD individual expects attacks; no one is immune from being viewed as mistreating the PPD individual. The PPD individual's foundation is built upon fear and hate, nondisclosure, and mistrust. The fear and distancing of the self are self-protective in response to the abuse, but the PPD individual also identifies with the parent figure that was harsh, intimidating, and cruel. As these become internalized, the PPD individual develops an interactional style that mimics the parent's behaviors and presents as self-righteous, controlling and judgmental, and willing to abuse others for self-protection.

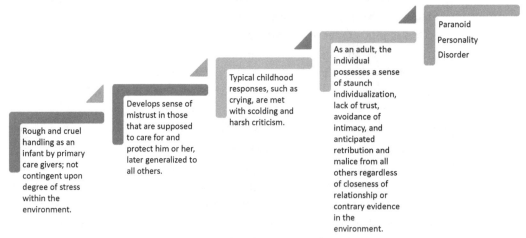

Proposed Pathogenesis of PPD

Within the family environment, the PPD individual suffered frequent comparisons to other family members and was often scapegoated. The child might have been perceived as bad, arrogant, stubborn, "stuck up," emotional, or intractable within the family. Benjamin (1996) goes on to describe that regardless of the offense, harsh punishments were administered without due process or consideration of forces beyond the child's control. Siblings of the PPD individual were usually preferred within the family and blatantly showered with privileges, affection, and acknowledgement. The PPD individual's parents would often talk negatively about him as if he were not present, building within the individual hypersensitivity and anger about whisperings, humiliations, and exclusions, and increased sensitivity to disproportionate distribution of punishment and privileges to peers. These individuals have an intense ability to hold grudges and internally rage against the seemingly favored individual.

There are more contemporary cognitive models to explain the etiology of PPD. The PPD individual tends to make misattributions by reading cruel or biased intentions into seemingly harmless remarks or statements, focusing on signs within the environment that could pose threat or harm, and holding onto past misdeeds or behaviors that offended or hurt him (Williams et al., 1997). It has been suggested that the core cognitive schemas in PPD are related to feelings of inadequacy in combination with poor social skills and the external attribution of blame to reduce anxiety (Beck et al., 2004).

The research being conducted today on PPD cannot isolate a definable cause. Currently most professionals subscribe to a biopsychosocial model of causation, which postulates that biological and genetic factors, social factors (such as how a person interacts in early development with family and friends and other children), and psychological factors (the individual's personality and temperament, shaped by environment and learned coping skills for dealing with stress) are contributory. This suggests that no single factor is responsible and that it is the complex interplay of all three factors that is important. Current research on genetics and paranoia conducted by Simons and colleagues (2009) concluded that gene-environment interactions and response to life stressors may lead to the development of paranoia. Brain chemistry, including the effects of neurotransmitters and the effects of drugs such as cocaine, marijuana, and methamphetamines on the brain can produce paranoid beliefs. Traumatic life events, such as unresolved childhood trauma, and its impact upon cognitive processing and environmental interpretation, and stress reactions, including paranoid beliefs derived from prolonged and intense stress, such as war and torture, have all been postulated as precursors to the development of paranoia, but the inherent challenge of working with and understanding PPD individuals remains.

PREVALENCE

Paranoid personality disorder is most often diagnosed in males. This discrepancy may largely be due to societal allowances for the expression of anger in men, but in recent years females have increasingly been diagnosed with PPD (Buss 2005; Coie & Dodge 1998). Females are not necessarily less aggressive but tend to be more subtle in their aggression. For example, they are more likely to engage in social rejection (Hines & Saudino, 2008). Thus, the small difference in prevalence between males and females may be due to different manifestations of the disorder. Nestor (2002) found that the combination of a paranoid cognitive personality style and narcissistic injury increases the risk for violence. According to the DSM-5 (2013), the prevalence of PPD, based upon National Comorbidity Survey Replication (NCS-R; Lenzenweger, Lane, Loranger, & Kessler, 2007), is approximately 2.3% and based upon the National Epidemiologic Survey and Alcohol and Related Conditions (NESARC) is approximately 4.4% in prevalence rate at 4.4% in the general population.

Using the International Personality Disorder Examination (IPDE), which is a standardized interview of 537 questions used for the screening of candidates for personality disorders, Samuels and colleagues (2002) found a prevalence rate of 0.7% for paranoid personality disorder. Using the Structured Clinical Interview for DSM-IV Axis II personality disorders, a standardized instrument for diagnosis of the 10 DSM-IV Axis II personality disorders, plus depressive personality disorder, passive-aggressive personality disorder, and personality disorder-not otherwise specified, Crawford and colleagues obtained a prevalence rate for PPD of 5.1%. Lenzenweger and colleagues (2007) obtained a prevalence rate for PPD of 2.3% using the IPDE. In the UK, PPD was reported as a primary diagnosis in 236 admissions, with 129 (55%) males and 107 (45%) females (UK Department of Health, Hospital Episode Statistics, 2010).

ATTACHMENT

In tracing the development of an individual with PPD, it can often be seen that the child had a disturbed attachment to parents and caregivers. The bond between caregiver and child can be quite distorted in PPD individuals. Sperry (2003) noted a correlation between fearful attachment style and a sense of unworthiness, intertwined with the presumption of rejection and mistrust of others in PPD. Rejection and consequent mistrust foster a deficient sense of trust in self and in internal thoughts and beliefs, as well as feelings regarding others' intentions. Contrary, but inherent, is the belief that they are special and different from others, while guarding against threat, and not believing others can protect them and keep them safe.

Crawford and colleagues (2006) showed that symptoms of cluster A personality disorders were more severe in individuals with higher ratings of avoidant attachment. In the classic study: "the strange situation" (Ainsworth et al., 1978) avoidantly attached infants actively turned away from the mother when she returned following the final and most stressful situation posed in the experiment. These infants maintained both emotional and physical distance from others, even though they had elevated heart rates indicating underlying anxiety or distress. It is easy to see how this framework fits neatly into the PPD individual's presentation and attachment pattern of attempting to maintain distance even though that distance creates increased tension. The lack of trust and connection in these individuals' overall cautious approach to the world are both a cause and a result of this tension.

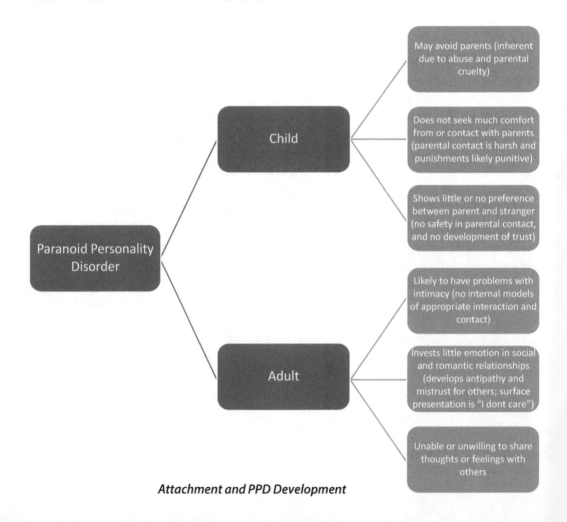

Attachment and PPD Development

This figure shows the different aspects of the PPD individual from an attachment standpoint of how interpersonal behaviors, beliefs, and emotions are exhibited and internalized. A better understanding of the attachment pattern of the PPD individual allows the clinician to examine a client's life and approach to others and situations and provides invaluable information on how to build or reconstruct interpersonal dynamics. For example, knowing that the PPD individual has intimacy problems due to a lack of internal models of appropriate interaction and contact, the therapist can engage in social skills training, modeling of appropriate behavior, "people-watching" with the client to identify the best-fitting or appropriate interaction styles and how they differ in the PPD client's understanding and expectation of those interactions.

DIAGNOSIS

The criteria most often used to diagnose PPD are the seven listed in the DSM-5 (2013) and shown below in Table 1.

TABLE 1: DSM-5 DIAGNOSTIC CRITERIA FOR PARANOID PERSONALITY DISORDER
A. A pervasive distrust and suspiciousness of others such that their motives are interpreted as malevolent, beginning by early adulthood and present in a variety of contexts, as indicated by four (or more) of the following: (1) Suspects, without sufficient basis, that others are exploiting, harming, or deceiving him or her   (2) Is preoccupied with unjustified doubts about the loyalty or trustworthiness of friends or associates   (3) Is reluctant to confide in others because of unwarranted fear that the information will be used maliciously against him or her   (4) Reads hidden demeaning or threatening meanings into benign remarks or events   (5) Persistently bears grudges, i.e., is unforgiving of insults, injuries, or slights   (6) Perceives attacks on his or her character or reputation that are not apparent to others and is quick to react angrily or to counterattack   (7) Has recurrent suspicions, without justification, regarding fidelity of spouse or sexual partner
B. Does not occur exclusively during the course of schizophrenia, a bipolar disorder or depressive disorder with psychotic features, or another psychotic disorder and is not attributable to the physiological effects of another medical condition.
Note: If criteria are met prior to the onset of schizophrenia, add "premorbid," e.g., "paranoid personality disorder (premorbid)."

Each of these criteria assists in identifying the disorder, and it is suggested that the DSM-5 criteria be used as guidelines and not hard and fast rules. Criterion one identifies the aspect that focuses on being exploited, harmed, or deceived by others regardless of evidence in the environment. This is based in the delusion that others have already harmed them through their conspiratorial nature. This delusion will prevent these individuals from developing close relationships with others, causing them to be constantly vigilant, difficult to live with, and causing friends and relatives to avoid them, hence proving that they were only out to do harm. The second criterion centers upon the idea that others are plotting against them, justifying attack toward others. They harbor a deep and irreversible sense of having been injured by others, and they are cognitively focused upon unjustified doubts regarding the loyalty or trustworthiness of friends, family members, or associates. Individuals with PPD are constantly requiring others to prove and demonstrate their loyalty and trustworthiness. Criterion three addresses PPD individuals' tendency to remain distant from others and not confide in or become close as they fear information they provide will be used against them. The delusional belief is that all information, even the most mundane, is critical and can be distorted or used against them in some way. The fourth criterion pertains to PPD individuals' tendency to read hidden meanings into any statements made or questions asked and feel that all information is "nobody's business." Individuals with PPD can take even the most authentic compliment as a manipulative attempt to gain favor or as an attempt to "get their guard down" or be taken advantage of by others. Criterion five addresses the tendency to hold and bear grudges and reluctance to forgive any insults, injuries, or slights they believe they have experienced. Their hyper-vigilance for transgressions against them, even if they are benign, insignificant, and unintentional mistakes, will produce gross exaggeration and again reinforce their untrusting stance towards others whose implicit agenda, the PPD individual believes, is to inflict harm and misery on him or her. The sixth criterion focuses on the PPD individual's rapidity to counterattack with anger in reaction to perceived insults. Individuals with PPD have their defense mechanisms ready to be unleashed upon the perpetrator, and all *others* are likely perpetrators, in the anticipation of hurtful behavior. The attack is typically swift, sharp, and emotionally painful to the identified other, usually an unsuspecting friend or family member. The final criterion addresses the PPD individual's pathological jealousy regarding infidelity by a spouse or significant other without any evidence or justification; if the PPD individual believes it, that is enough to make it true. This is central to PPD individuals' difficulty in maintaining long-term healthy relationships, as every relationship failure only proves that the significant other(s) was out to harm them anyway. This perpetual cycle is a recapitulation of earlier developmental issues and is best for treatment if viewed as such.

The DSM-5 (APA, 2013) criteria should be considered starting points to gain better understanding and a basic clinical picture of PPD. They illustrate many critical aspects of the PPD individual, such as the pervasive suspiciousness and mistrust of others and their motives, hypersensitivity to slight criticism, and inherent vigilance to protect oneself. Benjamin (1996) pairs past experiences and interpersonal history with each criterion of the DSM, providing greater understanding. The DSM item number 1 is likely derived from cruel, shaming, and controlling parenting that leads the PPD individual to expect to be exploited and harmed by others. Numbers 2, 5, 6, and 7 come from past unfavorable comparisons with other family members and being the target of grudges, creating a foundation of mistrust and suspicion. Numbers 3 and 4 address PPD individuals seeing harmful outcomes and fear of exploitation as a recapitulation of past experiences with family members and others who have violated their trust and harmed them.

The individual with PPD does not present with a simple linear pattern of symptoms that neatly fit into four of the seven criteria for diagnosis. The most common PPD type is the anger- and rage-filled individual who is also withdrawn and fearful, whereas the atypical type is more anxiety driven where rage is supplanted by worry and tension. Both types still have socioeconomic dysfunction and poor interpersonal interactions, but the underlying drive is different and impacts pathological presentation leading to possible misdiagnosis and poor treatment response and outcome.

Bernstein and Useda (2007) note that the DSM-IV criteria for PPD is skewed toward more cognitive traits, specifically mistrust and suspiciousness, leaving out behavioral, affective, and interpersonal expressions that are more likely to be encountered. Whereas six of the seven traits address mistrust and suspiciousness, only one of the seven is related to rigidity (bears grudges). The strong cognitive emphasis leaves out many crucial aspects of the disorder. For example, the PPD individual's difficulty with social skills and argumentativeness through constant complaining or quiet brooding is not discussed but is in fact a central feature. The individual's cold or aloof interpersonal manner is not discussed, but is again a central factor.

The DSM does not mention that the PPD individual's maladaptive patterns tend to occur within a more global presentation of relatively adaptive behavior. Higher functioning PPD individuals are typically able to present themselves as rational and "able to control their emotions," but, once slighted or perceiving harm in some way, they will likely revert to a labile range of affect, with hostility, stubbornness, and sarcasm being central modes of relaying venomous retaliation. Individuals with PPD may produce a hostile response in others, as a result of wearing them down with accusations and suspicions. When the other individual attempts to defend himself or herself, that is used as evidence of their intended harm. The PPD individual is typically self-sufficient and autonomous, and demands a high degree of control at all times. Inflexibility makes him or her exceptionally difficult to collaborate with even on the most basic of tasks. PPD individuals are often in legal disputes and are highly litigious. Their thoughts and fantasies tend to focus on grandiose ideas centered on power and rank.

Individuals with PPD are likely to hold negative stereotypical views of others, specifically those visibly different from them in race, socioeconomic status, ethnicity, etc. These individuals are typically attracted to simple aspects of the world in which to frame their view and experience and distance themselves from nebulous ones. A job as an accountant that is very straightforward and driven by logical numerical outcomes, or a job as an IRS agent would be ideal.

When the PPD individual experiences a high degree of stress, he or she is at a higher likelihood of experiencing a psychotic break or episode lasting anywhere from minutes to hours. PPD could be a premorbid condition to delusional disorder or schizophrenia. Distinguishing PPD from other severely debilitating mental illnesses is crucial to making the proper diagnosis.

In examining personality disorder components, Skodol and colleagues (2011) identified four prominent personality domains and one trait within each domain for PPD. Within the domain of negative emotionality, the trait of suspiciousness; within the domain of detachment, the trait of intimacy avoidance; within the domain of antagonism, the trait of hostility; and within the domain of schizotypy, the trait of unusual beliefs is present.

Differential Diagnosis

Paranoid personality disorder has considerable overlap with other mental illnesses that are also in Section II, Diagnostic Criteria and Codes in the DSM-5 (APA, 2013). Central to accurate diagnosis is distinguishing PPD from the schizophrenia spectrum and other psychotic disorders. Delusional disorder and schizophrenia involve false beliefs that reach the level of psychosis. Individuals who are paranoid go to great lengths to hide their paranoid or "crazy beliefs." An individual with PPD is likely to possess delusions that will be difficult to distinguish from actual "real world" events: For example, the grandmother who feels that her family is only out to get her money, because her children come by to check on her weekly to see if she is dead so they can get their hands on it. This is not psychotic, but extreme in its paranoid belief and is therefore difficult to rule out, as opposed to individuals who think that the CIA has linked their phone to a monitoring device to track where they go and who they talk to.

In a sample of almost 300 outpatients, 22% qualified for the PPD diagnosis. However, substantial overlap was found with borderline personality disorder (48.4%), avoidant personality disorder (48.4%), and narcissistic personality disorder (35.9%) illustrating that the DSM criteria, though useful, have inherent limitations (Morey, 1988). Lenzenweger and colleagues (2007) found significant diagnostic overlap between PPD and schizoid, antisocial, borderline, avoidant, and obsessive-compulsive disorders. Interestingly, PPD was not found to greatly correlate with schizotypal personality disorder which is within the same cluster, but warrants distinction diagnostically. Individuals with PPD must be distinguished from other individuals with cluster A (schizotypal and schizoid) personality disorders. Schizotypal personality disorder (SZT) and PPD share a commonality in that they both possess strong traits of suspiciousness, detached interpersonal style, and paranoid beliefs, but the SZT individual is likely to possess magical thinking, unusual perceptual experiences, and odd thinking and speech, e.g., the man who thinks that his wishing his neighbor dead caused his heart attack. Schizoid personality disorder (SPD) individuals are often seen as eccentric, cold, and aloof but without marked paranoid ideation. Individuals with avoidant personality disorder (AVD) are likely to be reluctant to confide in others, but typically out of fear of embarrassment, as opposed to fear of malevolent retribution. Individuals with both borderline personality disorder (BPD) and PPD have violent outbursts as a reaction to a minor stressor, but the BPD individual is likely to be acting-out as a reaction to fear of abandonment to keep others close, whereas the PPD individual tries to limit closeness and contact and is comfortable with interpersonal distance. Individuals with PPD are likely to exploit others as someone with antisocial personality disorder (APD) may do, but they are not likely to do it for personal gain but more often for revenge and payback for feeling harmed in some way. Obsessive-compulsive personality disorder (OCPD) and PPD are likely to overlap due to the demand for clear and stringent rule adherence, but the PPD individual does this out of a need to keep him or her safe as opposed to a need for their world to be perfect.

Assessment

Psychological assessment can provide highly valuable information to accurately diagnose PPD and determine a course for treatment. Sperry (2003) stated that the Minnesota Multiphasic Personality Inventory, Second Edition (MMPI-2); Millon Clinical Multiaxial Inventory, Third Edition (MCMI); Rorschach Psychodiagnostic Test; and the Thematic Apperception Test (TAT) can be useful diagnostic tools. He goes on to indicate that the PPD individual is likely to score high on scales 1 (hypochondriasis), 3 (hysteria), 6 (paranoia), and K (correction) due to a tendency to be hyper-alert, utilize denial and projection, an inclination to focus on somatic complaints, and an inherent need to present a false sense of competence. On the MCMI scale, P (paranoia) will accurately identify the PPD individual's suspiciousness, defensiveness, vigilance toward criticism, as well as the tendency to externalize blame, attack and humiliate those they feel are trying to control or influence them, and other critical aspects of PPD. Scale 6B (aggressive-sadistic) will show an elevation due to the PPD individual's hostile and combative style, retaliatory actions, and tendency to occupy socially approved roles to disguise aggression. On the Rorschach, PPD individuals are likely to have more P (popular) and A (animal) responses than C (color) and M (human movement) due to resentment toward ambiguous stimuli and a testing approach style that is highly critical and condescending, which causes them to respond in a more D (detail) manner (Meyer & Deitsch, 1996). On the TAT, the PPD individual is likely to respond with a theme of suspiciousness throughout his or her responses that focus largely on manipulation and being taken advantage of by others.

The Paranoid Personality Disorder Features Questionnaire (PPDFQ, Useda, 2002 as cited in Bernstein & Useda, 2007) is a measure of the following six main traits: mistrust/suspiciousness, antagonism, introversion, hypersensitivity, hypervigilance, and rigidity that have been identified as fundamental components of PPD based upon past research (Cameron,1963; Millon, 1969, 1981; Shapiro, 1965; Sheldon & Stevens, 1942, Turkat & Maisto, 1985) and the DSM-IV (APA, 1994). The PPDFQ can serve as a diagnostic tool in conjunction with other assessments, and clinical interview, as a means to best identify areas of focus for therapy and appropriate treatment planning.

CASE EXAMPLE – MALE

Paul is a 20-year-old male who has come to the university counseling center at the request of his parents for academic accommodations due to failing grades. Paul is reluctant to discuss his concerns during intake, often responding with evasive or non-specific information, even regarding where he grew up and his home town. Paul shows no signs of attending to internal stimuli, but when asked if he had ever "seen or heard anything that no one else did" he scoffed and replied, "Is that what they told you to look for? It's never happened." After two sessions of limited interactions in their final session, Paul reports that he feels that his parents are working with his roommate to prevent him from graduating. He reports instances where his roommate will stay up late "studying" with the light on over his desk to keep Paul awake or purposefully call or text him with distracting news so that he (Paul) cannot focus. Paul further reports that his parents are hoping for his failure by doing things such as sending payments late to school, which serve to make his brother look good. Paul then states that the university has set him and everyone else up for failure with this "three-for-free" session deal, as most people would not talk to a stranger until they felt at least a modicum of comfort and he doesn't see how that is possible in "just three sessions."

After obtaining proper release from Paul, with the stipulations that he be able to see the case notes and the conversation be held with him in the room, the therapist contacted Paul's parents. Paul's parents report that Paul has always kept to himself and often has short, distant friendships. He is happiest when alone or engaging in solitary activities. He excels at math because "it is a singular triumph" as Paul always says. Lastly, his parents report that Paul will often "blow-up" in anger without their or anyone knowing what "set him off," although he is quick to name the individual who has done him wrong. Paul has never worked and it is his parents' hope that he can do well enough in school to graduate and live independently. At the conclusion of the phone conference, Paul said "I told you they would lie about me, all of it to get me kicked out of school so he [the brother] can continue to excel. What's the use?" and walked out, not returning to the counseling center.

CASE EXAMPLE – FEMALE

Maggie has worked in a department store for the last three years; Maggie tends to stay at her register and vigilantly watch her coworkers and the customers. Her breaks consist of walking on her own around the store (at times returning to check her register) or through the mall. When coworkers attempt to engage her, she is terse in her response and never mixes business with pleasure. She is certain they are talking about her and making fun of her, as they are usually laughing and looking around, sometimes in her direction. Maggie has never received a promotion. She is always polite with her boss and never takes much of his time. She considers herself a good employee. She sees her boss walking and talking with the other employees and it builds nothing but greater rage inside her. She was recently moved from china and dishware to appliances for higher commissions for good loyal services, or so her boss told her. Maggie knows the truth: she was moved so the other girls could "cash in" on the commissions.

At the end of Maggie's shift, she always checks and rechecks her register as she is sure that the other employees are just waiting for her to let her guard down to take from her till. What bothers Maggie most is when her coworkers use the customers to manipulate her. She will watch customers approach the other employees who often send them over to her to answer their questions regarding china and other dishware just to rub it in her face. One day while Maggie was driving off in heavy rain, she saw one of her coworkers standing with her back to the street next to a large puddle. Maggie pressed a little harder on her gas pedal and steered her car slightly to the right causing the puddle to splash the girl, who recently started in the china and dishware department.

TREATMENT

Treatment of the individual with PPD should largely focus on individual therapy. Group therapy is likely to only increase the PPD individual's suspiciousness and cause him or her to sabotage the group. General treatment goals should be to develop trust, decrease aggression, both implicit and explicit, and improve and develop positive relationships. General treatment strategies to achieve these goals would include the following: accept that the client will mistrust you, scale trust periodically, and always "do what you say and say what you're going to do."

Benjamin (1996) outlines her five categories of correct response when working with individuals with PPD. Facilitating collaboration is the first step and likely the most trying. Once you are able to establish collaboration, the paranoia has started to recede to some degree. We alert that individuals with PPD are going to be hypervigilant to criticism and judgment, always looking for fault, and seeing themselves as frustrating the therapist . As this may very well be true, use this moment as a here-and-now intervention. The second step is facilitating pattern recognition through learning that expectations of attacks and abusiveness are understandable as they are derived from earlier experiences, but this is taken with the understanding that these expectations are not always appropriate and should be evaluated on a case-by-case basis. The therapist needs to work with PPD individuals to attempt to get them to recognize that hostility breeds hostility and that their tendency to engage in avoidance, control, and "anticipatory retaliation" brings about attack and retaliation. It is important to couch this in a framework that explains to them that by lessening attacks on others, they, in turn, gain greater control over themselves and their environment.

The third category of correct response is teaching the PPD individual to block maladaptive patterns. The therapist needs to get the PPD client to notice patterns and interactions are "worsened when he or she has contact with the persons or situations similar to those in which the patterns were generated" (Benjamin, 1996, p. 333). Transference matters that arise, and they will, need to be dealt with in the here-and-now and immediately. Most PPD individuals will respect this honesty and it should be couched in a way that they can hear the message and digest the proposed outcome. The fourth response category is strengthening the will to give up maladaptive patterns. This step entails identifying and strengthening the wish to break past behavior of alienation, hostility, grudge harboring, etc., and to gain a sense of safety. The PPD individual must distance himself or herself from earlier controlling and attacking figures, while building comforting contacts with a significant other or a child, as well as with the therapist. It is essential that the therapist be consistent in presentation and seen as a reliable figure. In distancing himself or herself from the identified abuser, the PPD individual will likely experience ambivalence, and the therapist must not seem critical of the abusing parent or figure, but rather appear as a source of support and encouragement to differentiate from the abuser. Once a connection is made with the significant other or child, the PPD individual can start to channel his or her anger in a manner that encourages separation from old destructive maladaptive patterns. The PPD individual must loosen himself or herself from the need to be affirmed by an abuser. The final step in Benjamin's correct responses is facilitating new learning. This is likely to include social skills training, relationship development skills, and stress management skills, accepting and providing genuine positive feedback, and building trust. It is here that most therapeutic interventions begin, and sometimes fail, assuming that the previous four categories have been achieved.

Additional modes of therapy include utilizing a psychodynamic or object relations approach. A psychodynamic approach would utilize empathy, patience, and sensitivity to the vulnerability with which the PPD client is contending. Treatment will be slow and long-term and should include meaningful therapeutic alliance, treatment strategies to convert paranoid ideations and beliefs into depression and work through the underlying mourning. It is additionally important for the clinician to possess a staunch sense of respect for the PPD individual's fragile and threatened sense of individuality (Meissner, 1986, 1989).

A cognitive-behavioral approach as outlined by Beck, Freeman, and colleagues (2004) requires self-disclosure, trust, and recognizing weakness. The authors go on to state that less sensitive issues should be addressed first or in a circuitous manner. Focusing on problem-solving utilizing more behaviorally focused methods is likely to lessen the inherent stress of the key factors that make up PPD. Utilizing a guided discovery approach to identify paranoid patterns that keep the PPD individual constantly in his or her pathology is more likely to be efficacious than addressing the issues of suspiciousness, malevolence, and contempt for others directly (Sperry, 2003). Treatment should grow to include addressing specific goals and enhancing the client's self-efficacy before working on more salient and foundational matters, such as interpersonal conflicts, behaviors, and automatic thoughts (Sperry, 2003). Cognitive-behavioral techniques, such as assertiveness communication training and behavioral rehearsal, can be useful to reverse the tendency toward hostile reactions in those persons that the PPD individual sees as threatening and harmful. Sperry (2006) recommended using structured skills treatment interventions for altering the PPD individual's affective, behavioral, and cognitive style. Schema therapy can be utilized to address the maladaptive schemas held by the PPD individual that may include mistrust and personal defectiveness. Schema therapy focuses on four main strategies: cognitive, experiential, behavioral, and the therapeutic relationship, and has been used to treat personality disordered individuals in both couples and individual therapeutic settings (Young & Klosko, 2005).

Psychopharmacology

There are no studies that directly assess the efficacy of medication for PPD. This lack of research has been attributed to the very basic components of the disorder, since only about 1 in 10 is willing to submit to any form of treatment (Tyrer et al., 2003). In addition, one of the greatest hurdles to overcome regarding medication treatment for personality disorders has been to determine efficacy and separate personality components from mental state such as depression, anxiety, paranoid or suicidal ideation. Accordingly, there is considerable doubt regarding medication effectiveness in treating personality disorders or answering the question: is the medication treating mental state components that underlie the personality structure that constitute the personality disorder? (Tyrer & Bateman, 2004)

Paranoid personality disorder is often viewed as sub-syndromal to a schizophrenia spectrum or other psychotic disorders, though the individual is not psychotic. The link between personality and its neurobiological dimensions was studied by Cloninger (1987) and has provided some justification to medication treatment. Low activity of the neurotransmitter dopamine has been linked to the cognitive personality dimension related to high novelty-seeking behavior, as well as low dopamine activity, which could be a potential connection between paranoid personality disorder and schizophrenia spectrum and other psychotic disorders. The theoretically appropriate drug treatment would be an antipsychotic medication to reduce the novelty-seeking behavior. Soloff (1998) postulated that changing neurotransmitter physiology paired with a particular dimension of personality disorders would produce medication-responsive results. For example, the cognitive/perceptual components of suspiciousness and paranoid ideation can be addressed with antipsychotic medication, as suggested by Cloninger's earlier work. It is further believed that affective dysregulation, such as lability of mood (anger outbursts), 'rejection sensitivity,' inappropriate intense anger, and temper outbursts can be best treated with selective serotonin reuptake inhibitors (SSRIs). Mood stabilizers could potentially be utilized with the PPD individual to target sensation-seeking or reckless behavior, low frustration tolerance, impulsive aggression, recurrent assaultiveness, and threat-making.

One study found that using fluoxetine hydrochloride (Prozac) has been beneficial in reducing suspiciousness (Fieve, 1994). Coccaro and Kavoussi, (1997) furthered this finding by conducting a double-blind placebo controlled trial using Prozac in 40 personality disordered individuals with no Axis I (clinical disorders) diagnosis and a current history of impulsive aggressiveness and irritability (28% of the sample met criteria for a cluster A personality disorder). Prozac, but not placebo, produced a sustained reduction in irritability and aggression which led the authors to conclude that treatment with Prozac can produce a reduction in impulsive aggression in personality-disordered individuals.

FILM AND POPULAR MEDIA EXAMPLES

The Caine Mutiny (1954) – Phillip Queeg, played by Humphrey Bogart

The Conversation (1974) – Harry Caul, played by Gene Hackman

Falling Down (1993) – William "D-Fens" Foster, played by Michael Douglas

The Treasure of the Sierra Madre (1948) – Fred Dobbs, played by Humphrey Bogart

CHECKLIST: PARANOID PERSONALITY DISORDER

Below is a complete list to best identify and diagnose Paranoid Personality Disorder. DSM-5 (APA, 2013) criteria are first, followed by discernible components, and lastly, associated features.

- ❑ A pervasive distrust and suspiciousness of others such that their motives are interpreted as malevolent, beginning by early adulthood and present in a variety of contexts*
- ❑ Suspects, without sufficient basis, that others are exploiting, harming, or deceiving him or her*
- ❑ Is preoccupied with unjustified doubts about the loyalty or trustworthiness of friends or associates*
- ❑ Is reluctant to confide in others because of unwarranted fear that the information will be used maliciously against him or her*
- ❑ Reads hidden demeaning or threatening meanings into benign remarks or events*
- ❑ Persistently bears grudges, (i.e., is unforgiving of insults, injuries, or slights)*
- ❑ Perceives attacks on his or her character or reputation that are not apparent to others and is quick to react angrily or to counterattack*
- ❑ Has recurrent suspicions, without justification, regarding fidelity of spouse or sexual partner*
- ❑ No psychosis is evident (if present, brief psychotic reaction lasting minutes to hours)
- ❑ Absence of a bipolar disorder with psychotic features
- ❑ Absence of a depressive disorder with psychotic features
- ❑ No identifiable physiological effects of another medical condition
- ❑ Poor interpersonal skills rooted in paranoia
- ❑ Significant relationship difficulties centered on mistrust and infidelity
- ❑ Suspiciousness/hostility expressed in overt argumentativeness
- ❑ Hypervigilant to potential threats
- ❑ Tendency to display labile range of affect, with hostility, stubbornness, and sarcasm predominating
- ❑ Elicits hostile responses in others due to combativeness and suspiciousness
- ❑ Excessive need to be self-sufficient
- ❑ High degree of control in his or her environment
- ❑ Rigid and critical of others and unable to collaborate
- ❑ Difficulty accepting criticism
- ❑ Tendency to blame others for his or her shortcomings
- ❑ Frequent legal disputes related to counterattacking in response to real or perceived threats
- ❑ Seeks to confirm preconceived adverse notions related to people or situations
- ❑ Often attuned to issues of power and rank

*distinguishing characteristics

THERAPIST CLIENT ACTIVITY

Use these probes to explore your PPD client's suspiciousness and paranoia that are central to the pathology and enhance the socioeconomic dysfunction.

- ➢ What are your concerns regarding what will happen if people talk behind your back?
- ➢ Who betrayed you most?
- ➢ What is it like for you when someone has slighted you and how important is it that you get that person back?
- ➢ What is the proper consequence for being dishonest and untruthful?
- ➢ If you could do one thing differently, what would it be and how would you have changed it for yourself?
- ➢ What is the most important part in your life in which to feel successful?
- ➢ How will you know you are successful?
- ➢ What would it take for you to forgive someone?
- ➢ Has anyone ever been upset at you for reasons you could not easily identify?
- ➢ How can therapy help you most?
- ➢ How far do you see our therapy going?
- ➢ What would be most helpful for me to do to help you in therapy?
- ➢ Can you agree to let me know if I ever do anything to make you uncertain of our relationship?
- ➢ How will we know when therapy is successful for you?

CLIENT QUESTIONNAIRE

The following questions are to be given to your client to help him or her identify past challenges and provide guidance for treatment.

What is your earliest recollection? Please describe as much as you feel comfortable.

Describe, with as much detail as you feel comfortable, when you were hurt most by someone else:

What has been your greatest obstacle and how has it blocked or hindered your success?

In what working environment do you see yourself succeeding most and how do you plan to get there?

Schizoid Personality Disorder

Schizoid personality disorder (SPD) is characterized as a disorder in which the individual lacks interest in aspects of life that most find enjoyable and intriguing, such as social relationships, a tendency toward a solitary lifestyle, secretiveness, emotional coldness, and sometimes (sexual) apathy. In addition, a limited range of affect is also present in these individuals. Schizoid personality disorder has been a difficult and nebulous disorder to categorize, making it among the most complex of the personality disorders and presenting a significant diagnostic challenge for the last 100 years (Beck, Freeman, & Davis, 2004). In 1908, Eugene Bleuler called individuals whose focus was inward to an extreme schizoid personality (Akhtar, 1987). Bleuler (1924), using a classical psychoanalytic or object-relations viewpoint, examined the schizoid structure from unconscious motivations that encompassed the characterological structure and hypothesized that the schizoid individual and schizoid pathology are intertwined.

In 1925, Ernest Kretschmer described observable behaviors in schizoid individuals, in the descriptive psychiatric tradition, organized into three groups (Kretschmer, 1925):

> Unsociable, quiet, reserved, serious, eccentric

> Timid, shy in feeling-expression, sensitive, nervous, excitable

> Flexible, honest, indifferent, silent, emotionally cold

Groups of SPD Observable Behaviors

Kretschmer's observable characteristics were the precursors to the Diagnostic and Statistical Manual's schizoid criterion in the fourth edition, and though he divided the character structure into three seemingly separate components, he noted that these facets are typically present in one individual simultaneously moving along a single dimension. In other words, these traits are present but expressed at various points depending upon what situations, views, and experiences the individual has had in the past or is currently experiencing. However, it was not Kretschmer's or Bleuler's work that set the foundation for understanding SPD, but Fairbairn (2002) in 1940 as he described the four central components of the schizoid individual:

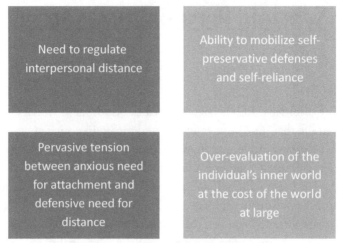

Components of the SPD Individual

From these four components research continued and the criteria were subsequently included in the very first *Diagnostic and Statistical Manual* (APA, 1952). DSM-I (APA, 1952), under personality pattern disturbance, describes SPD:

> Inherent traits in such personalities are (1) avoidance of close relationships with others, (2) inability to express directly hostility or even ordinary aggressive feelings, and (3) autistic thinking. These qualities result early in coldness, aloofness, emotional detachment, fearfulness, avoidance of competition, and day dreams evolving around the need for omnipotence. As children they are usually quiet, shy, obedient, sensitive, and retiring. At puberty, they frequently become more withdrawn, then manifesting the aggregate of personality traits known as introversion, namely, quietness, seclusiveness, "shut-in-ness," and unsociability, often with eccentricity (p. 35).

One of the key points regarding SPD within the DSM-I and past literature is that it is often mentioned in context with schizophrenic and dissociative reaction, as well as paranoid personality disorder (APA, 1952; Campbell, 1989; Silverberg, 1947; Tidd, 1937). From its inception to its formal placement in the DSM-I, schizoid personality patterns have been linked to psychosis in some way. Schizoid personality disorder is often considered a schizophrenia spectrum disorder, as it addresses the separation of the personality that is characteristic in individuals with schizophrenia and the SPD's behavior can be seen as indicative of a genetically determined vulnerability to schizophrenia or a psychotic disorder (Campbell, 1989). This link has led many to distinguish SPD from psychosis and even to identify four subtypes delineated by Millon and Davis (1996) and later used by Millon (1996) to suggest treatment approaches based upon the subtypes. However, little empirical data has been found to support this approach (Beck, Freeman, & Davis, 2004):

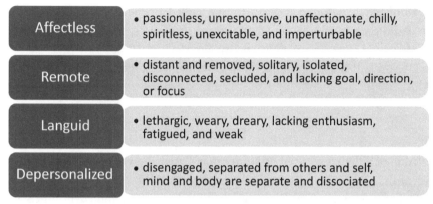

Affectless	• passionless, unresponsive, unaffectionate, chilly, spiritless, unexcitable, and imperturbable
Remote	• distant and removed, solitary, isolated, disconnected, secluded, and lacking goal, direction, or focus
Languid	• lethargic, weary, dreary, lacking enthusiasm, fatigued, and weak
Depersonalized	• disengaged, separated from others and self, mind and body are separate and dissociated

Millon and Davis's Subtypes of SPD

The *Diagnostic and Statistical Manual, Fourth Edition, Text Revision* (DSM-IV-TR; APA, 2000) is consistent with the historical perspective of SPD, but some crucial components are lacking (Mittal, Kalus, Bernstein, & Siever, 2007). One aspect is the "contradictory affective and cognitive states in schizoid personality disorder that were not recognized in the DSM-III" (Mittal et al., 2007, p. 64) that the authors believe was subsumed into schizotypal or avoidant personality disorders. In part, this could have been due to the *Diagnostic and Statistical Manual, Third Edition* (DSM-III; APA, 1980) introducing diagnostic criteria as opposed to only providing descriptions, as it did in earlier versions. In the DSM-III (APA, 1980) a new disorder, Avoidant personality disorder (AVD) was added. AVD possessed a critical similarity, but a crucial difference from SPD. The AVD individual was hypersensitive to rejection and belittling as opposed to indifferent. The root of the AVD individual's social isolation was social anxiety; the SPD individual isolated himself or herself due to social aloofness and indifference. Within the description of SPD in the DSM-III-R (APA, 1987) an emphasis was placed on emotionality, but later deemphasized in the DSM-IV (APA, 1994). Currently, there is so much debate about SPD and the similar AVD that some consider it to be the same disorder though they reside in separate clusters within the DSM-IV-TR (APA, 2000) and DSM-5 (APA, 2013) due to theoretical distinction (Miller, Useda, Trull, Burr, & Minks-Brown, 2004) and odd and eccentric presentation.

Many studies have explored the possible link between SPD and Asperger's syndrome (DSM-5 renamed autism spectrum disorder; Attwood, 2007; Raja, 2006; Wolff, 1998; Wolff, 2000). The schizoid spectrum disorders have been found to share commonalities with both in that both have impaired social relationships and developmental delays, as well as eccentricity, a tendency to be socially isolated, and the potential for bizarre behavioral expression (Attwood, 2007). Wolff (1998) reported that in the 1960s approximately 4% of children were presenting to psychiatric facilities with an "unusual clinical picture" of continual social isolation and peculiar behavior. He followed a group of these children, who were diagnosed with SPD using earlier psychiatric descriptions, from the 1960s until adulthood. More boys than girls were impacted at a ratio of 3.4:1 (Wolff & McGuire, 1995, as cited in Wolff, 1998). A 10-year follow-up study was conducted using a "blind" interviewer focusing on the key features of the children: solitariness, lack of empathy, emotional detachment, increased sensitivity with paranoid ideation, rigidity in ideas and views, and a unique style of interaction with others to distinguish between a group of schizoid boys and a matched control group. The interviewer identified 18 of the 22 schizoid individuals and only 1 of the 22 individuals in the control sample as "definitely schizoid." Wolf (1998) stated that "the syndrome was very clearly long-lasting, as one would expect from a personality disorder" (p. 125).

The DSM-5 (APA, 2013) criteria for SPD were not changed from its predecessor, DSM-IV-TR (APA, 2000).

Etiology

The origination of SPD has received little attention. Based upon the paucity of research and the complexity of the SPD, it is certain that the etiology of SPD is complex and likely driven by the individual's experience and the influences of both heritability and environmental exposure to varying degrees.

It has been speculated that SPD develops from early experiences that include peer rejection and bullying, as well as being separate from the family or compared to others as less than worthy. The SPD individual has internalized this view and sees the self as negative, others as insensitive and insignificant, and social interaction as harmful and complicated (Beck et al., 2004).

Benjamin (1996) described a theoretical hypothesis for the etiology of SPD. The SPD individual is likely to have a home that is highly structured and formal where basic needs are met. These basic needs would include physical, educational, and social aspects. Parental goals for the child would have been to prepare him or her to attain basic adult functioning, not to make the family proud or acquire fame. The SPD individual is socialized to perform rudimentary social functions, but remains detached emotionally and physically. The family would be rather stoic in forms of interaction and concretely goal focused. The SPD individual, through observational learning, would build the tendency to withdraw and/or engage in orderly, singular, and quiet pursuits. Benjamin (1996) goes on to discuss that the link between the SPD individual and withdrawn parents provides the foundation to expect nothing and give nothing.

Individuals with SPD often report that their parents were cold and unaffectionate toward them, though this has not been empirically examined. No currently available studies link parent aloofness and lack of emotional connection with the development of schizoid personality traits (Millon, 1981). Martens (2010) applied Kernberg's work (1968) on borderline personality organization and splitting as a defense mechanism to schizoid personality development as a foundational state of unreality and diffusion leading to chronic feelings of emptiness, which in turn result in internalized fear, paranoia, social withdrawal, and loneliness. It is further hypothesized that internal makeup of the schizoid individual involves hypersensitivity, paradoxical conflicts regarding basic needs, such as food and affection, as well as social rejection and isolation, trauma, jealousy, self-hatred, and low self-esteem as opposed to the presenting apathy and social aloofness typically seen with SPD. It is the intertwining of these factors that the individual with SPD is contending with and the social isolation that entrenches him or her into the schizoid pathology (Martens, 2010).

Prevalence

According to the DSM-5 (APA, 2000), SPD is uncommon in clinical settings but prevalence is estimated, based upon the National Epidemiologic Survey and Alcohol and Related Conditions

(NESARC) to be at approximately 3.1%, whereas the National Comorbidity Survey replication lists SPD prevalence at approximately 4.9%. Miller, Useda, Trull, Burr, and Minks-Brown (2001) stated that SPD is considered one of the least frequently encountered personality disorders but gives prevalence rates between 0.5% and 7.0% based on past research (Drake & Valliant, 1985; Reich, Yates, & Nduaguba, 1989; Zimmerman & Coryell, 1990).

In one study that used the International Personality Disorder Examination (IPDE) to determine DSM-IV and ICD-10 personality disorders, between 0.9% and 1.1% of a weighted prevalence was found for SPD in the community (Samuels et al., 2002). Again using the IPDE, SPD was diagnosed in 279 (4.9%) individuals from a sub-sample gathered from the National Comorbidity Survey Replication (NCS-R; Lenzenweger, Lane, Loranger, & Kessler, 2007). Using the Structured Clinical Interview for DSM-IV-TR personality disorders (SCID-II) it was found that out of a sample size of 644 youths from the Children in Community Study (Cohen & Cohen, 1995), 11 (1.7%) were diagnosed with SPD. Cohen and colleagues (2005) found that paranoid and schizotypal symptoms tend to be more stable over time than SPD as the individual moves into adulthood and after, which may account for the difficulty in accurately diagnosing SPD depending upon the point at which the individual is assessed.

ATTACHMENT

Attachment is the connection between people within relationships. Individuals with SPD are inherently adverse to connection and relationships. Avoidant attachment has been associated with SPD (Mikulincer & Shaver, 2007). The avoidantly attached child is likely to show little affect during play, little or no distress upon the caregiver's leaving with no visible response upon the caregiver's returning, no effort to maintain contact if picked up, and no distinction between her treatment of care givers and strangers. In response to the avoidant child, the caregiver tends to provide little or no response when the child is in distress and discourages crying while encouraging independence (Ainsworth, Blehar, Waters, & Wall, 1978). According to Bartholomew and colleagues (2001) there is no evidence of negative models of self or fear of rejection; instead there is a severe form of "dismissing avoidance" (Bartholomew, 1990), which is a denial of attachment needs as opposed to fear of connecting with others and being rejected, as in the case of the avoidant personality disordered individual. Studies have been conducted that show that individuals with SPD symptoms score high on measures of attachment avoidance or dismissing styles (Brennan & Shaver, 1998; Lyddon & Sherry, 2001; West, Rose, & Sheldon-Keller, 1994), adding to the finding that specific attachment securities are present in distinct personality disorders.

Object-relations theorists believe that SPD individuals avoid interpersonal closeness due to fear of connection and being overrun with such a degree of emotional pain that collapse or trauma ensues. The desire for, and fear of, connection cause the individual to withdraw into basic forms of functioning, mimicking autism spectrum behaviors (Martens, 2010). Due to the intense need for intimacy and the experiences of intrapsychic conflict that thwart "normal" development of interpersonal needs and skills, there is an ever-present fear of connection, loss, anxiety, and sexual tension (Alperin, 2001). Theories suggest that the experience of loss and the inability to cope with a rejecting mother or caregiver is central to SPD issues and concerns (Guntrip, 1991; Mahler, Pine, & Bergman, 1975; Waska, 2002). The lack of connection between caregiver and child happens at a time when the child does not have adequate resources to combat the separation and trauma. It builds within the individual and represents a failure to resolve past attachment conflicts of interactions and intimacy as he or she develops and separates from the caregiver. These emotional experiences, and the subsequent deprivation, cause an inability to develop a secure base. A lack of satisfaction in interpersonal relationships develops along with maladaptive schemas and cognitive behaviors that are highly associated with attachment malformation and the severe loneliness that are at the root of SPD (Fairbairn, 1952; Guntrip, 1991).

DIAGNOSIS

The criteria most often used to diagnose SPD are the seven listed in the DSM-5 (APA, 2013) and recreated below in Table 1.

TABLE 1: DSM-5 DIAGNOSTIC CRITERIA FOR SCHIZOID PERSONALITY DISORDER
A. A pervasive pattern of detachment from social relationships and a restricted range of expression of emotions in interpersonal settings, beginning by early adulthood and present in a variety of contexts, as indicated by four (or more) of the following: (1) Neither desires nor enjoys relationships or human interaction, including being part of a family (2) Almost always chooses solitary activities (3) Has little, if any, interest in having sexual experiences with another person (4) Takes pleasure in few, if any, activities with other people (5) Lacks close friends or confidants other than first-degree relatives (6) Appears indifferent to the praise or criticism of others (7) Shows emotional coldness, detachment, or flattened affect
B. Does not occur exclusively during the course of schizophrenia, a bipolar disorder or depressive disorder with psychotic features, another psychotic disorder, or autism spectrum disorder and is not attributable to the physiological effects of another medical condition.
Note: If criteria are met prior to the onset of schizophrenia, add "premorbid," e.g., "schizoid personality disorder (premorbid)."

The criteria related to SPD are not concrete, but provide guidelines to diagnose the SPD individual. Cultural and other aspects will be imperative to consider when attempting to diagnose SPD. The first criterion has been identified as the critical criterion to accurately diagnose SPD (Allnutt & Links, 1996). The first criterion identifies the lack of interest in initiating, developing, and maintaining close relationships. These individuals tend to lack interest in their family of origin, do not find membership in social groups interesting or desirable and will actively avoid social gatherings. The second criterion relates to the SPD individual's introverted style, due not to shyness but by choice. These individuals prefer solitude to the company of others and find pleasure in their isolation, and are not outwardly distressed by being alone. They are not fleeing social contact or connection due to a perceived threat or an anxiety-producing context; instead, they do not find others interesting. Criterion three addresses the SPD individual's lack of sexual desire toward someone else; he or she finds the greatest erotic satisfaction from masturbation. It has been found that individuals with SPD tend to dislike the physical and emotional closeness of sex, but having an average sex-drive, find masturbation fulfilling (Nannarello, 1953). Akhtar (1987) proposes that the SPD individual experiences both covert and overt sexual states that include overt asexuality, free of romantic interests, and sexually distant; whereas the covert state involves voyeurism, possible erotomania, and a tendency towards compulsive masturbation.

The fourth criterion examines the individual's tendency to have few if any activities that he or she finds pleasurable. Those activities that he or she does engage in tend to be solitary and passive and the approach can be obsessive, such as playing video games and listening to music. Criterion five pertains to the individual's lack of close friends or acquaintances. He or she separates from others and finds no need to connect, but may have one or two confidants, usually a sibling or cousin. If he or she does connect with another, it is likely to be on an intellectual level or within the same academic club, such as a debate or chess club. The sixth criterion discusses the SPD individual's outward indifference to praise, criticism, or opinions of others. If praised or congratulated for a job well done, the SPD individual is likely to show little response, though he or she may value the test score or whatever was at the root of the compliment or congratulations. The final criterion identifies the tendency to move through life without affective response: he or she is expressionless and will show no sadness, glee, fear, disgust, anger, or surprise in response to stimuli. This criterion is critical to the overlap between SPD and autism spectrum disorder and schizophrenia spectrum and other psychotic disorders.

The DSM-5 (APA, 2013) identifies other crucial features of SPD. The SPD individual is likely to have difficulty expressing anger or other emotional response, even when provoked. He or she may appear to lack direction and goals, appear indifferent to adverse situations, and encounter problems responding sufficiently to critical life events. Occupational functioning may be adversely affected if there is an interpersonal component, but the SPD individual is likely to find work that is solitary and has limited social interaction. The SPD individual is at risk for a brief psychotic episode lasting from minutes to hours if he or she encounters a high degree of stress.

In addition to the DSM-5 (APA, 2013), Millon and colleagues (2004) and Guntrip (1969) identified additional subtypes of SPD useful in diagnoses. Millon and colleagues (2004) identified four subtypes:

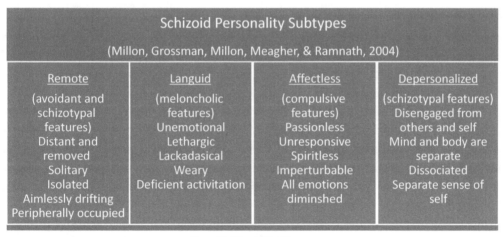

Schizoid Personality Subtypes			
(Millon, Grossman, Millon, Meagher, & Ramnath, 2004)			
Remote	Languid	Affectless	Depersonalized
(avoidant and schizotypal features) Distant and removed Solitary Isolated Aimlessly drifting Peripherally occupied	(meloncholic features) Unemotional Lethargic Lackadasical Weary Deficient activitation	(compulsive features) Passionless Unresponsive Spiritless Imperturbable All emotions diminshed	(schizotypal features) Disengaged from others and self Mind and body are separate Dissociated Separate sense of self

Four Schizoid Subtypes

The four subtypes listed provide a greater understanding and clearer picture of the SPD individual, aiding the clinician in accurate diagnosis and greater understanding of the within-disorder differences. Guntrip (1969) expanded the understanding of the schizoid personality by breaking the diagnosis into nine different characteristics:

TABLE 2: NINE CHARACTERISTICS OF SCHIZOID PERSONALITY	
Introversion	Cut off from the outside world. Interests and focus are inward.
Withdrawnness	Detached from the outside world, though may interact within it.
Narcissism	Love object and identification are inward.
Self-sufficiency	Emotional connections are inward and great focus on doing for self.
Sense of superiority	Due to degree of self-reliance, little to no need for others and tendency to see others as disposable and unnecessary.
Loss of affect	Due to high degree of self-sufficiency, little desire to feel empathy and sensitive to others leading to a loss of affect.
Loneliness	Underlying intense feeling for love and belonging, but this is thwarted by introversion and the loss of external relationships.
Depersonalization	Experience is vague, dreamlike, and blunted in significance; typically arises out of high anxiety state.
Regression	Revert to a basic form of fantasy closing oneself off, as well as moving backward to withdrawal to a safe environment.

The SPD individual presents a complex set of mechanisms developed to manage and maintain intrapsychic distance and a harmonious ego state. As noted previously, the DSM-5 (APA, 2013) is a starting point, but accurate diagnosis involves greater understanding of the disorder to be a springboard for appropriate treatment as well as to distinguish it from other mental health disorders.

No changes were made to the SPD criteria in the DSM-5 (APA, 2013) from the previous volume, DSM-IV-TR (APA, 2000).

Differential Diagnosis

Schizoid personality disorder is within the cluster A of the DSM-5 that is defined as "odd and eccentric." SPD has great overlap with the other two disorders that share this cluster, paranoid personality disorder and schizotypal personality disorder. Lenzenweger and colleagues (2007) found considerable comorbidity between SPD and the other personality disorders.

As evidenced by Table 3, SPD correlates most strongly with the other cluster A personality disorders (paranoid and schizotypal) in the positive direction, while most negatively correlated with antisocial and dependent personality disorders. Considering the great overlap within cluster A, variation tends to be very difficult to distinguish. Paranoid personality disorder individuals will possess a strong sense of suspiciousness in conjunction with paranoid ideation. Schizotypal personality disorder individuals will possess positive symptoms in the form of cognitive and perceptual distortions (e.g., magical thinking) not seen in schizoid pathology. Distinction from avoidant personality disorder is warranted as both it and SPD have similar

TABLE 3: SPD AND OTHER PERSONALITY DISORDERS	
Personality Disorder	**Correlation with SPD***
Paranoid	0.77
Schizotypal	0.96
Antisocial	-0.84
Borderline	0.56
Avoidant	0.55
Dependent	-0.84
Obsessive-Compulsive	0.40
* From Lenzenweger et al. (2007)	

presentation styles, including removal from social encounters, and tendency to isolate. However, the rationale for these overlapping behaviors are entirely different. Avoidant personality disorder individuals avoid others out of fear of being embarrassed or being found to be incompetent and subsequently being rejected, whereas SPD individuals find little interest in others and tend not to seek out social interaction for that reason, so they tend not to care what others think of them. Individuals with obsessive-compulsive personality disorder (OCPD) may present in a manner similar to individuals with SPD, but though the OCPD pathology tends to cause them to show social detachment due to dedication to task completion and discomfort with their emotions, they are able to connect with others on an intimate and social level, whereas the SPD individual will not and in some cases cannot, due to stunted emotional development.

Kasen and colleagues (2001) found that Axis I (clinical disorders) disorders in adolescents were associated with later SPD and PPD in early adulthood. Adolescents who tend to act out are at a six times greater risk for SPD in early adulthood, possibly due to underlying Asperger's-like symptoms (criteria are equivalent to autism spectrum disorder in DSM-5, APA, 2013) and avoidant anxiety (Cohen, Crawford, Johnson, & Kasen, 2005). It is critical to separate the SPD individual from someone with an autism spectrum disorder. An individual with autism spectrum disorder will show earlier and more severe social difficulties, depending upon the severity level, as well as deficits in nonverbal communication (e.g., lack of eye contact), speech clarity, and a dedication to rituals and routine not typically seen in the SPD person.

Under stress, the individual with SPD is at a higher likelihood to experience a brief psychotic episode (Campbell, 1989). Individuals with cluster A disorders are at a higher probability to have come from a family with a history of schizophrenia, leading many researchers to believe there may be a genetic link (Campbell, 1989; Miller et al., 2004). One study using the SCID-II (First, Gibbon, Spitzer, Benjamin, & Williams, 1997) to interview 40 parents and outpatients diagnosed with schizophrenia found that 27.5% met criteria for premorbid SPD (Solano & De Chávez, 2000). In addition to schizophrenia spectrum and other psychotic disorders, the DSM-5 (APA, 2013) lists delusional disorder and bipolar or depressive disorders with psychotic features as important mental health conditions that warrant differentiation from SPD. All of these disorders have persistent psychotic symptoms, such as hallucinations or delusions, which the clinician is not likely to see in the SPD individual. However, to give the diagnosis of SPD, in addition to a schizophrenia spectrum and other psychotic disorder, the personality disorder must have been present prior to the onset of the psychosis or must continue when psychosis remits. Another and often confusing aspect of accurate diagnosis of SPD is the possible presence of seemingly negative symptoms. It is possible to see restrictions in affect and range in intensity of emotions, as well as a paucity of speech, but the SPD individual is presenting this way due to lack of interest, not as a result of a psychotic state. In addition, negative symptoms in SPD can include lack of goal-directed behavior. In the SPD individual, goal-directed behavior should not be greatly impaired; if present, it is typically due to apathy and not a volition, as in the case of the psychotic individual.

Assessment

Considering the rarity of SPD individuals in treatment, assessment is a crucial and valuable plan to accurately identify schizoid traits and SPD, and to determine the most effective method for treatment. There are no specific measures to assess SPD, though there are several comprehensive structured interviews with scales that address aspects of SPD (Mittal et al., 2007). The SCID-II (First et al., 1997) and Structured Interview for DSM-IV Personality Disorders (SIDP-IV; Pfohl, Blum, & Zimmerman, 1997) have produced reliable outcomes based upon past studies (Auther, 2003; Maffei et al., 1997 as cited in Mittal et al., 2007).

Sperry (2003) discussed possible results using several popular assessment methods to identify the SPD individual and similar traits. The Minnesota Multiphasic Personality Inventory, Second Edition (MMPI-2) is likely to produce a "normal" profile with an elevated O (Social Introversion); however, when in distress the SPD individual is likely to show elevations in F (Frequency), 2 (Depression), and 8 (Schizophrenia). Infrequently, a 1-8 code (Hypochondriasis-Schizophrenia) type may be produced illustrating the tendency to harbor feelings of hostility and aggression, and an inability to express these feelings in a proper way. The unexpressed feelings remain under the surface or in some cases may be expressed in a belligerent manner. Lastly, individuals with this code type tend to be socially inadequate, particularly around those of the opposite sex, lack trust in others, keep people at a distance, and possess a general feeling of isolation and alienation (Graham, 2011). Based upon what the psychological community knows of the SPD individual, it is easy to see that a person with this disorder would produce such a profile, but it is important to note that assessment should never stand alone and be the only means of diagnosis.

The Millon Clinical Multiaxial Inventory (MCMI) is used to identify psychopathology, as well as disorder within the DSM-IV. An SPD individual is likely to show an elevation on scale 1 (Schizoid) and low scores on 4 (Histrionic), 5 (Narcissistic), and N (Bipolar-Manic) (Choca & Van Denburg, 1997 as cited in Sperry, 2003). The Rorschach, when given to the SPD individual, is likely to produce a high percentage of A (Animal) and few C (Color) responses. Overall, the results tend to show a restricted or rejecting response pattern. It may take the SPD individual more time to answer with some cards, a higher experience potential as opposed to actual, and M (human movement) production will be elevated when compared to the overall protocol (Exner, 1986; Sperry, 2003). On the Thematic Apperception Test (TAT), the clinician should expect to see constricted responses in addition to a lack of theme, as well as a flat explanation of characters within the story (Bellak & Abrams, 1997 as cited in Sperry, 2003).

CASE EXAMPLE – MALE

Mike is a 23-year-old white male who works in a busy record store. Mike loves music but hates his job. He tends to stay away from his co-workers, and when he does interact, his responses tend to be negative and short. As a result, his co-workers stay away from him and do not interact much with him; he likes this aspect very much. Mike becomes visibly tense when customers approach him and he appears frustrated and annoyed to discourage further interaction; this works well. Mike was recently offered a promotion that came with more money and a greater discount on CDs, so he took it. On his first night as assistant manager, he had to deal with complaints from staff about their schedule and customers regarding returns. Mike responded in his usual fashion, terse and annoyed. After several weeks of this, Mike began to have difficulty sleeping and was losing interest in playing his video games. Mike's behavior at work began to be agitated and visibly disheveled. During a conversation with his manager regarding his behavior, he told her that he was fine to end the conversation as quickly as possible. The next day Mike found a new job as a vender for Frito-Lay, where he restocked vending machines in his own truck with no assistant. He never told the record store he had quit, thinking "they'll figure it out."

CASE EXAMPLE – FEMALE

Betty is a 35-year-old female who has been married for 5 years and has one child, age 2. She is a stay-at-home mom and spends most of her time reading books and watching TV. She keeps her 2-year-old son on a schedule and will read one book to him in the morning, and attend to him for meals, but tends to leave him to play on his own most of the time. Betty believes that all children should learn to control themselves, so when her son is crying she will check and make sure he does not need to go to the restroom and is not hurt. Otherwise, she will ignore him. Her husband is a gregarious man, who often "steals the spotlight" and enjoys not having to compete with her for attention with friends and family, as she typically does not attend gatherings with family or friends and, if she must, she will remain quiet and stay at a physical distance. Betty recently found out that her husband is having an affair. When her husband confronted her with the news, she felt a sense of relief, as she often did not enjoy sex or intimacy with him and viewed their marriage as a necessity in her life, a role she had to fill. Soon after, her husband divorced her and obtained custody of their son without any contention from Betty. Betty is currently pleased with her life, living alone in a small apartment, and receiving a monthly alimony check that covers her basic needs so she can continue to read her books and watch TV.

TREATMENT

It is very rare to encounter SPD individuals within a clinical setting as they tend to be treatment-rejecting and not likely to seek therapy. The majority of research on treatment within cluster A, the cluster that houses SPD, has been on schizotypal disorder (Koenigsberg, Woo-Ming, & Siever, 2007) so research is limited and no well-controlled studies of therapeutic efficacy have been conducted (Crits-Christoph & Barber, 2002; Miller et al., 2004). The individual with SPD is likely to have a poor prognosis as it would require significant change to how they see the world, function within it, and feel comfortable with themselves and others (Millon, Davis, Millon, Escovar, & Meagher, 2000). The SPD individual is most likely to enter treatment due to anxiety, depression, or some other mental health disorder. The approach to treatment will likely not include increasing interpersonal interaction and building outward support systems, as this is contrary to the SPD individual's very makeup.

Individual therapy can be beneficial for the SPD client whether using a psychodynamic or cognitive-behavioral approach. In the psychodynamic approach, both expressive and supportive forms of treatment are recommended based upon the SPD individual's levels of functioning, as well as adopting a short-term or long-term modality (Sperry, 2003). Long-term treatment is best for individuals who possess some degree of empathy, emotional warmth, and motivation for improved functioning. The frequency of sessions should be one to two times per week (Stone, 1983). The short-term modality is for attending to crises, situational problems, and to follow up on past treatment (Sperry, 2003). The clinician is tasked with working with the client to change internal object-relations through corrective emotional experience. Therapy should work to replace maladaptive internalized relationship models (Gabbard, 1994a). Utilizing a supportive therapeutic approach, the therapist needs to develop a "permissive, accepting attitude, and must be exceedingly patient with these individuals" (Sperry, 2003, p. 230). Counter transference will be a key aspect of treatment, and silence becomes critical to demonstrating to the SPD client that it is accepted and legitimate to possess a private and silent self. Treatment should include techniques to encourage greater activities with others until a level of ease is attained, such as participating in a chess club or online video gaming as opposed to solitary activities (Sperry, 2003). Periodically testing the limits of social interaction can be beneficial with therapy being the safe haven for the SPD individual to retreat to process the experience.

The cognitive-behavioral approach should focus largely on building social motivation and increasing social interaction, though it may be slight and slow (Beck et al., 2004). Some therapeutic interventions have been suggested in regard to treating the SPD individual. Due to the foundational nature of therapy, being interactive and social, the SPD individual is likely to have difficulty establishing the collaborative therapeutic relationship (Beck et al., 2004). A key area of treatment will be the SPD individual's belief about himself or herself and others, and a very basic approach to treatment will be best. In order to encourage the client to participate, it will be beneficial to write out the pros and cons of treatment and, as Beck and colleagues (2004) illustrate through case example, the advantages should appear to outweigh the disadvantages. They describe their client "Derek," who was eventually able to engage in therapy. However, it took five consecutive sessions to even get to that point. The pace of therapy will be considerably slower than with "typical clients," even those with other personality disorders. Therapy is likely to be a combination of negotiation and atypical assessments of interactions and the client's problems. In developing a problem list, it is best created through a collaborative and Socratic approach drawn from the client. The therapist should not look for "appropriate goals," which typically entails building social alliances and relationships, as this may thwart the therapeutic process (Beck et al., 2004). As greater self-awareness is achieved in interpersonal interactions, the focus can turn to social skills training with practice taking place in treatment and in the outside world. Due to the SPD individual's inherent lack of expression, feedback on the level of anxiety may reduce the possibility of early termination (Sperry, 2003). The dysfunctional thought record, social skills training through role-playing, real-life exposure, and homework have been found to be effective techniques with this population (Beck et al., 2004). Near the end of therapy, relapse (back into an isolative lifestyle) prevention is discussed. Relapse is thwarted through the use of "booster sessions" (Beck et al., 2004).

Although group therapy would seem counter to progress in treatment, there is evidence that the socialization aspect of group, providing exposure to, and feedback from others within a safe environment, can foster gains in the SPD individual (Appel, 1974; Sperry, 2003) as well as provide fertile ground to build trust in others and move from an overly protective secluded style to one of interpersonal engagement. Of course, this is based upon the individual's level of isolation and pathology (Leszcz, 1989). Schizoid clients can be expected to attend groups regularly; they may experience some shame about attending, but can become a valuable part of the group process even though they may not be very active. Support is recommended to overcome issues of shame about group therapy and their role within the group. Support and explanation regarding the slow process of therapy, particularly for these individuals due to their limited participation, is very important (Yontef, 2001). Group can also be a safe environment in which to challenge beliefs that keep these individuals in the schizoid process, such as when the group challenges them to be more expressive. However, be aware that the group's anger or blaming may cause SPD individuals to get caught up in a "role lock" (Bogdanoff & Elbaum, 1978). A useful intervention to deal with role lock would be for SPD individuals to individualize responses to particular group members, increase awareness of avoidance strategies, be more here-and-now in attending to feelings, and self-monitor body responses (Yalom & Leszcz, 2005).

There is no available data on the frequency with which individuals with SPD marry; although rare, it does happen. As noted earlier, SPD, like all mental health disorders, exists on a continuum. Those with milder forms of SPD would have a greater likelihood of marrying. Marital therapy should focus on clarification and understanding to de-escalate confrontations, and it should explore vulnerabilities, the value of having needs, and the risk and reward of examining them (McCormack, 1989).

The schizoid individual is most likely to remain at home with his or her parents and, at the behest of family members, may be brought in for treatment. Family therapy can be an effective treatment modality and should address issues of familial tension and impatience on the part of the parents concerning the desire to have their child leave home and be more independent (Anderson, 1983).

Psychopharmacology

There are no controlled studies that examine the efficacy of medication to treat SPD (Crits-Christoph & Barber, 2002). There is some speculation that dopaminergic dysregulation underlies the cluster A symptoms that are related to schizophrenia, both the positive and negative (Siever & Davis, 1991). The schizoid individual is likely to show mainly negative symptoms of the schizophrenia spectrum or other psychotic disorders, as discussed earlier. Sadock and Sadock (2007) postulate that small dosages of antipsychotics, antidepressants, and psychostimulants may prove beneficial to "some patients" and that serotonergic medications may lessen the sensitivity to rejection, whereas benzodiazepines could attenuate interpersonal anxiety.

FILM AND POPULAR MEDIA EXAMPLES

Remains of the Day (1993) – James Stevens played by Anthony Hopkins

The English Patient (1996) – Count Laszlo de Almásy

Holden Caulfield, main character in Catcher in The Rye by J.D. Salinger

Author – J.D. Salinger

Author, *To Kill A Mockingbird* – Harper Lee

Famous Businessman – Howard Hughes

Famous Chess Player – Bobby Fischer

CHECKLIST: SCHIZOID PERSONALITY DISORDER

Below is a complete list to best identify and diagnose Schizoid Personality Disorder. DSM-5 (APA, 2013) criteria are first, followed by discernible components, and lastly, associated features.

❑ A pervasive pattern of detachment from social relationships and a restricted range of expression of emotions in interpersonal settings, beginning by early adulthood (age 18 or older) and present in a variety of contexts.*

❑ Neither desires nor enjoys relationships or human interaction, including being part of a family.*

❑ Almost always chooses solitary activities.*

❑ Has little, if any, interest in having sexual experiences with another person*

❑ Takes pleasure in few, if any, activities with other people.*

❑ Lacks close friends or confidants other than first-degree relatives.*

❑ Appears indifferent to the praise or criticism of others.*

❑ Shows emotional coldness, detachment, or flattened affect.*

❑ Does not meet criteria for schizophrenia spectrum or another psychotic disorder.

❑ No psychotic symptoms associated with a bipolar disorder or depressive disorder with psychotic features.

❑ Does not meet criteria for an autism spectrum disorder.

❑ Home life, growing up, that was highly structured and formal.

❑ Excessive masturbatory behavior.

❑ Difficulty expressing anger, even if provoked.

❑ Appears directionless without life goals.

❑ History of passive reaction to adverse situations, such as being laid off.

❑ Employment choice tends to be isolative, such as computer technician.

❑ History of brief psychotic reaction to prolonged stress. Psychotic episode typically lasts minutes to hours (not prolonged).

*distinguishing characteristics

THERAPIST CLIENT ACTIVITY

Use these probes to explore your SPD client's pathology and enhance socioeconomic functioning:

- ➤ What do you like best about being alone?
- ➤ What is the closest relationship you have ever had, with whom, and what was it about that person that you responded to?
- ➤ Where do you see yourself in 3, 5, or 10 years?
- ➤ If you had to be with one person, who would it be?
- ➤ Do you think there is a benefit in engaging more with others?
- ➤ Do other people have something to offer you?
- ➤ What is or was your most intimate relationship?
- ➤ Do you fantasize about sex with someone else, and if so, how would you describe it? (expect very logical and affectless responses)
- ➤ Do you think other people have benefit?
- ➤ When was the last time you felt happy?
- ➤ When was the last time you felt sad?
- ➤ What is your ideal job and why?
- ➤ How long do you think our sessions should last?
- ➤ How can I make therapy useful for you?
- ➤ How will you know this process has been beneficial for you?

CLIENT QUESTIONNAIRE

The following questions are to be given to your client to help him or her identify past challenges and provide guidance for treatment.

What is your earliest recollection? Please describe as much as you feel comfortable.

Describe, with as much detail as you feel comfortable, when you were hurt most by someone else:

Describe your closest friendship, and how would you classify that relationship now?

Provide three reasons to participate in treatment and identifiers of success (how will you know you have achieved these goals)?

Schizotypal Personality Disorder

This is that odd and peculiar individual you just cannot put your finger on. Schizotypal personality disorder (SZT) has its roots as a schizophrenia-spectrum disorder that developed out of the terms schizotype and schizotypal. The term schizotype was coined by Sandor Rado as an abbreviation of a schizophrenic genotype (Rado, 1953), which referred to the genetic makeup that predisposed an individual to schizophrenia. Schizotype is derived from a combination of the terms *schizo*phrenia and pheno*type* (Miller et al., 2004). However, even before Rado used the term, Kraepelin (1919/1971 as cited in Bollini & Walker, 2007) and Bleuler (1924) described relatives who were not psychotic, but possessed odd behavioral inclinations that were lasting and representative of schizophrenia. Meehl (1962) expanded on the definition and understanding of Rado's concept titled schizotypy to represent less overt expressions of aspects of schizophrenia. He further postulated four traits associated with the schizotype: cognitive slippage (mild thought disorder or associative loosening), social aversiveness, anhedonia, and ambivalence. He wrote that an individual with particular constitutional strengths, such as a high threshold for anxiety and stress, will be less likely to develop mental disease, but those that experience cognitive slippage or other aberrant neurological impairment are at a high risk for schizophrenia.

It has been postulated that 10% of those who carry the dominant schizotype gene will develop schizophrenia, whereas 90% of those individuals will have differing degrees of personality dysfunction (Meehl, 1990). The variability in premorbid and full presentation of schizophrenia continues to be researched. It has been found that those who develop schizophrenia experience premorbid signs, such as increased thought blocking, mental fatigue, visual illusions, misidentification of people, inability to focus attention, impaired comprehension of speech, and acute auditory perceptual abnormalities (Freedman & Chapman, 1973). It was not until 1980, with the third edition of the *Diagnostic and Statistical Manual of Mental Disorders* (APA, 1980) that SZT was introduced.

Schizotypal personality disorder was derived from the early, ill-defined schizoid and borderline personality disorders that were too broad in definition. A new diagnosis was needed that encompassed affective instability and schizophrenic-like symptoms (Sperry, 2003). However, a further complication was present and a distinction had to be made between borderline personality disorder (BPD) and SZT, as both exhibit thought disorder. Spitzer, Endicott, & Gibbon (1979) conducted a study with one group that consisted of individuals diagnosed with "borderline personality, borderline personality organization, and borderline schizophrenia" (Spitzer, Endicott, & Gibbon, 1979, p. 20) and the second group, a control group, was composed of individuals who were moderately to severely ill, but did not have a diagnosis of psychosis or fit into a borderline category. The findings of this study illustrated the difference between BPD and SZT by emphasizing the psychotic aspect of the latter disorder and assisted in defining SZT and BPD in the DSM-III, and solidified SZT as a characterological variant of schizophrenia (APA, 1980; Benjamin, 1996). Further distinction was made between BPD and SZT by McGlashan (1987) through statistical analyses that identified odd speech, paranoid ideation, and social isolation as characteristics of SZT, whereas core symptoms of unstable relationships, impulsivity, and self-defeating acts were associated with BPD.

From DSM-III (APA, 1980) to DSM-III-R (APA, 1987), only one criterion was added that focused on odd and eccentric behavior or appearance. Several research studies were conducted examining the link between SZT and schizophrenia (Battaglia et al., 1991; Condray & Steinhauer, 1992; Gruzelier & Raine, 1994; Torgersen et al, 1993; Webb & Levinson, 1993) that caused a debate about moving SZT from Axis II (personality disorders) to Axis I (clinical disorders), with the other psychotic disorders (Siever, Bernstein, & Silverman, 1991) in the DSM-IV. SZT remained on Axis II (personality disorders) as it is believed to be a set of behavioral inclinations. The criteria remained unchanged from the DSM-IV to the DSM-IV-TR, as no significant research findings have been presented to consider making changes (Bollini & Walker, 2007).

Though the criteria were not changed in the DSM-5 (APA, 2013), SZT is in two locations. It is now in the schizophrenia spectrum and other psychotic disorders and the personality disorder section. It is included in the schizophrenia spectrum and other psychotic disorders, "Because this disorder is consider part of the schizophrenia spectrum of disorders, and is labeled in this section of ICD-9 and ICD-10 as schizotypal disorder, it is listed in this chapter [schizophrenia spectrum and other psychotic disorders] and discussed in detail in the DSM-5 chapter 'Personality Disorders'" (APA, 2013, p. 90).

ETIOLOGY

Genetics continues to be a strong consideration when examining the etiology of SZT. Ericson and colleagues (2011) conducted a longitudinal study investigating the environmental and genetic etiology of schizotypal personality traits and found "moderate stability" as the adolescents matriculated and that genetic and non-shared environmental factors influence schizotypal trait development and expression. Kety and colleagues (1994) replicated a study originally conducted in 1968 in Denmark that examined biological and adopted relatives of schizophrenic adoptees. Results showed that SZT individuals are at a higher risk to develop SZT than control subjects, even without familial interaction with the schizophrenic relatives. The environment has also been found to play a key role. Berenbaum and colleagues (2003) found that experiencing childhood neglect increased the probability that females would experience SZT symptoms, more specifically exhibiting post traumatic stress disorder symptomatology, depression, dissociation, and poor ability to accurately identify their own emotions. This was not directly linked to SZT, but illustrated a strong relationship showing environmental influence. An example of a possible etiological process for SZT is shown below:

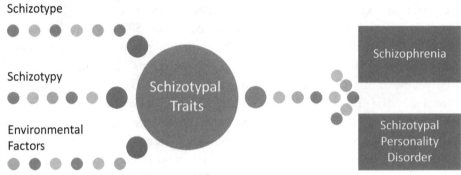

Possible Etiology of Schizotypal Personality Disorder

It has been found that individuals who had traumatic births tended to develop schizophrenia more often than those who experienced fewer birthing complications which resulted in SZT as compared to those who did not develop either disorder and experienced a "normal" birth without any disruption during birth or fetal development (Mednick, Parnas, & Schulsinger, 1987). Individuals who later develop SZT and schizophrenia show signs in childhood of greater social maladjustment, specifically more often in boys than girls, with a tendency for over-reactivity, less positive emotionality, greater passivity, disengagement, and hypersensitivity to criticism (Done, Crow, Johnstone, & Sacker, 1994; Olin, Raine, Cannon, Parnas, et al., 1997; Walker, Grimes, Davis, & Smith, 1993). When these individuals reach adolescence, adjustment problems including social withdrawal, irritability, negative affect, and noncompliance increase (Walker, Baum, & Diforio, 1998).

Benjamin (1996) proposed a set of hypotheses to account for the SZT individual's manner of functioning and relating to the world. The SZT child was punished by the parent for autonomous behavior that the parent was actually engaging in; Benjamin gives the example of the absent father who physically punishes the child for not staying home. The parent models illogical or "knowing" behavior so that even when the child is not present the parent "knows" something critical about the child and he or she is punished for it. Reality testing is undermined due to the incongruous nature of the punishment and behavior leading the adult SZT to imitate this "knowing" through claimed telepathy, ESP, or the ability to gather information about instances that will impact others.

The second aspect of the hypothesis is the disproportionate dependence on the SZT child to perform household tasks as though "life itself was at stake" (2002, p. 347). For example, the child is told that if he or she does not vacuum the house or do the laundry it would cause great stress and cause the parent to have a fatal heart attack or other debilitating reaction. The child is taught that if he or she does as requested, adverse consequences can be avoided. However, with such seemingly critical tasks being placed on the young child associated with looming threat and odd outcome, the child's reality is negated and ignored. The child learns how to control and defer into adulthood utilizing a paradoxical tendency to achieve power through deference to capricious actions and rituals. Due to this, the SZT individual remains detached from the world around him or her.

Benjamin's third hypothesis is that the SZT individual experienced a history of severe abuse that leads to a paranoid removal as an adult, and a tendency to identify with the aggressive parent. Typically, the SZT individual is highly restrained and not likely to act out, but does tend to possess a sense of vulnerability to feeling invaded and abused by outside forces, and as a result works hard to control anger. The final hypothesis discusses the SZT individual as being conflicted or blocked from leaving the home to connect with friends or for other purposes; being solitary provided a sense of safety. While in the home, the SZT child learns to avoid the aggressive parent and subsequent violent environment. This prevented the child, and later the adult, from learning and utilizing social skills. This removal from peer interaction and experiences outside the home reinforced the SZT individual's finding "safe haven" alone and encouraged the creation of his or her own world and fantasy.

PREVALENCE

The DSM-5 (APA, 2013) reports that SZT occurs between 0.6% in a Norwegian sample and 4.6% in the U.S. general population and 1.9% in clinical populations. The DSM-5, (APA, 2013) goes on to report that according to the National Epidemiologic Survey and Alcohol and Related Conditions (NESARC), the prevalence rate for SZT is approximately 3.1%. Lifetime prevalence rates from a national sample have been found to be 3.9%, with the greatest rate among men at 4.2% and women at 3.7%. There is an increased probability of SZT traits in black women, those with lower socioeconomic status, and those individuals who have experienced divorce, separation or widowhood (Pulay et al., 2009). A study conducted by McGlashan (2005) to assess the stability of DSM-IV diagnoses found that 83 of 571 (14.5%) participants met criteria for SZT using the Diagnostic Interview for personality disorders (Zanarini, Frankenburg, Chauncey, & Gunderson, 1987). For those diagnosed with SZT, the most common and trait-like criteria were paranoia, ideas of reference, odd beliefs, and unusual experiences. These aspects are presumed to represent milder variations of cognitive distortions of reality as seen in the schizophrenia spectrum and other psychotic disorders, but in SZT the disorder is less severe and only intermittently expressed as an outward coldness or oddness.

A study that used the International Personality Disorder Examination (IPDE) to determine DSM-IV and International Statistical Classification of Diseases and related Health Problems, 10th Revision (ICD-10) (World Health Organization, 1993) found a prevalence rate of 0.6% in the community (Samuels et al., 2002). Again, using the IPDE, SZT was diagnosed in 187 (3.3%) individuals from a sub-sample gathered from the National Comorbidity Survey Replication (NCS-R; Lenzenweger et al., 2007). Using the Structured Clinical Interview for DSM-IV-TR personality disorders (SCID-II) it was found that, out of a sample size of 644 youths from the Children in Community Study (Cohen & Cohen, 1995), 7 (1.1%) were diagnosed with SZT. It is believed that estimates for SZT are much higher due to the isolative nature of the disorder, and that prevalence could be as much as three to four times above current estimates for schizophrenia (Bollini & Walker, 2007). Though not all individuals with SZT develop schizophrenia, they are at a higher risk to develop it (Miller et al., 2002).

ATTACHMENT

Bowlby (1980) postulated that avoidant defenses can develop early on and include the exclusion of attachment- and threat-related content from consciousness and the creation of a broken or split mental system that precludes the development of a stable and coherent sense of identity. This describes the SZT individual very well and fits nicely into past theories already discussed on the etiology of SZT (Benjamin, 1996) Meehl, 1990; Miller et al., 2004). Positive symptoms, negative symptoms, and paranoia have been found to be associated with avoidant attachment (Berry, Barrowclough, & Wearden, 2008). Paranoia as a positive schizotypal signs was found to be predictive of attachment anxiety, but negative schizotypal signs were associated with both attachment anxiety and avoidance (Meins, Jones, Fernyhough, Hurndall, & Koronis, 2008). Tiliopoulos & Goodall (2009) examined a non-clinical sample to determine the relationship between SZT and attachment. Findings revealed that attachment anxiety, specifically social anxiety, may be more predictive of SZT than avoidant attachment as it tended to encompass both positive and negative symptomatology, whereas avoidance attachment was only associated with negative symptomatology.

	Thoughts of Self — Positive	Thoughts of Self — Negative
Thoughts of Partner — Positive	Secure comfortable with intimacy and autonomy	Preoccupied Preoccupied with relationships
Thoughts of Partner — Negative	Dismissive Dismissing of intimacy Strongly independent	Fearful Fearful of intimacy Socially avoidant

Attachment Styles of SZT

The model shown in this figure depicts attachment style and its four components based upon Bartholomew & Horowitz (1991, p. 227). Studies that utilize these four aspects of attachment to examine personality disorders have found in nonclinical samples a relationship between a fearful attachment style and several aspects of psychopathology and personality disorders, including SZT (Anderson & Alexander, 1996; Carnelley, Pietromonaco, & Jaffe, 1994; Diehl, Elnick, Bourbeau, & Labouvie-Vief, 1998; Onishi, Gjerde, & Block, 2001; Riggs et al., 2007). Using the Millon Clinical Multiaxial Inventory, Third Edition, the personality dimensions of high anxiety and/or deficient self-worth, which includes SZT, were associated with a negative self-model, but not the negative other-model that may show the SZT individual's tendency to focus inward and to be "out of touch" with reality and the world around him or her (Riggs et al., 2007). Anglin, Cohen, & Chen (2008) conducted a 20-year longitudinal study with a sample pulled from upstate New York counties and found that early maternal separation and longer duration of separation were highly associated with odd and eccentric behaviors and beliefs, suspiciousness, unusual perceptual experiences, and inappropriate affect over the lifetime; these aspects are central to SZT. SZT individuals possess a fearful-dismissing attachment style that is indicative of their negative view of self and others, using others to meet their needs and being cautious and dismissive of them as well (Sperry, 2003).

DIAGNOSIS

The criteria most commonly used to diagnose SZT are the nine listed below in Table 1 from the DSM-5 (APA, 2013):

TABLE 1: DSM-R DIAGNOSTIC CRITERIA FOR SCHIZOTYPAL PERSONALITY DISORDER
A. A pervasive pattern of social and interpersonal deficits marked by acute discomfort with, and reduced capacity for, close relationships as well as by cognitive or perceptual distortions and eccentricities of behavior, beginning by early adulthood and present in a variety of contexts as indicated by five (or more) of the following: (1) Ideas of reference (excluding delusions of reference) (2) Odd beliefs or magical thinking that influences behavior and is inconsistent with subcultural norms (e.g., superstition, belief in clairvoyance, telepathy, "sixth sense," or bizarre fantasies or preoccupations) (3) Unusual perceptual experiences, including bodily illusions (4) Odd thinking and speech (e.g., vague, circumstantial, metaphorical, or stereotyped speaking) (5) Suspiciousness or paranoid ideation (6) Inappropriate or constricted affect (7) Behavior or appearance that is odd, eccentric or peculiar (8) Lack of close friends or confidants other than first degree relatives (9) Excessive social anxiety that does not diminish with familiarity and tends to be associated with paranoid fears rather than negative judgments about self.
B. Does not occur exclusively during the course of schizophrenia, a bipolar disorder or depressive disorder with psychotic features, another psychotic disorder, or autism spectrum disorder.
Note: If criteria are met prior to the onset of schizophrenia, add "premorbid," i.e., "schizotypal personality disorder (premorbid)."

Consistent with all of the criteria listed in the DSM, these are not hard and fast rules of diagnosis but guidelines and criteria to make diagnoses, as individual differences will impact presentation and expression of SZT. The key criterion for diagnosing SZT is odd thinking and speech and behavior or appearance that is odd, eccentric, or peculiar (Allnutt & Links, 1996 as cited in Sperry, 2003). The first criterion, "ideas of reference (excluding delusions of reference)," pertains to the tendency of the individual to perceive events as meaningful when most others would see them as odd. The SZT individual further inaccurately interprets events in a manner that is unique and divergent from what others have experienced when encountering the exact same event. However it is important to note that the SZT's individualized interpretation is not based in delusion. Criterion two addresses odd or magical thinking that influences the individual's behavior and exists outside cultural expectations and norms. The individual who meets this criterion will wholeheartedly believe that he or she possesses paranormal abilities. In addition, the individual believes he or she influenced others' behavior or knew something specific was going to happen, and/or following an event that someone experienced, the SZT individual may tell that person he or she caused the incident to take place. It is important to take into account cultural, racial, and ethnic influences when assessing this criterion in the patient.

The third criterion pertains to unusual perceptual experiences, including bodily illusions. The individual in this case may present as though he or she is experiencing a hallucination and may believe that someone else is present in the room, though no one is there. This is one of the difficult aspects that confuse the diagnosis of SZT with that of the schizophrenia spectrum and other psychotic disorders, but the individual must meet five or more criteria, not just this one. The overlap with a schizophrenia spectrum disorder is further illuminated in the second criterion, which includes odd or magical thinking. This is similar in individuals who may have a schizophrenia spectrum disorder. In the latter case, the individual speaks in a way that is not consistent with the situation, but in contrast, the SZT individual is focused on the issue and not incoherent. He or she expresses ideas or thoughts differently than most others, or may talk as if "thinking out loud." Suspiciousness and paranoid ideation constitute the sixth criterion. The SZT individual is aware that other people avoid him or her, but has poor insight into why and is likely to ascribe malicious intent when encountering other peoples who tend to avoid him or her due to odd presentation, manner, or speech.

Criterion seven addresses the SZT individual's tendency to exhibit odd or peculiar appearance or behavior. He or she may wear clothing inappropriate to the setting, as in shorts on a cold day or a dirty, odd-fitting shirt. She may appear very different from others within the same environment, for example, wearing all white to a funeral. He or she may appear disheveled or have body odor or long, untrimmed fingernails with days-old caked dirt under them. Socially inappropriate and offensive behavior is also exhibited under this criterion: The SZT individual may laugh while others cry, pick his or her nose in a crowd, belch in a quiet restaurant, and sit on the floor when others are sitting on chairs. Other people are likely to find these individuals rude, weird, or "playing to their own tune." The SZT individual possesses poor insight into why others have issue with his or her presentation or behavior.

The eighth criterion pertains to the lack of close friends aside from first-degree relatives (typically parents and siblings). Due to the presentation of odd behavior and appearance, mixed with strange ideas of reference, those not in direct contact with the individual for a period of time keep their distance. The final criterion for SZT is the presence of intensive intractable social anxiety that does not diminish with greater familiarity and is likely to be associated with paranoid fears as opposed to negative judgments about self. The SZT individual has enough insight to recognize that others avoid him or her, but cannot ascertain why. This distance causes increased anxiety over time and, paradoxically, may even increase as familiarity grows; typically social anxiety lessens with familiarity. The increase in anxiety induces paranoid ideations. Whereas many individuals may engage in self-exploration to determine why others are distant and avoidant, the SZT person believes that others are conspiring against him or her and is likely to withdraw and fall deeper into isolative behaviors, as opposed to examining the root of the negative perceptions and judgments.

The DSM-5 (APA, 2013) describes associated diagnostic features for SZT. SZT individuals are not typically treatment-seeking and are likely to present for treatment of anxiety or depression, rather than SZT features or issues. Due to the stress associated with such a divergent view of the world and interacting within it, these individuals are likely to experience brief psychotic episodes (lasting minutes to hours) associated with stress. It is important to note that the psychotic episode is typically not long enough in duration to classify for an additional diagnosis of brief psychotic disorder which requires an episode lasting at least one day but less than one month or schizophreniform disorder which requires an episode lasting at least one month but less than six months, as depicted below.

Schizotypal Personality Disorder (psychotic episode minutes to hours)	Brief Psychotic Disorder (psychotic episode at least one day, less than one month)	Schizophreniform Disorder (psychotic episode at least one month, less then six months)

SZT Psychotic Episodes, Duration, and Disorders

SZT is best differentiated from delusional disorder, the schizophrenia spectrum and other psychotic disorders, and bipolar and depressive disorder with psychotic features by the presence of psychotic symptoms (e.g., delusions and hallucinations; APA, 2013).

In examining personality disorder components, Skodol and colleagues (2011) identified several prominent personality domains and traits for SZT and broke them down by schizotypy, detachment, or negative emotionality. They found that eccentricity, cognitive dysregulation, unusual perception, and unusual beliefs are all related to the schizotypy factor of SZT. The detachment of SZT is related to social withdrawal, restricted affectivity, and intimacy avoidance. Negative emotionality was found to be associated with SZT in the domain of suspiciousness and anxiousness. These components are proposed to be crucial to creating a clearer description and rationale for SZT. Additional criteria that have been found to be the most prevalent and stable for SZT include paranoid ideation and ideas of reference, whereas odd beliefs and unusual experiences have been found in other studies to be highly related to SZT (McGlashan, et al., 2005; Skodol et al., 2011).

Benjamin (1996) proposed a link between DSM criteria and the SZT individual's interpersonal history. Ideas of reference and suspiciousness are derived from chronic and invasive abuse mixed with assigned responsibility for the parent's life. Odd beliefs, unusual perceptions, and odd thinking and speech compose the thought disorder aspect of the SZT individual. The thought disorder is hypothesized to originate from early learning in which the SZT individual is encouraged to be separate and is told he or she had power to help or hurt another, but was not permitted to do this playing or interacting with other children. The subsequent social isolation caused the SZT individual to engage in fantasy and imagination resulting in the odd and unusual experiences inherent in the SZT individual's pathology. Due to a lack of social learning, isolation, deference, and detachment, in combination with magical and odd thinking, social anxiety, lack of close friends, and unusual perceptual experiences, the SZT individual developed inappropriate and constricted affect and is perceived as odd by others. Odd presentation and behavior stems from not receiving appropriate feedback on social norms.

(Millon, Grossman, Millon, Meagher, & Ramnath, 2004) proposed two subtypes of SZT:

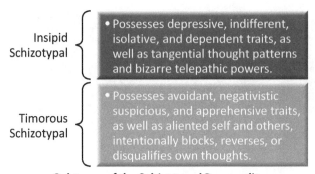

Insipid Schizotypal — • Possesses depressive, indifferent, isolative, and dependent traits, as well as tangential thought patterns and bizarre telepathic powers.

Timorous Schizotypal — • Possesses avoidant, negativistic suspicious, and apprehensive traits, as well as aliented self and others, intentionally blocks, reverses, or disqualifies own thoughts.

Subtypes of the Schizotypal Personality

These two subtypes add additional aspects to the SZT diagnosis and provide an integrative formulation by adding a greater degree of clarity to criteria that may assist in understanding this complex diagnosis.

The cognitive behavioral diagnostic formulation of SZT identifies expected patterns of automatic thoughts and cognitive distortions. Beck and colleagues (2004) identify suspicious or paranoid thoughts, ideas of reference, magical thinking, and illusions as automatic thoughts associated with SZT individuals. These include such thoughts as "why are they watching me?" "I know they aren't going to like me," and "they are going to hurt me." The cognitive peculiarities are most evident in speech that is circumstantial, odd, vague, or over-elaborated, in conjunction with constricted and inappropriate affect. Cognitive distortions are present as in the belief that a negative emotion is proof of a threatening or negative environment or situation, and explains his or her negative emotion(s).

Differential Diagnosis

The DSM-5 (APA, 2013) notes a high degree of similarity between SZT and delusional disorder, schizophrenia spectrum disorders, and bipolar or depressive disorder with psychotic features, which must be ruled out.

| Schizotypal Personality Disorder | Delusional Disorder | Brief Psychotic Disorder | Schizophreniform | Schizophrenia |

SZT and the Schizophrenia Spectrum

To diagnose an individual with SZT in addition to a schizophrenia spectrum disorder or bipolar or depressive disorder with psychotic features, the PD must have been present prior to the onset of the psychotic symptoms and the SZT traits must continue even when the psychotic symptoms remit (APA, 2013). In this instance, the SZT should be followed by "premorbid" when diagnosed.

As there is considerable overlap among personality disorders, SZT must be distinguished to be accurately diagnosed. Cluster A comprises paranoid personality disorder (PPD) and schizoid personality disorder (SPD), as well as SZT, so clarity is especially important. PPD and SPD are likely to present with social detachment and restricted affect, but not cognitive or perceptual distortions and eccentricity or oddness as evident in SZT. Avoidant personality disorder (APD) is characterized by limited close relationships. However the AVD individual will want interpersonal closeness but be restricted by fear of rejection, as opposed to the SZT individual who has no desire for such connection to others (APA, 2000). Individuals with narcissistic personality disorder (NPD) and SZT both tend to display suspiciousness, social withdrawal or social isolation but the NPD individual engages in these behaviors out of fear of having his or her inadequacies and imperfections exposed, whereas the SZT individual does not possess the required level of insight, in most cases, to note inadequacies and imperfections that could lead to embarrassment or social humiliation. Both the individual with borderline personality disorder (BPD) and the SZT individual may experience psychotic-like symptoms, but the BPD individual is usually responding to intense stress and affective changes and tends to exhibit derealization or depersonalization. Social Isolation in the BPD individual is typically due to interpersonal breakdowns as a result of anger and mood shifts, in contrast to the SZT who does not desire social contact or intimacy (APA, 2000).

Lenzenweger and colleagues (2007) found considerable overlap between SZT and SPD, AVD, and dependent personality disorder (DPD). PPD did not have a strong relationship to SZT even though they are within the same cluster. The strongest relationship was between SPD and SZT, which is not surprising as these two disorders share considerable traits: lack of emotional closeness, preference for solitude, lack of interest in sex, detachment, and clear divergent criteria such as oddness and eccentricity. AVD and SZT also share many similar traits, so overlap and comorbidity is not surprising. The AVD individual is socially isolative and withdraws, but for different reasons. A strong negative relationship was found between SZT and DPD, which is not too surprising as the DPD individual has an intensive desire to connect and depend on others, whereas the SZT person is solitary in activities and autonomous. Differential diagnosis and teasing out criteria that assist in accurately identifying SZT is a constant challenge for the clinician.

ASSESSMENT

There is a wide variety of assessment measures, both objective and projective, used to asses SZT. The Schizotypal Personality Questionnaire (SPQ; Raine, 1991) is a self-report measure derived from the DSM-III-R criteria (APA, 1987) and consists of 74 items. In 1995, an abbreviated version was devised (SPQ-B; Raine & Benishay, 1995) that covers the nine symptoms from the DSM-IV (APA, 1994). From the SPQ-B, a child version, called the SPQ-C, was devised in 2003 and developed for the Southern California Twin Project, but is unpublished. Fourteen of the original items from the SPQ-B were maintained, and eight items were adjusted for children (Raine & Baker, 2003, as cited in Ericson et al., 2011). The Minnesota Multiphasic Personality Inventory, Second Edition (MMPI-2) has been used to identify particular traits. Using the MMPI-2, SZT individuals are likely to display a 2-7-8 code (Edell, 1987). The 2-7-8 code type identifies significant turmoil and a tendency toward a "schizoid lifestyle" (Graham, 2011, p. 114). According to Graham (2011), these individuals also tend to feel anxious, fearful, depressed and hopeless, have problems concentrating, and often ruminate about suicide. Their affect is likely to be blunted or inappropriate. In females, there is a tendency towards more somatic complaints and eating issues. In inpatients, this code type has been associated with a history of sexual abuse. The SZT individual tends to be introverted, passive and lacking in social skills in relationships. Their tendency is to withdraw socially.

The Millon Clinical Multiaxial Inventory, Third Edition (MCMI) is likely to show elevations on S (schizotypal), 2 (avoidant), 7 (obsessive-compulsive), and 8A (passive-aggressive) when given to an individual with SZT (Edell, 1987; Choca & Van Denburg, 1997). Individuals with this type of response pattern are likely to be cognitively dysfunctional, detached, may appear self-absorbed and ruminative, behaviorally eccentric, perceived by others as odd, utilize a tangential communicative style, and be emotionally bland. In addition, they may be vigilant to their surroundings, possess a sense of unease, tend to overreact to minor events, be preoccupied with intrusive and disruptive thoughts, indirectly express negative emotion, and be passively compliant as well as resentful, moody, complaining, and chronically pessimistic. Counter-intuitively, they may be meticulous, have a high demand on self, fear disapproval, and be overly passive.

Huprich (2006) states that the Rorschach Inkblot Method is more effective than self-report, structured interviews, and forced-choice questionnaires due to being less sensitive to "the mild or moderate thought disturbances" (p. 121) found in SZT as these individuals may be able to mask their peculiar way of seeing the world or lessen their pathology due to the direct nature of such questions. Using the Rorschach, Exner (1986) found that schizophrenics and SZT individuals have some strong similarities, such as a preference for an internally focused coping style and an intensive determination to delay decision-making and be reserved in their behaviors.

CASE EXAMPLE – MALE

Troy is a 20-year-old male who recently graduated from high school; he was held back in the 3rd and 9th grade due to a reading disability. He spends the majority of his day in his room making papier-mâché body parts that he tends to paint in fluorescent colors. When asked about this he says that the "b-parts need to be bright so no one gets hurt." Troy has no friends and does not desire other human contact, but is "pleasant and polite" with his parents and siblings. He has worked at approximately three fast food restaurants and was fired from all three due to "doing things my own way." These included putting all the dirt on the floor while sweeping into a long straight line so he could determine the large and small pieces to place in the trash by size, neatly folding all of the hamburger wrappers into small diamond shapes to store "more efficiently," and washing only the upper portions of the window to dim the restaurant and add to the "edible ambiance." Troy has never been married and has never had a romantic relationship with another person. He has been seen by a psychiatrist on and off throughout his life starting at age 14. His first visit was due to his tying the family's cat to the exhaust pipe of his father's car to see if it would prevent it from starting. Troy reports anxiety in the form of constant fears of not being recognized and then injured, being mugged, and having his room vandalized by terrorists. He has taken a wide variety of medications throughout his life and he considers them "lightly to mildly effective."

Case Example – Female

Tanya is a 34-year-old female still living at home. She has never worked and has been going to college on and off since graduating from high school. Tanya has no friends and limits her contact with her family, preferring her room, which she refers to as her "outer sanctum of experience." When asked about this, she says her inner sanctum is much too private and valuable to share with others, even her parents. She is able to make an income by designing websites for various artists that respond to her postings on Craigslist. She was once nominated for an award for creativity for one of her websites, but this did not impact her in any way and she felt that the award was given to "everyone who makes websites for people who get paid and share their finger tapping." The term "finger tapping" refers to using the keyboard. Tanya does not have a bed and prefers to have no furniture in her room as she feels it lessens the "usable space to breathe." She has been to several mental health clinics and hospitalized one time at age 21 for auditory hallucinations that consisted of the "pod people who were trying to steal her vagina." This was in response to her parents' short-lived separation and family problems at that time within the household. Tanya is not permitted to use nail clippers as she will try and remove her toe and finger nails because she feels that hard skin is indicative of "serious malignant disease." She refuses all medication and prefers to wear only blue clothing as it matches the ocean and sky and is the "purest form of covering a person can buy." She buys her own clothing on the Internet, but demands it be shipped Federal Express and overnight "to prevent contamination from the other colors of the rainbow."

Treatment

Treatment of SZT is largely dependent upon the degree of social anxiety. Individuals with SZT tend to be treatment-rejecting and may only end up in therapy at the demand of a family member or due to hospitalization. Each patient/client must be seen as unique and treatment must be specialized to match symptom presentation (Miller et al., 2004). SZT individuals who have thought disorder issues are likely to gain great benefit from the combination of traditional therapy methods in conjunction with psychopharmacology. This will be discussed in the psychopharmacology section as individuals with SZT can benefit from therapy alone that addresses their ability to function consistently, as opposed to augmenting their personality to fit more into society's mainstream (Sperry, 2003).

There is no data to support using cognitive-behavioral therapy (CBT) to treat SZT (Miller et al., 2004). One of the difficulties with utilizing this modality with SZT individuals is that they are not bothered by their odd thoughts and peculiar presentation and lack insight into problems these may cause. (Beck et al., 2004) identify several methods of employing CBT with the SZT individual. The therapeutic relationship and trust between the client and therapist is central to progressive treatment, but when working with the SZT individual there must be clarity regarding the level of trust, and creating a "two column consideration of the evidence for and against the belief" is recommended (p. 154). The cost and benefit of various symptoms should be laid out to attenuate any ambivalence regarding lessening symptoms, such as paranoia. A critical component of CBT in working with SZT individuals is to create alternative approaches that may be more beneficial and useful.

Beck and colleagues (2004) list five methods to employ when working with SZT individuals. Collaborating and compromising on a problem and goal list is the first step. The list would include specific, measurable, and concrete goals, such as reducing social anxiety, decreasing drug use, stabilizing sleep patterns, and developing social relationships. This list dictates the course of therapy and even the slightest movement towards change or a decrease in symptomatology should be seen as significant. After approximately ten sessions, the list should be reviewed and assessed for accuracy and applicability.

The second method is to lessen anxiety. It is likely that the SZT individual will have a significant degree of anxiety, though it may not be as evident as in someone without a personality disorder. The basis for the anxiety should be ascertained, and the root examined to determine the best approach. For example, if it is based upon social dysfunction (unlikely in an SZT individual), or derived from fears related to persecution or suspiciousness, utilizing a Dysfunctional Thought Record could prove to be valuable in addressing anxiety and paranoia.

The third component is facilitating change in the individual's paranoid beliefs. The therapist needs to examine these beliefs from a goal-oriented perspective, which is to say that if the beliefs did not serve a need, they would not be present. What is the purpose of the paranoia and how does it serve him or her? The client should be encouraged to develop reality-based alternatives to suspicious and paranoid beliefs, and the benefit should be clearly stated.

The fourth method is employing behavioral experiments. It is crucial at this point in treatment to elicit internal motivation for change and enough that the individual wants to engage in change. Utilizing behavioral experiments helps to solidify change and, with a positive outcome, can assist in cementing long-term movement toward larger goals. The final step involves addressing the stigma of having a mental disorder and related problems. Educating the client on SZT and how it impacts his or her life is critical. Once at this stage of therapy, the client is prepared to challenge and address the issues in a more realistic manner. Connecting previous life experiences as the basis for his or her thinking and life experiences allows for greater change and lessening of stigma, as opposed to identifying it as part of his or her personality which makes it appear more firm and intractable, and less likely to change. At the conclusion of treatment, the maintenance goals should be addressed and delineated, as well as identifying potential triggers for relapse and effective coping mechanisms.

Interpersonal therapy for the treatment of SZT has been described by Benjamin (1996) and includes her five categories of correct response. The first and most critical is developing collaboration, and this sometimes calls for early termination of the session and allowing the client to feel efficacious within the therapeutic process. The therapist should respect the SZT individual's need for interpersonal distance and the tendency to feel humiliated. Caution regarding examining sensitive topics and delusions should be consistently employed by the therapist. The second step is to encourage pattern recognition of how the inappropriate placement of responsibility in an abusive situation in which he or she had no control influenced the belief in magical thinking. The SZT individual is likely to be aware of his or her history of abuse, will discuss it in detail, and is likely to have little to no affect regarding the abuse (Benjamin, 1996). A critical step at this point is to help the SZT individual to express empathy and sympathy for others who have also been abused. The therapist must be careful here not to inappropriately attack the vulnerability the SZT individual has to his or her abusers. Underlying emotions, such as guilt and pain, can be brought up and it is the therapist's responsibility to expect this and work within it to move the allegiance from the abuser to a more healthy self. If the therapist remains steadfast in caring and commitment to a positive change, it is hoped that the SZT individual will internalize this and move away from pathological social interactions and presentation.

The third step entails blocking maladaptive patterns carefully while maintaining the therapeutic relationship and respect for the client. It is here that the client is likely to terminate treatment due to feeling betrayed and humiliated, or perceiving the process as dangerous. A slow and methodological approach is key to success. Supporting the client to recognize reality distortions and consciously blocking psychotic thought processes through self-talk that is focused on the here-and-now is critical (Benjamin, 1996). Magical thinking should be examined for its probability and challenged for its lack in basis of fact; this is done in a careful, encouraging, and thoughtful manner so as to protect the client as well as challenge him or her. The fourth step is to strengthen the desire to let go of maladaptive patterns and define boundaries of self and others within a framework of trust. The therapist should connect fantasies, suicidal or otherwise, to underlying wishes for relief and provide greater opportunities for a different choice, which moves the client to the final stage, facilitating new learning. The SZT individual at this point is ready to engage in a reconstruction of his or her personality and new approach to the world in which they live. It is here that most therapies begin and routine therapeutic techniques can be used.

Group, marital, and family therapy have been used to treat SZT, though efficacy and outcome data is very limited or nonexistent. Group therapy can be utilized to build awareness of other people's fantasies and self-criticisms likened to the SZT individual and challenge the view that he or she is "unlikeable" (Stone, 1985). The shyness of the SZT individual can be effectively treated through group therapy, but paranoid ideations and suspiciousness can cause him or her to feel overwhelmed within the group setting and leave prior to adjusting and reaping benefit (Stone, 1985). Data on marital and family therapy with the SZT individual is not available, since the individual with SZT is likely to be single and avoid committed relationships (Sperry, 2003).

Psychopharmacology

It is hypothesized that dopamine antagonism is an effective treatment for the psychotic-like symptoms of SZT and, noting that it is a schizophrenia-spectrum disorder, antipsychotic medication may be beneficial as well (Koenigsberg et al., 2007). Buspirone, citalopram, dextroamphetamine and amphetamine, and methylphenidate have been found to effectively treat SZT and have a positive impact on self-report, peer interaction, and psychological assessment (Nathanson & Jamison, 2011). Utilizing the atypical antipsychotic risperidone, at a low dose, 25 individuals who were diagnosed with SZT using the DSM-IV-TR criteria were placed in a placebo-controlled double-blind study and rated using four measures: the Positive and Negative Syndrome Scale (PANSS), Schizotypal Personality Disorder Questionnaire (SPQ), the Hamilton Rating Scale for Depression (HAM-D), and the Clinical Global Impressions scale (CGI). Results showed a reduction in scores on the PANSS, SPQ, HAM-D, and CGI in the risperidone group (Koenigsberg et al., 2003). This result illustrates the beneficial use of a low-dose antipsychotic in individuals with SZT. This study is of particular benefit as it studied SZT individuals only.

Most studies that have focused on borderline personality disorder (BPD) and included individuals who met criteria for SZT as well (Koenigsberg et al., 2007). Three double-blind studies showed lessening of psychosis, anxiety, depression, aggression, and sensitivity to rejection with a low-dose antipsychotic compared to placebo (Cowdry & Gardner, 1988; Goldberg et al, 1986; Soloff, George, Nathan, Schulz, et al., 1989). Using the Structured Clinical Interview for DSM-III-R Disorder (SCID-II) seven of 11 individuals met criteria for SZT, though comorbid with BPD, and were prescribed olanzapine, an antipsychotic. Results showed a "significantly reduced" result on the global measures of the Brief Psychiatric Rating Scale (BPRS), Buss-Durkee Hostility Inventory (BDHI), Barratt Impulsivity Scale (BIS 11), Global Assessment of Functioning scale (GAF), and Hopkins Symptoms Checklist-90 (SCL-90) (Schulz, Camlin, Berry, & Jesberger, 1999). Antipsychotic and antidepressant medications are likely to be useful, in conjunction with psychotherapy, in the treatment of various aspects of SZT, such as ideas of reference, illusions, and depressive symptoms (Sadock & Sadock, 2007). It is clear from these studies that the SZT individual may benefit from antipsychotic and other medications, but as with all medication and treatment, efficacy must be assessed on a continual and routine basis.

FILM AND POPULAR MEDIA EXAMPLES

Taxi Driver (1976) – Travis Bickle, played by Robert DeNiro

The Apostle (1997) – Euliss "Sonny" Dewey, played by Robert Duvall

Willy Wonka & The Chocolate Factory (1971/2005) – Willy Wonka, played by Gene Wilder in 1971 and Johnny Depp in 2005

Harry Potter movies (2004, 2007, 2011) – Professor Sybil Trelawney, played by Emma Thompson

CHECKLIST: SCHIZOTYPAL PERSONALITY DISORDER

Below is a complete list to best identify and diagnose Schizotypal Personality Disorder. DSM-5 (APA, 2013) criteria are first, followed by discernible components, and lastly, associated features.

- ❑ A pervasive pattern of social and interpersonal deficits marked by acute discomfort with, and reduced capacity for, close relationships as well as by cognitive or perceptual distortions and eccentricities of behavior, beginning by early adulthood and present in a variety of contexts*
- ❑ Ideas of reference (excluding delusions of reference)*
- ❑ Odd beliefs or magical thinking that influences behavior and is inconsistent with subcultural norms (e.g., superstition, belief in clairvoyance, telepathy, "sixth sense" or bizarre fantasies or preoccupations)*
- ❑ Unusual perceptual experiences, including bodily illusions*
- ❑ Odd thinking and speech (e.g., vague, circumstantial, metaphorical or stereotyped speaking)*
- ❑ Suspiciousness or paranoid ideation*
- ❑ Inappropriate or constricted affect*
- ❑ Behavior or appearance that is odd, eccentric or peculiar*
- ❑ Lack of close friends or confidants other than first-degree relatives*
- ❑ Excessive social anxiety that does not diminish with familiarity and tends to be associated with paranoid fears rather than negative judgments about self*
- ❑ Criteria for a schizophrenia spectrum disorder or other psychotic disorder is not met
- ❑ Absence of a bipolar disorder or depressive disorder with psychotic features
- ❑ Criteria for an autism spectrum disorder is not met
- ❑ No identifiable physiological effects of another medical condition
- ❑ Tangential thought patterns
- ❑ Believes he or she has bizarre telepathic powers
- ❑ Avoidant, negative, and apprehensive traits

*distinguishing characteristics

THERAPIST CLIENT ACTIVITY

Use these probes to explore your SZT client's odd and eccentric views and presentation that are central to the pathology and enhance the socioeconomic dysfunction.

➤ Do you think people around you are talking about you?

➤ Do you feel you can read other people's minds, and if so, how does it feel to be able to do that?

➤ Do people stop talking or act differently when you enter the room?

➤ To what degree do you feel your thoughts influence others?

➤ Have rules ever been changed for you?

➤ Have you ever sensed some unusual force or presence around you?

➤ How have you influenced others just by willing it or thinking about it?

➤ Do you feel that special messages are coming just to you from the TV, newspaper, etc.?

➤ Do you tend not to give information to others because you feel it may be used against you?

➤ Do you feel that others are trying to take advantage you; if so, how?

➤ Whom do you trust most and why?

➤ Where do you feel safest?

➤ Do other people make you feel anxious or nervous?

➤ When and where do you feel most relaxed?

CLIENT QUESTIONNAIRE

The following questions are to be given to your client to help him or her identify past challenges and provide guidance for treatment.

What is your earliest recollection? Please describe as much as you feel comfortable.

What you think would help you interact best with others?

Can you draw a picture of yourself in relation to the world around you?

Can you make two lists of things that would make you most happy; include one that only pertains to you and on the other list include at least one other important person in your life.

You	Important Other

Antisocial Personality Disorder

Antisocial personality disorder (ASPD) pertains to an individual who does not conform to rules and regulations, regardless of setting, and tends to act out for benefit to self without care or thought for others. ASPD can be examined from many angles and has been referred to using alternate terms such as sociopathy and psychopathy interchangeably (e.g., Stout, 2005). Sociopathy and psychopathy have been seen as variants of a broader disorder of acting-out and misbehavior known as ASPD (Lykken, 1995). For the purpose of this chapter, ASPD will be seen as a broad disorder, with sociopathy and psychopathy as variants.

Going back to the 1800s, Pinel (1806) noted that individuals who possessed "insanity without delirium" would act out repeatedly toward themselves or others though no cognitive impairment existed. There is further documentation of individuals who were not cognitively impaired, but possessed socially deviant behaviors and willfully engaged in immoral and abnormal conduct (Rush, 1835). This can be seen as the beginning of a clinical/medical approach to the ASPD individual. Research and psychiatric exploration of these individuals continued and are best described by Henry Maudsley (1874), a British psychiatrist: "as there are persons who cannot distinguish certain colours, having what is called colour blindness, so there are some who are congenitally deprived of moral sense" (p. 11). The term "moral insanity" was often used, but was changed to "psychopathic inferiority" in the *Short Textbook of Psychiatry PsychopathischeMinderwertigkeite* by J.L.A. Koch. Gutmann, (2006) also expanded the understanding of those engaged in deviant behavior into congenital and acquired typologies with varying severity. He used the term "psychopathic inferiority" in reference to the mental capabilities, regardless whether acquired or congenital, which caused the individual to be not in full control of his or her mental condition. Koch devised three subcategories that are listed below (Gutmann, 2006):

Psychopathic Disposition	Psychopathic Taint	Psychopathic Degeneration
• Tension and high sensitivity. Mildest form eventually turning into "normality."	• Peculiar, egocentric, and highly impulsive.	• Seen mostly in impaired cognitive functioning or in moral behavior, or both. Believed to turn to psychosis.

Three Sub-categories of Psychopathy

From Koch's work, the field was further expanded and continued to grow. Cesare Lambroso postulated that immoral behavior is housed in the brain within the "born" criminal and he further identified physical traits, such as retreating forehead and protruding lower jaw; and emotional traits, such as emotionally hyperactive, easily angered, and lacking in humane feelings (Lombroso, 1911).

Adolf Meyer, in line with Koch's theory in a general sense, believed that neurosis was derived from the mind and not physiology (Meyer, 1904). He worked to draw clear distinctions between genetic or physical aspects and psychogenic aspects. This line of thinking continued in American psychiatry for some time. The term "inferiority" was later dropped, as it tended to be disparaging, and replaced by "constitutional psychopathic state" and "psychopathic personality" as well-known designations in the early part of the 20th century (Millon, Simonsen, & Birket-Smith, 1998). Emil Kraepelin (1904) used the term "psychopathic personalities" and devised four groups of individuals: (1) "Morbid liars and swindlers" who were charming, deceitful, and fraudulent con artists, who lacked loyalty to others and responsibility; (2) "criminals by impulse" who were urged by the inability to control themselves and were arsonists, rapists, and kleptomaniacs; (3) "professional criminals" who appeared well-mannered and socially appropriate, but implicitly calculating, manipulative, and self-serving; and, (4) "morbid vagabonds" who were aimless, lacking in self-confidence, and irresponsible. In the next and final edition of *Psychiatry: A Textbook*, Kraepelin (1915) revised his psychopathic personalities, removing "professional criminal" and added four types: excitable, eccentric, antisocial, and quarrelsome. The antisocial and quarrelsome types, which were representative of an individual who is callous, destructive, socially removed, and lacking connection to others, are very similar to the diagnostic criteria in the DSM.

The first edition of the DSM (DSM-I; APA, 1952) lists four separate disorders that can be seen as aspects of the current singular diagnosis, ASPD. Sociopathic personality disturbance encompasses individuals who are "ill primarily in terms of society and of conformity with the prevailing cultural milieu, and not only in terms of personal discomfort and relation to other individuals" (p. 38). This diagnosis is seen, in this volume, as being "symptomatic of severe underlying personality disorder, neurosis, or psychosis, or occurs as the result of organic brain disease" (p. 38). The global sociopathic personality disturbance can be diagnosed with further definitions of antisocial and dissocial reactions, and sexual deviation, which is meant to supply greater clarification. Antisocial reaction would be diagnosed if the individual is continually in trouble and does not alter behavior based upon experience or punishment. The DSM-I identifies this clarifier as being previously classified as "constitutional psychopathic state" and "psychopathic personality," referring back to the work of Kraepelin (1904) and Meyer (1904). The dissocial reaction pertains to individuals who are callous and hedonistic, lack in responsibility, but who may be loyal and only show allegiance to their criminal behavior or code. This term is related to "pseudosocial personality" and "psychopathic personality with asocial and amoral trends" (p. 38). The final clarifier, sexual deviation refers to "psychopathic personality with pathological sexuality" (p. 39) and includes such behaviors as rape and sexual assault.

In the DSM-II (APA, 1968) sociopathic personality disturbance is no longer a diagnosis, but rather a global term only with antisocial personality first appearing.

This version borrows from Cleckley's (1941) description of psychopathy and describes individuals who are "unsocialized and whose behavior pattern brings them repeatedly into conflict with society" (APA, 1968, p. 43). It goes on to describe an inability to be loyal to groups, individuals, and social values, and refers to one who is callous, irresponsible and selfish, but feels no guilt and does not learn from experience. It adds a specifier in that "a mere history of repeated legal or social offenses is not sufficient enough to justify this diagnosis" (p. 43). A problem arises with the DSM-II in that the criteria were being applied unreliably within research and clinical settings so that the validity of the diagnosis for the manual was in question (Spitzer, Endicott, & Robins, 1975). Due to this, the authors of the DSM-III (APA, 1980) developed more specific criteria that were created for research purposes by Feighner and colleagues (1972) and Spitzer, Endicott, and Robins (1978).

The DSM-III (APA, 1980) developed criteria addressing ASPD's severity and chronicity and refers to the individual's irresponsibility, impulsiveness, irritability, aggressiveness, and lack of remorse. The criteria were successful in providing improved levels of reliability, but problems arose regarding behaviorally specific criteria that were included in the other personality disorders (Widiger & Trull, 1987). Criticism regarding the DSM-III criteria centered around its lack of inclusion of the psychopathy features identified by Cleckley (1941), such as low anxiousness, arrogance, lack of remorse and empathy, and superficial charm (Widiger, 2006). In the DSM-III-R (APA, 1980), in response to the criticism, lack of remorse was added to the criterion set (Widiger, Frances, Spitzer, & Williams, 1988).

The DSM-IV differed from the DSM-III-R in that an ASPD diagnosis must be preempted by evidence of conduct disorder with onset prior to 15 years of age. In developing the criterion sets for the DSM-IV (APA, 1994) two aspects were considered: greater emphasis on traits of psychopathy and simplifying the criteria without changing the diagnosis, in addition to deleting two criteria, parental irresponsibility and failure to sustain a monogamous relationship for more than one year, which did not adversely affect diagnostic reliability (Widiger et al., 1996). With a strong emphasis on research outcome data, ASPD criteria in the DSM-IV continued to receive criticism stating that psychopathy was not sufficiently addressed and that a call to study psychopathy as a separate construct was merited (Newman & Brinkley, 1998). The DSM-IV-TR (APA, 2000) only updated the associated features to clarify that aspects that are part of the traditional concept of psychopathy may be more predictive of recidivism based on the setting, such as prison, where criminal acts are highly likely to be more non-specific. The DSM-5 (APA, 2013) criteria for ASPD were not changed from its predecessor, DSM-IV-TR (APA, 2000).

ETIOLOGY

Antisocial personality disorder has many hypothesized roots; it is typically recognized as being derived from a myriad of occurrences throughout the individual's life. The transmission of antisocial behavioral disorders has to consider both nature and nurture without bias toward a greater influence of either one (Cloninger, Reich, & Guze, 1978). The origin of ASPD has been examined using twin, family, and adoption studies, with separation of adopted twins being the greatest paradigm to separate genetic and biological influences. Abundant evidence shows that antisocial spectrum disorders and psychopathic traits are inheritable and that genetic or neurological factors play as important a role as shared and non-shared environmental aspects (Cadoret, Cain, & Crowe, 1983; Rhee & Waldman, 2002; Walsh & Wu, 2008).

Several studies have found neurological markers for ASPD and psychopathy. Raine, Lee, Yang, and Colletti (2010) examined those with cavum septum pellucidum (CSP), an indicator of neural maldevelopment in the limbic system, and those without. They used anatomical magnetic resonance imaging in a community sample of individuals with ASPD and psychopathy and found abnormal neurodevelopment. They further hypothesized that limbic and septal structural abnormality is indicative of limbic neural maldevelopment and predisposes an individual to antisocial spectrum behaviors. Verona, Sprague, and Sadeh (2012) examined event-related brain potentials in individuals identified with psychopathy or ASPD and controls during an emotional-linguistic go/no-go task, using finger press when emotionally neutral (e.g., lamp), general negative (e.g., poison), and offender-relevant (e.g., scum) words were presented. Results showed that control group individuals showed an appropriate prioritization of inhibition over emotional processing, whereas the psychopathy group had blunted processing of negative emotional words irrespective of inhibitory demands, and the ASPD group illustrated increased processing of negative emotional words in both trials, which is indicative of a failure to control negative emotional processing when inhibitory control is needed.

Twin studies are often used to illustrate the significant role genetics has on an ASPD or psychopathic individual. Eysenck & Eysenck (1978) found that 55% of monozygous (MZ) twins were similar for criminal conduct, whereas dizygous (DZ) twins accounted for only 13%. Utilizing a sample from the Twin Study of Child and Adolescent Development, Forsman and colleagues (2010) found that antisocial behavior in early adulthood was highly associated with psychopathic personality in adolescence. Genetic variance accounted for 2.9% of adult antisocial behavior in psychopathic personality. When reared in separate environments, psychopathic personality contributed to antisocial behavior, but to a lesser degree (1.2%). Adolescent psychopathic personality was genetically related to adult rule-breaking behavior (6.7%) but not as significantly soto adult aggressive behavior (1.8%). The authors conclude that these results illustrate a strong pathway between psychopathic personality and antisocial behavior, placing those predisposed to a higher degree of risk involvement in antisocial behavior. Several studies have shown a developmental pathway from attention-deficit/hyperactivity Disorder (ADHD) hyperactive-impulsive type or combined type to oppositional defiant disorder (ODD) in preschool, early-onset conduct disorder CD, typically in adolescence, and late adolescent and adult substance use disorders (SUDs), which predisposes the individual to ASPD and antisocial spectrum disorders (Kim-Cohen et al., 2003; Loeber, DeLamatre, Keenan, & Zhang, 1998; Loeber, Green, Keenan, & Lahey, 1995; Loeber & Hay, 1997;

Lynam, 1998; Ridenour et al., 2002). Thehypothesized pathway to ASPD is depicted below:

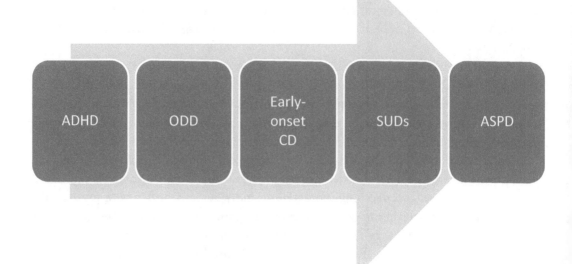

Hypothesized Pathway of ASPD Development

Studies have found that individuals who are later identified as antisocial have experienced childhood abuse or neglect and, as infants, were difficult to soothe and comfort (Meloy, 1988; Thomas & Chess, 1977). Family environmental factors, such as single-parent families and poverty, could possibly influence the expression of antisocial behaviors in siblings or other relatives (Carey & Goldman, 1997; Glueck & Glueck, 1950). Neighborhood violence and deviant peer group affiliation have also been found to contribute to ASPD and antisocial spectrum behaviors (Dishion, McCord, & Poulin, 1999; Ingoldsby, 2002). Personality features, such as stress reaction and harm avoidance, have a weak relationship when analyzing mating conditions. However, robust results have been found with self-reports of specific antisocial actions, such as theft and fraud, and peer delinquency (Krueger, 1998). This result shows the importance of the propagation of antisocial traits through connecting or lack of aversion to partnering with an individual who is not deterred by antisocial spectrum behavior or ASPD.

Benjamin (1996) proposes a pathogenic hypothesis for the development of ASPD. She postulates that the ASPD individual comes from a "broken home" filled with alcoholism, violence, and parental neglect. However, she clarifies that these factors alone, or in subtle combination, would not fully account for the development of ASPD. She notes, mitigating factors, such as a caring mother, that may to some degree protect against harshness and possible abuse from an alcoholic or abusive father, may perhaps lessen the expression of ASPD features. From the interpersonal standpoint, the neglect of the parent toward the child at crucial developmental stages is critical. Economic standing would not factor into the degree of parent neglect, as ASPD individuals have been derived from all socioeconomic levels and "walks of life." Benjamin cites a finding by Pollock, Briere, Schneider, and Knop (1990), who conducted a study with 131 participants with alcoholic fathers and 70 controls to attempt to predict antisocial spectrum behaviors. The results showed that males whose fathers were alcoholics did not engage in more antisocial acts, but that those who experienced physical abuse reported more frequent violent acting-out to express disagreement. Uncontrolled aggression is derived from a lack of attachment to others. Benjamin cites Harlow and Harlow's work with rhesus monkeys (1962) which showed uncontrolled hostility due to a lack of attachment even in monkeys who never actually had been treated aggressively. Violent acting-out in the ASPD individual is seen as a learned behavior. Benjamin (1996) reports that as the child sees his father violently attack his mother, he internalizes these behaviors and is at a greater likelihood to imitate such behavior. The ASPD individual internalizes parental abandonment and neglect, fails to learn self-care, and develops no awareness of others due to a failure to be taught to do so. An effect of their not having learned to consider others and their feelings is an inability to control their behavior, especially during a violent attack, as well as the ability to be emotionally removed when exploiting others.

Benjamin (1996) proposes that ASPD individuals protect their autonomy due to inconsistent control by the parent, which could be due to intervals of sobriety or physical presence and attempts to enforce rules that are typically ignored. This inconsistency creates the need in the ASPD individual to stay distant, because if he or she does not they are subject to "arbitrary control." However, the ASPD individual internalizes this controlling and acts it out in his or her relationships and encounters with others. The modeling of inept caring by the ASPD individual's parent results in his or her doing the same, and in combination with the desire for control, he or she develops methods to "con" or trick others into seeing him or her as helpful and possibly caring, but in the end only victimize and take advantage. The end result of these developmental experiences is the creation of an individual who possesses a strong need for control, is detached, and exploitive of others to meet his or her own needs and goals.

As evidenced by the research discussed previously, ASPD, psychopathy, and antisocial spectrum behaviors have various causal attributes. The one that is certain is that as crime and aggression toward others increase, mental health professionals will encounter these individuals more readily. But how prevalent are these disorders?

PREVALENCE

Psychopathy has been found to have a lower prevalence rate (0.5–1.0%) than ASPD (Hare, 1996, 1999). The DSM-IV-TR (APA, 2000) estimated ASPD to be prevalent in approximately 2% in the general population, with 3% among males and 1% among females. Within clinical settings, the rate is reported to range from 3% to 30%, which is dependent upon the characteristics of the sample that is derived. To account for the gender difference, it is hypothesized that men are traditionally encouraged to be aggressive whereas females are not (Patrick, 2007). ASPD tends to be more prevalent within forensic settings than in the community. This is due to the criterion set of ASPD being seen as biased toward "criminally-deviant behaviors that most individuals who run into serious trouble with the law will be diagnosed with [ASPD], even though such individuals vary widely in the expression of their deviance and in the underlying variance of it" (Patrick, 2007, p. 120). Patrick goes on to describe this misdiagnosis as the ASPD "wastebasket," due to a wide variety of deviant individuals being lumped together without specific regard for history of offense, degree of violence, or other critical aspects. Within forensic or prison settings, the prevalence of ASPD has been found to range from 50% to 80% (Hare, 2003), which goes back to Patrick's "wastebasket" label. He contends that this finding is too extreme and nonspecific and that ASPD should be considered a more "broad trait factor." When more stringent methods are applied, such as using the Hare Psychopathy Checklist, Revised (PCL-R), 15% of inmates in a North American prison are identified as psychopaths.

Research findings on psychopathy should not simply be applied to ASPD individuals, and those who use the DSM criteria must expend effort to discriminate ASPD from psychopathy (Hare, 1996; Rogers, Salekin, Sewell, & Cruise, 2000). Psychopathy, as defined by a PCL-R high score (30 or above), has been found to be present in approximately 15% of male prisoners, 10% of forensic patients, 7% of female prisoners, and 1% of those involuntarily committed to psychiatric centers (Cunningham,1998; Hare, 2003). Eaton and colleagues (2012) utilized a national sample to determine gender differences in prevalence rates for common mental disorders. DSM-IV diagnoses were made based upon results from the Alcohol Use Disorder and Associated Disabilities Interview Schedule – DSM-IV Version (AUDADIS) (Grant, Harford, Dawson, & Chou, 1995) that includes ASPD as a diagnostic consideration. Results showed a lifetime prevalence of 1.9% for females and 5.5% for males. The DSM-5 (APA, 2013), reports prevalence rates of ASPD between 0.2% and 3.3%, with a rate greater than 70% being found in "substance abuse clinics, prisons, or other forensic setting" (APA, 2013, p. 661). The DSM-5 goes on to state that prevalence is also higher within lower socioeconomic status individuals or those with adverse sociocultural factors.

ATTACHMENT

As previously noted in this chapter, individuals with ASPD tend to grow up in homes fraught with maltreatment of varying degrees (Benjamin, 1996; Meloy, 1988; Thomas & Chess, 1977) and have been shown to thwart secure attachment (Alexander, 2009; Bowlby, 1989). The living environment of neglect, disorganization, and instability has been found to be a strong component of the anxious-resistant pattern of attachment (Ainsworth, Blehar, Waters, & Wall, 1978). Bowlby (1944) wrote about 14 children who he deemed as "affectionless" that were characterized by "their remarkable lack of affection or warmth of feeling for anyone" (p. 23). This group did not respond to either kindness or punishment; some were gang-affiliated, glib or superficial in their interactions, aggressive or bullies. Bowlby goes on to define them as "delinquent characters" (p. 25) and as a separate identification class from the other participants in the study. What Bowlby was examining, within the construct of attachment, was the fledgling psychopath, though he does not use this exact term. Meloy (1988, 1992) postulated the notion of a "biopsychoanalytic" concept that states that without normal attachment, greater psychological identification with others and the internalizing of values is not possible.

It has been found that the ability to form an emotional bond, such as attachment, is suggestive of a less severely psychopathic criminal as compared to the more extreme cases of the ASPD individual and the genuine psychopath (Fonagy et al., 1997; Frodi, Dernevik, Sepa, Philipson, & Bragesjö, 2001; Meloy, 2003). Using the Rorschach and the Exner scoring system, attachment deficits were found in 88% of children diagnosed with conduct disorder (CD), 86% of adolescents diagnosed with CD, 71% of antisocial female inmates, and 91% of ASPD male inmates who were also identified as primary psychopaths (Gacono & Meloy, 1991; Gacono & Meloy, 1997; Smith, Gacono, & Kaufman, 1997; Weber et al., 1992). Anxious attachment has been found in individuals with ASPD and psychopathy in many studies (Bekker, 2007; Gacono, 1992; Weber, Meloy, & Gacono, 1992). Mack, Hackney, and Pyle (2011) examined the relationship between attachment and psychopathic traits using 209 college students who were assessed on the Experiences of Close Relationships-Revised (ECR-R; Fraley, Waller, & Brennan, 2000) questionnaire to assess attachment, and the Levenson Self-Report Psychopathy Scale (LSRP; Levenson, Kiehl, & Fitzpatrick, 1995) to assess psychopathic traits. Results showed that individuals who were high in attachment avoidance and attachment anxiety scored higher on primary psychopathic traits, including both interpersonal and affective psychopathic traits (inheritable affective deficits), and participants who were high in attachment anxiety and high in attachment avoidance had higher secondary psychopathy scores (environmentally acquired). Attachment and ASPD and psychopathy remain complex constructs to study, but it is clear that they are important in understanding the ASPD diagnosis.

DIAGNOSIS

The criteria most commonly used to diagnose ASPD are the seven listed below in Table 1 from the DSM-5 (APA, 2013):

TABLE 1: DSM-5 DIAGNOSTIC CRITERIA FOR ANTISOCIAL PERSONALITY DISORDER
A. There is a pervasive pattern of disregard for and violation of the rights of others occurring since age 15 years, as indicated by three or more of the following: (1) Failure to conform to social norms with respect to lawful behaviors as indicated by repeatedly performing acts that are grounds for arrest (2) Deception, as indicated by repeatedly lying, use of aliases, or conning others for personal profit or pleasure (3) Impulsiveness or failure to plan ahead (4) Irritability and aggressiveness, as indicated by repeated physical fights or assaults (5) Reckless disregard for safety of self or others (6) Consistent irresponsibility, as indicated by repeated failure to sustain consistent work behavior or honor financial obligations (7) Lack of remorse, as indicated by being indifferent to or rationalizing having hurt, mistreated, or stolen from another
B. The individual is at least age 18 years.
C. There is evidence of conduct disorder with onset before age 15 years.
D. The occurrence of antisocial behavior is not exclusively during the course of schizophrenia or bipolar disorder.

Reprinted with permission from the *Diagnostic and Statistical Manual of Mental Disorders, Fifth Edition*, (Copyright ©2013). American Psychiatric Association. All Rights Reserved.

Consistent with all of the criteria listed in the DSM, these are not hard and fast rules of diagnosis but guidelines and criteria for making diagnoses, as individual and cultural differences will impact presentation and expression of the ASPD. The first criterion pertains to the individual who engages in behaviors well outside simple social norm violation, such as smoking in a restricted area. His or her behavior is a significant offense, such as breaking into and entering a home, assault with a weapon, or murder. Individuals with ASPD do not always commit physical or overtly heinous crimes, but some carry out economic crimes that can impact millions of people. Corporate executives who embezzle millions or billions could fall under this criterion.

Criterion two includes the pathological liar or con-man or woman who makes someone believe that by giving them their personal or private information they will benefit, but only lose in the end. The individual who meets this criterion is not who he or she says they are. The third criterion is related to the difficulty in controlling behavior and not fully grasping its consequences. As a result, he or she continues to get into legal problems, physical altercations, or financial straits. Criterion four is related to the individual's difficulty controlling his or her temper and the tendency to engage in physical violence, typically to resolve stress or tension. Due to the lack of less violent alternatives, in his or her eyes, the ASPD individual is likely to assault and intimidate through whichever means will help him or her achieve the end goals.

The component of disregarding self and others to his or her own benefit is the central point in criterion five. This behavior typically manifests by the ASPD individual's performing reckless or violent acts to meet his or her needs. An example would be the kidnapper who has taken someone from his or her life, without regard to how that person feels or long-term impacts. Engaging in sensation-seeking behavior falls under this criterion and includes cases where the individual is seeking stimulation in an adventurous and reckless manner, such as drag racing, unsafe sexual acts, and drug abuse. The sixth criterion pertains to the individual's tendency to not follow through and not be dependable. This behavior adversely impacts work and social relationships. He or she will have many jobs, typically of short duration, and when asked why a job was lost, the response will deflect responsibility to the business owner or manager. In addition, these individuals are likely to default on loans, business deals, or any agreement made. The final criterion is associated with the lack of remorse following an act that has negatively affected another person. The impetus guiding the ASPD individual's behavior is the attainment of his or her goal, regardless of who is harmed along the way. The drug dealer who sells to elementary school-aged children would meet this criterion. A typical response when asked why, would be: "If their parents were looking out for them, they wouldn't need to get high. I only provide a service. No business, no need for the service."

The DSM-5 (APA, 2013) reports additional, more atypical, features of ASPD. The ASPD individual may have an inflated view of himself or herself, and possess narcissistic components. Due to this expanded feeling of self-worth, he may feel that particular work is beneath him. She is likely to be strongly opinionated and may present as glib or charming, and use "four-dollar words" to impress others into believing she is highly intelligent. The ASPD individual may be exploitive and unfaithful in his or her sexual relationships, irresponsible as a parent, and may not be self-supporting, becoming homeless or spending time in prisons. The ASPD individual is at a greater probability of dying by violent means, as compared to individuals in the general population.

In examining personality disorder components, Skodol and colleagues (2011) identified several prominent personality domains and traits for ASPD and psychopathy and broke them down by antagonism and disinhibition. Traits under antagonism include callousness, aggression, manipulativeness, hostility, deceitfulness, narcissism, and oppositionality. The disinhibition traits were irresponsibility, recklessness, and impulsivity. These traits were examined to differentiate ASPD and psychopathic traits from the other personality disorders to provide greater specificity in classification.

Millon and colleagues (2004) have identified five subtypes of ASPD, which are shown below:

Nomadic	Malevolent
(schizoid, avoidant features)	(sadistic, paranoid features)
Feels jinxed, doomed, and cast aside. Tends to be a vagrant, misfit, and vagabond.	Belligerent, resentful, vicious, brutal, desires revenge, callous, and guiltless.

Covetous	Risk-Taking
(variant of "pure" pattern)	(histrionic features)
Feels intentially denied and deprived. Envious, seeks retribution, derives more pleasure from taking than having.	Dauntless, venturesome, bold, audacious, impulsive, pursues perilous ventures.

Reputation-Defending
(narcissistic features)
Needs to be thought of as unflawed, invincible, and formidable. Inflexible when status is quesitoned and overreactive to slights.

Subtypes of ASPD

It is Millon's (2004) view that there are few pure personality prototypes and that instead there are mixed variants of one major type with one or more secondary or subsidiary subtypes.

Benjamin (1996) proposes a link between the ASPD individual's interpersonal history and the DSM criteria. The ASPD individual does not see a strong need to submit to social or legal norms due to a weak conscience intermixed with a controlling household while growing up (criterion 1), which results in deceitfulness (criterion 2) and a resistance to being predictable or responsible in regard to employment or financial issues (criterion 6). Neglectful parenting is derived from "pseudo-attachment to self and others" (p. 201). This ineptitude in caring produces recklessness with self and others (criterion 5). An additional outcome of poor attachment and little to no consistent discipline is the ill-formed or unformed conscience (criterion 7). "Meeting one's needs of the moment in very concrete and immediate terms is all that can be counted on" (p. 201) is the lesson the ASPD individual learns as the foundation for his or her impulsivity, irresponsibility, and failure to plan ahead (criterion 3). Due to poor ability to bond and repeated exposure to random and extreme attacks from the parental figure, he develops a high level of aggressiveness (criterion 4), which is a tool whereby he attempts to maintain control.

Psychopathy

Psychopathy has taken up volumes of literature and will only be discussed, in a cursory fashion, as it pertains to ASPD to expand clinical awareness and usage. There are many research studies that have explored the overlap and distinction between ASPD and psychopathy (Chapman, Gremore, & Farmer, 2003; Edens, Poythress, & Watkins, 2001; Hare, 1996, 2003), but the issue continues to confound clinicians and researchers alike. Findings tend to illustrate that individuals diagnosed with psychopathy within prison settings will also meet criteria for ASPD. However, approximately half of ASPD individuals will meet criteria for psychopathy (Hare, 1996, 2003). Typically, two correlated factors on the PCL-R are found to provide the discrimination between psychopathy and ASPD (Hare, Hart, & Harpur, 1991; Harris, Rice, & Quinsey, 1994; Lilienfeld, 1994. Factor one pertains to glibness, pathological lying, manipulative behavior, lack of remorse or guilt, shallow affect, and failure to accept responsibility. Factor two pertains to the need for stimulation, proneness to boredom, a parasitic lifestyle, poor behavioral control, impulsivity, juvenile delinquency, and early behavioral problems (Hare et al., 1991, 2003). The first factor is related to specific aspects of psychopathy, whereas factor two has a greater relationship to "social deviance" (Hare, 2003, p. 79). Studies have illustrated a greater relationship between ASPD and factor two due to the ASPD criterion set being broad and including criminal and antisocial individuals who are psychologically heterogeneous, and leaving out the personality components of the psychopath (Hare et al., 1991).

From a more global perspective, psychopaths can be seen as individuals who engage in immoral behavior while having no regard for the individuals they harm and feeling no association with the adverse outcomes their victims experience. Their relationships are variant and typically short-lived and they tend not to learn from past experiences (Karpman, 1948, 1955). From this view, two components, primary and secondary psychopaths can be derived and distinguished. Primary psychopaths are born with emotional deficits, whereas secondary psychopaths acquire this irregularity through harsh emotional experiences, such as parental abuse, neglect, and rejection (Karpman, 1948, 1955).

Differential Diagnosis

It is possible for an adult to be given a diagnosis of conduct disorder, but only if the ASPD criteria have not been met. In these cases, the individual would have been aggressive towards animals, destroyed property, engaged in theft or deceitfulness, and seriously violated rules, but has not graduated to "the pervasive pattern of disregard for and violation of the rights of others, occurring since age 15..." (APA, 2013, p. 659). There is extensive literature regarding ASPD and substance-related disorders (Krueger et al., 2002; Lewis, 2011; Mueser et al., 2012; Robins, Tipp, & Przybeck, 1991), but the disorders are only diagnosed when criteria for each are present. Though some ASPD criteria can be met as a result of addiction to drugs and alcohol, the antisocial spectrum behavior is not as prevalent.

Hodgins and colleagues (2010) examined a population of 279 inmates in penitentiaries in Quebec to explore anxiety disorders and ASPD. All participants met criteria for ASPD. Results showed that 68.5% of individuals with ASPD met criteria for an anxiety disorder, with the highest percentage (48.4%) meeting criteria for generalized anxiety disorder. In addition, the researchers examined suicidal ideation and attempts and found that 75.9% of the sample had suicidal ideations and 43.7% had made suicide attempts. Lastly, 78.5% of the sample met criteria for alcohol abuse or dependence and 76.4% met criteria for drug abuse and dependence.

Behavior that occurs during a psychotic or manic episode will not qualify for ASPD. Individuals who engage in illegal activity for monetary or other personal gain, aggressive or other antisocial behavior do not simply qualify for ASPD. Additionally, those who do not have the personality characteristics should receive a diagnosis of adult antisocial behavior.

Individuals with ASPD can be confused with individuals with other personality disorders, especially those within its same cluster, cluster B (Sutker & Allain, 2001). The ASPD individual is similar to the individuals with narcissistic personality disorder (NPD) in that they both lack empathy and possess glib, superficial, stubborn, and exploitive features, but the NPD individual is not likely to be impulsive, aggressive, deceitful, in need of admiration and envy of others, and is unlikely to have been previously diagnosed with CD. Histrionic personality disorder (HPD) is similar to ASPD in that both are likely to be impulsive, superficial, sensation seeking, irresponsible, provocative, and manipulative, but tend to be more florid in their emotional expression and are unlikely to engage in antisocial spectrum behaviors. The ASPD individual shares manipulativeness with both HPD and borderline personality disorder (BPD) but the end goal is different, as the HPD and BPD person is attempting to gain nurturance and emotional safety, as opposed to the ASPD individual who wants money, power, and control. The ASPD individual is also less likely to possess the emotional lability than the BPD individual and show heightened aggression.

Sprague and colleagues (2012) examined the interpersonal-affective and impulsive-antisocial traits of psychopathy and how it related to BPD in females. In two independent samples, one composed of male and female college students and the other of incarcerated females in a maximum security prison in Wisconsin, results showed, across both samples, that the two psychopathy factors were associated with BPD. The impulsive-antisocial traits of psychopathy were found to be associated with BPD symptoms in both genders, but the authors stipulate that this is likely due to the "overlapping symptoms clusters in psychopathy and BPD" (p. 134). The interpersonal-affective traits of psychopathy were related to BPD in women, but only in those who also had high impulsive-antisocial traits. Results support the notion of a BPD variant of psychopathy in women, similar to the secondary psychopathic component proposed by Karpman, (1948, 1955).

ASSESSMENT

The assessment of ASPD and psychopathy has been studied extensively, but this section will focus on assessment that is most useful in a clinical or therapeutic setting. On the Minnesota Multiphasic Personality Inventory, Second Edition (MMPI-2) a person with ASPD is likely to produce a 4-9/9-4 profile. This is considered the classic ASPD profile, showing elevations on the psychopathic-deviant and hypomania scales. Individuals who produce this result tend to show disregard for social standards and values, are highly likely to get into trouble with the law or have legal problems, as well as having a poorly developed conscience and vacillating ethical values. Alcoholism and marital/relationship problems are common, in addition to narcissistic views, impulsivity in getting needs met, poor judgment, and failure to reflect responsibility. Individuals with this code type are likely to harbor grudges, be energetic and restless, extroverted, and have superficial relationships with others (Graham, 2011). The MMPI-2 has a specific scale titled Antisocial Practices (ASP) scale, with two subscales to assess antisocial attitudes and behaviors. The Antisocial Attitudes (ASP1) Component scale and the Antisocial Behaviors (ASP2) Component scale are designed to assess antisocial personality constructs, beliefs, and behaviors. High scores indicate that an individual is likely to have been in trouble in school or with the law, hold beliefs that circumventing the law as long it is not broken is all right, enjoystories related to criminal acts, hold cynical attitudes about others, resent authority, blame others for his/her difficulties, is manipulative, cold-hearted, and self-centered. High scores on this scale are not indicative of identifying past antisocial behaviors. The MMPI-2 alone cannot fully address all aspects of psychopathy, but it can assist in the overall assessment of psychopathic personality. More specifically, scale 4 is not as good a measure of psychopathic characteristics as ASP (Lilienfeld, 1994; Sellbom, Ben-Porath, Lilienfeld, Patrick, & Graham, 2005).

When given to an individual with ASPD, The Millon Clinical Multiaxial Inventory, Third Edition (MCMI), results are likely to show elevations on scale 5 (narcissistic), 6A (antisocial), B (alcohol dependence), and/or T (drug dependence). An individual who produces this profile is likely to exaggerate his or her sense of self-importance, be hypersensitive to criticism, feel that conventional rules to not apply to him or her, present as arrogant or snobbish, and lack empathy. In addition, he or she is likely to engage in illegal behavior to exploit the environment for personal gain, be impulsive, potentially violent, ignore consequences of behavior, can be charming, and acknowledge drug and/or alcohol issues. It would be uncommon for the ASPD individual to produce elevations on A (anxiety), D (dysthymia), and H (somatoform) scales due to the these individuals' tendency not to be highly distressed (Choca & Van Denburg, 1997).

Using projective tests, such as the Thematic Apperception Test (TAT) and the Rorschach, can be helpful to identify the ASPD individual's superego development. Also, he or she is less likely to deceive the clinician in the same manner in a clinical interview as there are no "correct" answers (Gabbard, 2005). The Rorschach has been found to be useful in discriminating between personality disorders, including psychopathic and non-psychopathic ASPD individuals (Gacono & Meloy, 1997). On the Rorschach, ASPD individuals tend to produce a low to average number of responses or reject cards they would be able to cognitively handle. ASPD individuals tend to delay reaction to color cards, but when a response is given, their C (pure color) responses are primitive and impulsive. A high number of A (animal) and P (popular) responses are common, along with a low number of M (human movement) and W (whole) responses. One can expect an absence of shading (Y, YF, and FY) and a low number of Form plus (F+%) responses (Gacono & Meloy, 1997; Wagner & Wagner, 1981). On the TAT, the ASPD individual is likely to produce stories that are immature; the protagonist is typically caught in a negative act, and there tends to be little to no mention of consequences of the negative behavior (Bellak & Abrams, 1997).

Psychopathy

The Psychopathy Checklist, Revised (PCL-R; Hare, 1991, 2003) is a clinical rating scale of 20 items. It examines lifestyle, criminal behavior, glib and superficial charm, grandiosity, need for stimulation, pathological lying, conning and manipulating, lack of remorse, callousness, poor behavior controls, impulsivity, irresponsibility, failure to accept responsibility for one's action and others. This measure yields dimensional scores that may be used to classify individuals for both research and clinical purposes. Total scores can range from 0 to 40, which indicate the degree that an individual matches the classic psychopath, with a cutoff of 30 in North America, though cutoff scores vary depending upon reason for use. When used appropriately, the PCL-R provides a reliable and valid assessment of the clinical construct of psychopathy (Hare & Neumann, 2006). Results can be scored on two correlated factors, Factor 1 and Factor 2. Factor 1 has been identified with the core features of psychopathy, and Factor 2 is said to be more closely related to the ASPD criterion set in the DSM-IV-TR (Hare, 2003; Hart & Hare, 1989).

Levenson and colleagues (1995) developed the Levenson Primary and Secondary Psychopathy Scales (LPSP) to identify self-reported psychopathic features in non-institutional populations. The measure consists of 26 items that are rated on a 1 to 4 Likert scale and results have shown a two-factor structure, such as that found on the PCL-R. The primary scale is designed to identify aspects of Factor 2 on the PCL-R, whereas the secondary scale is designed to capture aspects of the PCL-R and Factor 2. The LPSP has some promise as a self-report measure of psychopathy, but construct validity is problematic as it tends to lean toward secondary psychopathy and antisocial behaviors as opposed to core affective and interpersonal features of psychopathy (Lilienfeld & Fowler, 2006).

The Psychopathic Personality Inventory (PPI) is a 187-item self-report measure that asks participants to respond on a 1 to 4 Likert scale. There are eight clinical scales: Machiavellian egocentricity, social potency, coldheartedness, carefree nonplanfulness, fearlessness, blame externalization, impulsive nonconformity, stress immunity; seven of these eight load on two higher order factors labeled fearless dominance (FD) and impulsive antisociality (IA).

As with any assessment measure, the clinician or researcher should be trained and skilled in administration, scoring, and interpretation of the particular measure before making any diagnostic determinations based upon testing data.

CASE EXAMPLE – MALE

James is a 21-year-old male who has never held "a real job." He earns money by stealing from stores and periodically he will sell drugs to the high school kids when he can get some. James has been in juvenile detention four times for fighting with neighborhood kids, stealing, and assault. James has been mandated for treatment as a condition of his recent release from prison. He served 3 years for vehicular assault, when he hit someone with his car in an act of aggression to get some money owed to him for half an ounce of cocaine. James is often vulgar and uses profanity often in session. He will make comments about the therapist's family pictures, calling the therapists wife "a cherry to be picked."

When the therapist tries to talk about James's mother and father, James becomes very upset and punches the coffee table in front of the couch in the therapist's office. When James is informed that the therapist is aware of his past abuse and admissions to the hospital for "suspected child abuse" perpetrated by both his mother and father, James begins to cry. The therapist presumes this to mean he is making headway, and brings up James's sister, who passed away due to a drug overdose at age 9. James abruptly stands with a clenched fist and walks toward the door, punches a hole in the wall, and knocks down a glass candy bowl as he walks out. James was picked up later that night and brought back to jail.

CASE EXAMPLE – FEMALE

Pam has never held a job and was kicked out of school in the 9th grade for fighting and sexually aggressive behavior towards a teacher. She was recently arrested for prostitution, her third arrest. Her previous two were for theft and assault with a deadly weapon. Pam has been a prostitute since she was 16 years old. She meets men and women from an ad she placed on the internet. She will typically perform the sexual act and then while the individual is distracted, usually in the bathroom, she will put several items in her purse. Her assault with a deadly weapon came after she was meeting with a man who caught her putting his watch in her purse. He grabbed her and slapped her across the face. She fell to the ground, grabbed her purse and pulled a 4-inch knife she kept for protection. She cut the man across his chest and ran out. She was picked up later that day by police, based upon the man's description of his "mugging." Pam is at intake in county jail. She answers most questions with, "it doesn't matter, it's all been done to me before." She refuses to give much information and when put in the holding cell with the other females, is in a fight within 5 minutes for being caught lying about why she is incarcerated.

TREATMENT

There are no controlled studies examining treatment of ASPD, and treatment is guarded in regard to applying most treatment modalities, unless the individual presents with other, more specific mental health concerns, such as depression (Crits-Christoph & Barber, 2002; Sperry, 2003). Most ASPD individuals are not going to be interested in treatment and typically enter therapy as mandated by the court or forced by family members (Reid, Balis, Wicoff, & Tomasovic, 1989).

Based upon a psychodynamic approach, treatment needs to be assessed regarding the time and effort expenditure that is going to be required, as therapy is typically going to be long term with a nebulous outcome (Gabbard, 1990). The more the ASPD individual resembles the profile of the psychopath, the less likely he or she is to respond to the psychodynamic approach

(Sperry, 2003). The five contraindications for psychotherapy with the ASPD client are listed below, based upon the work of Meloy (1988):

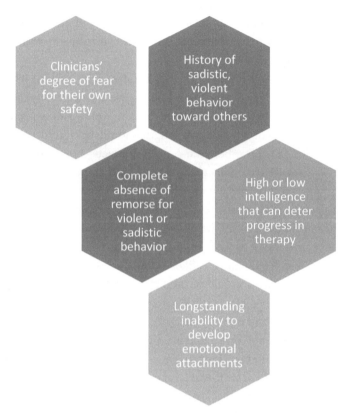

Contraindications to Treatment of ASPD Individuals

Meloy (1988) goes on to contend that the ASPD individual with narcissistic features may be "somewhat" amenable to treatment due to a tendency to reveal dependency in transferences and the "ideal object" being potentially less aggressive than in the psychopathic individual. From a psychodynamic perspective, the approach should be one of active engagement and confront the minimization and denial of the antisocial behavior (Gabbard, 1990). Confrontation should be grounded in the here-and-now as opposed to focusing on unconscious material. In addition, silence is seen as colluding with the ASPD client. Symington (1980) notes disbelief and collusion as concerns related to transference and ASPD clients. Disbelief includes rationalization by the clinician that the ASPD individual is not that bad and the minimizing of the antisocial acts he or she engages in. Collusion is a more extreme and serious issue as it entails the therapist's allowing himself or herself to be manipulated by the client and falling for the tactics that he employs to corrupt the clinician into aligning with him.

Beck et al. (2004) identify the twin issues of skills when using cognitive-behavioral therapy (CBT) with ASPD clients. These entail the therapist's having the skills necessary to work with these individuals, as well as the second issue of motivation, which includes the therapist's being motivated enough to enter and continue therapy and uphold the necessary relationship for effective treatment. The effectiveness of treatment is often limited to the balancing of disruptive behaviors to either function better within a prison setting or learning how to alter behavior to avoid such environments. The focus of treatment is not on building a better moral system through introducing anxiety or shame, but enhancing moral and social behavior through improved cognitive functioning. The authors suggest moving from concrete operations and self-determination to more abstract thinking and interpersonal consideration. This proposition entails viewing moral functioning as a dimension with a wider scope of thinking and knowing (Kagan, 1989).

The first step in CBT is to develop a collaborative relationship, which entails being open and honest about the ASPD diagnosis and setting clear requirements for the individual's participation in treatment. The therapist should outline limits and expectations of himself or herself and the ASPD client: the session length should be agreed upon in clear terms, cancellation policy, rules regarding between-session contacts, homework requirements, and how and when to use emergency contact numbers. The therapeutic contract should include number of sessions and expected behavioral change that is written in clear language; do not use jargon and do not try to impress these clients. The therapist must not only monitor his or her own counter transference issues, he or she must be aware of and appropriately respond to the ASPD client's transference as well. It is the job of the therapist to see the client from a standpoint of empathy and the therapist is likely to find some parallels between the client and himself or herself. These instances should be used to assist the client in making the most of the therapeutic sessions, but the therapist must always be cognizant of the level of familiarity and keep a healthy therapeutic boundary. The therapist must not get pulled into angry or violent outbursts and become judgmental or intractable during such episodes.

There are some specific interventions suggested by Beck and colleagues (2004) in treating the ASPD individual using CBT. The therapist should initiate problem-focused work through communicating the seriousness of the symptoms and how they have impacted the ASPD individual's life, and that therapeutic success may cause distance between the individual and friends, family, business associates, etc. The therapist should not allow himself or herself to be pulled into hearing "war stories" and gory details of brutal acts or conning as these are distraction tactics to thwart therapeutic movement. These stories are most likely to come out during periods of regression or high tension. It is the therapist's job to stay focused on treatment and the goals agreed upon. The ASPD individual has an internal need for control and may become aggressive or angry when he or she does not get a semblance of control, but the therapist must maintain structure and collaborate with the client.

Another specific intervention is linking distorted thoughts with maladaptive behaviors. Within the identified problematic behaviors it is helpful to the client to increase awareness of associated cognitive distortions. Most beliefs will be self-serving and one-sided. Beck and colleagues (2004) give the following example: "*Feelings make facts.* "I know I am right, because I feel right in what I do" (p. 175). The therapist should utilize the fact that ASPD clients' problems are long term and ego-syntonic, which tend to leave them confused about how they ended up where they are and how people are relating to them (Beck et al., 2004).

The next two interventions include building coping skills and the systematic approach to anger and impulsivity. For the ASPD individual, concerns that seem simple to most can generate significant problems. The building of adaptive problem-solving skills is central to potentially moving the ASPD client forward and teaching him or her to utilize other less previously utilized behaviors; skills include perspective taking, effective communication, response delay, etc. (Beck et al., 2004). The ASPD client has reaped many benefits from his or her anger and impulsivity, and it is up to the therapist to mirror these behaviors in a more responsible and clear manner so that the ASPD individual can attend to internal emotional and cognitive cues, assess how he or she sees the situation, determine whether a response is necessary, decide what are the alternative responses available, choose a response, and then respond (Beck et al., 2004).

Beck and colleagues' (2004) final three interventions include self-monitoring and functional motivation, broadening the base for attributions and appraisals, and making constructive choices. Most ASPD individuals lack the ability to introspect and are unaware of their choices to behave differently. The client must learn to listen to himself or herself, contend with the associated discomfort, and develop the skills to analyze these thoughts and feelings. If possible, the next step is to assist the ASPD individual in testing attributions, appraisals, and choices, and extend his or her range of interests from one solely about himself or herself to awareness of other people and situations. Ideally, the ASPD individual would begin to see how his or her behavior impacts others and develop an understanding of how it can affect him or her in the long term as well as others. To facilitate the ASPD individual's making constructive choices, the therapist works with the client to develop a "cost-benefit ratio" to show that antisocial behavior, while seemingly profitable in the short term, is actually detrimental and not cost effective in the long term. An example I like to use is the monetary cost of crime vs. imprisonment. A client has received a sentence of 60 months for Possession with Intent to Distribute Cocaine and would have made $2000 had he been able to successfully get the merchandise to the seller, but he was arrested at the border. The incarceration is 3,120 weeks and when we consider the payday of $2000 (had he received it), it equals $1.56 a week. This example can assist in getting the individual to think about behavior and consequences. In working with the ASPD individual, and especially the psychopath, interventions such as these have to be seen for what they are, small seeds that may incite moments of consideration. There are no silver bullets in treatment that will miraculously cause the development of intrinsic motivation for change, especially with these types of individuals.

Benjamin (1996) conceptualizes treatment of personality disorders using five categories of correct response. When this is applied to the ASPD individual, she recognizes the challenge and limitation as in the statement: "the effect of interventions is assessed in terms of the actual impact on the patient, not in terms of the therapist's intentions" (p. 213). According to her, the ASPD individual cannot be moved in a direction of betterment and treatment progress by way of typical means as it usually will take some type of coercion into treatment or some impetus that causes the ASPD individual to choose to participate in treatment. It is the therapist's job to "make the best" out of the treatment sessions. To build a sense of collaboration, the therapist may need to connect with the ASPD individual in his or her initial resistant stance and then slowly and methodically move him or her toward working together to resolve the issue, in some cases completing mandated treatment and meeting the requirements set by the court. Milieu treatment is recommended as a means to achieve a positive treatment outcome. The goal within this therapeutic community is for the client to build a bond with another and create a firm degree of interdependence; this is hypothesized to block maladaptive patterns and replace them with ones that move the ASPD individual toward discharge. Once the therapist and client have reached a point of bonding and interdependence, working to identify the adverse impact that antisocial behavior has had on the course of his or her life can be addressed. From here, skills such as delaying gratification, appropriate self-care, and empathy for others can be learned.

Open, exploratory, and nondirective groups have been found to be problematic as ASPD individuals tend to be very disruptive in these types of group settings (Sperry, 2003; Yalom & Leszcz, 2005). Walker (1992) notes three types of group treatment that have been used with ASPD individuals: psychoeducational, psychotherapy, and support groups. Content and agenda are highly structured in psychoeducational groups aimed at ASPD participants and session time is noted to be about 90 minutes in length, though psychoeducational groups have limited benefit for the ASPD individual. Psychotherapy groups should have two clinicians to decrease the potential for acting-out and making the clinician the target. The clinicians should determine the appropriateness of group members and the degree of ASPD and psychopathy before inclusion. Support groups can be useful for the ASPD patient who has had inpatient or outpatient group psychotherapy. The main focus of the group is relapse prevention and development of peer support.

Therapy with ASPD and psychopathic individuals must be seen as complex as the disorders themselves. Most treatments utilize a multimodal approach of both therapy and psychopharmacology to address specific features or issues that are present, such as impulse control and addictive urges (Patrick, 2007), but the therapist is never to forget that boundaries need to be solid, interventions and goals clear, and that an error in treatment with these individuals can have long-term and seriously detrimental consequences.

Psychopharmacology

The consensus within the field of psychology and psychiatry is that there are few controlled studies that examine ASPD and the efficacy of psychopharmacology (Koenigsberg, Woo-Ming, & Siever, 2002; Sperry, 2003; Walker, Thomas, & Allen, 2003). Medications are typically used in ASPD individuals to address symptoms, such as rage, anxiety, and depression, but due to comorbid substance abuse found in many of these individuals, medications must be used carefully (Sadock & Sadock, 2007). Individuals with ASPD have been prescribed methylphenidate (Ritalin) if symptoms of attention deficit hyperactivity disorder (ADHD) are present, or carbamazepine (Tegretol) or valproate (Depakote) to modulate impulse control issues (Sadock & Sadock, 2007).

Walker and colleagues (2003) examined data collected from four patients diagnosed with ASPD at a maximum security psychiatric facility who were prescribed quetiapine (Seroquel) at dosage ranges of 600 to 800 mg per day for 30 to 60 days. Results showed "substantial improvements in important behavioral aspects of psychopathy" (p. 566). Individuals with personality disorders who also exhibit aggressive behavior may benefit from mood stabilizing medication, such as valproate at mean dosages of approximately 1500 mg per day (Hollander et al., 2003; Hollander, Swann, Coccaro, Jiang, & Smith, 2005).

Eichelman (1988) developed four basic principles of clinical application of pharmacology for violent patients. This includes addressing the biological system, the anticipated action, and suggested medication to achieve the means of decreasing aggression and violence, depicted below:

PHARMACOTHERAPEUTIC EFFECTS ON VIOLENCE AND AGGRESSION		
Biological System	**Anticipated Action**	**Recommended Medication**
Y-Aminobutyric acid system	Inhibits affective aggression	Benzodiazepines
Noradrenergic system	Enhances aggression, inhibits predatory aggression	Lithium, propranolol
Serotonergic system	Inhibits predatory and affective aggression	Lithium, fluoxetine
Electrical "kindling"	Enhances predatory and affective aggression	Phenytoin, carbamazepine

PHARMACOTHERAPEUTIC EFFECTS ON VIOLENCE AND AGGRESSION

Utilizing medication to treat the behaviors associated with ASPD must include the assessment of the origin of the violent behavior in order to determine the best pharmacological treatment. For example, Barratt, Stanford, Felthous, and Kent (1997) examined whether phenytoin would decrease impulsive acts, both primarily impulsive aggressive acts and premeditated aggressive acts in incarcerated individuals. Results showed that phenytoin significantly reduced impulsive, but not premeditated, aggressive acts. Dysfunction within the serotonergic system is hypothesized to account for many of the most pronounced symptoms of ASPD, such as aggression (Carrillo, Ricci, Coppersmith, & Melloni, 2009), emotional dysregulation (Lewis, 1991), dysphoria (Moss, Yao, & Panzak, 1990), and Butler and colleagues (2010) showed marked reduction in irritability, anger, verbal assault, and indirect assault.

FILM AND POPULAR MEDIA EXAMPLES

A Clockwork Orange (1971) – Alex, played by Malcolm McDowell

American Psycho (2000) – Patrick Bateman, played by Christian Bale

Catch Me If You Can (2002) – Frank Abignale, Jr., played by Leonardo DeCaprio

Clay Pigeons (1998) – Lester Long, played by Vince Vaughn

Girl, Interrupted (1999) – Lisa Rowe, played by Angelina Jolie

Hannibal Lecter from books and movies

Monster (2003) – Aileen Wuornos, played by CharlizeTheron

Rounders (1998) – Lester 'Worm' Murphy, played by Edward Norton

The Fountainhead (book) – Ellsworth Toohey

The Talented Mr. Ripley (1999) – Tom Ripley, played by Matt Damon

Wuthering Heights (book) – Heathcliff

CHECKLIST: ANTISOCIAL PERSONALITY DISORDER

Below is a complete list to best identify and diagnose Antisocial Personality Disorder. DSM-5 (APA, 2013) criteria are first, followed by discernible components, and lastly, associated features.

- ❑ A pervasive pattern of disregard for and violation of the rights of others occurring since age 15*
- ❑ Failure to conform to social norms with respect to lawful behaviors as indicated by repeatedly performing acts that are grounds for arrest*
- ❑ Deception as indicated by repeatedly lying, use of aliases, or conning others for personal profit or pleasure*
- ❑ Impulsiveness or failure to plan ahead*
- ❑ Irritability and aggressiveness, as indicated by repeated physical fights or assaults*
- ❑ Reckless disregard for safety of self or others*
- ❑ Consistent irresponsibility, as indicated by repeated failure to sustain consistent work behavior or honor financial obligations*
- ❑ Lack of remorse, as indicated by being indifferent to or rationalizing having hurt, mistreated, or stolen from another*
- ❑ Individual meets criteria for conduct disorder with onset prior to age 15
- ❑ Client does not meet criteria for a schizophrenia spectrum behavior which caused him or her to engage in antisocial behaviors
- ❑ Client does not meet criteria for a manic episode which caused him or her to engage in antisocial behaviors
- ❑ Callous lack of concern for others
- ❑ Inability to maintain long-term relationships, though able to develop them
- ❑ Low frustration tolerance and easily induced into violent action
- ❑ Client does not experience guilt or profit from experience following punishment
- ❑ Tendency to blame others and offer rationalizations for his or her behaviors that have caused him or her to be in conflictual entanglements with society
- ❑ Superficial charm and inflated self-appraisal
- ❑ Parental irresponsibility
- ❑ Frivolously spending money that would be better spent on household needs (not during a manic/hypomanic episode)
- ❑ Inability to tolerate boredom
- ❑ Previous incarceration
- ❑ Dishonorable discharge from military

*distinguishing characteristics

THERAPIST CLIENT ACTIVITY

Use these probes to explore your ASPD client's malicious, blocking, and antisocial views and presentation that are central to the pathology and enhance the socioeconomic dysfunction.

➢ How do you feel when you hear that something you did has hurt someone else?

➢ Do you think there is anything to gain from treatment?

➢ Can you tell me about a time you helped someone?

➢ Can you tell me about a time someone helped you?

➢ Would you change your behavior if you knew there was more to gain from it?

➢ Have you ever damaged someone else's property by breaking windows, spray painting graffiti, etc.?

➢ What is the hardest thing you have to deal with in your life?

➢ Who would you say you care for most (and you cannot include yourself)?

➢ On a scale from one to ten, how much do you hate the world?

➢ If there were no consequences, what would be the one behavior you would engage in?

➢ How often did you get into fights growing up?

➢ If you knew you would be locked up the rest of your life for something you did, what is the one behavior you would change or not engage in?

➢ Where do you see yourself in 5 or 10 years? (And dead is not an answer).

➢ What is the one thing I could do to make the therapy easiest for you?

➢ Can you agree that anger is ok, but violence is not, especially in treatment?

➢ How many physical fights have you been in, why, and with whom?

➢ Did you pick on other kids when you were growing up?

CLIENT QUESTIONNAIRE

The following questions are to be given to your client to help him or her identify past challenges and provide guidance for treatment.

What is your earliest recollection? Describe only as much as you feel comfortable with.

List three things that have helped you in the past to avoid problems with others.

Will you draw a picture of how you see yourself and how others see you?

Will you draw me a picture of anger?

Will you draw me a picture of peace and calmness?

Borderline Personality Disorder

Borderline personality disorder (BPD) describes an individual with a history of emotional and behavioral instability that follows an identifiable trigger related to fear of abandonment, loss, or victimization. BPD is the most researched, clinically evident, and controversial personality disorder (Bradley, Conklin, & Westen, 2007; Sperry, 2003). Due to the extensive study of BPD and its specific treatments in books, articles, and other literature, this chapter will focus on condensing this information for the clinician in order to enhance its clinical utility.

The diagnosis "borderline" was first introduced in the 1930s to identify patients who seemed to be experiencing a mild form of schizophrenia and were on the borderline between neurosis and psychosis (Stern, 1938). Stern described character traits and reaction formations that included:

- narcissism
- psychic bleeding
- extreme hypersensitivity
- 'the rigid personality'
- negative therapeutic reactions
- deep-seated issues of inferiority
- masochism
- chronic and embedded insecurity or anxiety
- the tendency to utilize projection
- problems with reality testing, specifically in relationships

In the 1940s, Robert Knight combined the concept of ego psychology with borderline personality. Ego psychology examines how the individual interacts with the external world and how he or she responds to internal forces, which enables one to realistically perceive events and successfully integrate feelings and thoughts, as well as develop responses to the world around him or her in an effective manner. Knight believed that borderline personality individuals have impairments in this ability and called this inability "borderline states" (Friedel, 2004). The concept was later elaborated on by Kernberg (1967) to include enduring patterns of feeling, thinking, behaving, experiencing self and others, and contending with realities that are dissonant. Kernberg (1967, 1968) saw these patients as possessing a personality organization and system that tended to utilize drastic and immature ways of dealing with impulses and emotions. Kernberg (1975, 1984) is credited with the continued interest in borderline personality, especially by psychoanalytic theorists and clinicians.

The diagnosis BPD was not included in the first or second edition of the *Diagnostic and Statistical Manual of Mental Disorders* (DSM) as it was restricted to the psychoanalytic literature (Paris, 1999). Prior to that, borderline patients were typically diagnosed with schizophrenia, latent type (Sperry, 2003). The first study of borderline patients to develop diagnostic criteria was by Grinker, Werble, and Drye (1968), followed by the operational definition devised by Gunderson and Singer (1975) based upon findings in a literature review. The understanding of this construct and the discrimination of borderline patients from other groups diagnosed with mental illness (schizophrenia, neurotically depressed, and various other diagnoses) was furthered by Gunderson and Kolb (1978) in an effort to create a list of recognizable characteristics of the borderline patient. Research was later done to develop criteria for the borderline patient based upon mental status, history, interpersonal relationships, defense mechanisms, and other aspects of personality functioning in addition to research that further isolated characteristics of the borderline patient; these individuals were often not psychotic, but angry and demanding, and posed difficulties during the interview process (Perry & Klerman, 1978; Perry & Klerman, 1980). These research studies led to the formal and accepted diagnosis of BPD that appeared in the DSM-III (APA, 1980).

In the DSM-III, the BPD diagnosis tended to be given to those individuals who were more interpersonally unstable and affectively labile (Adams, Bernat, & Luscher, 2001). Problems arose out of the DSM-III and DSM-III-R (APA, 1987) criteria due to the failure to include the BPD individual's tendency for brief psychotic episodes, which was later added in the DSM-IV (APA, 1994) by including transient, stress-related paranoid ideation or severe dissociative symptoms (Sperry, 2003). Though the disorder seemed clear with solid empirical and clinical utility, concerns continued as to whether or not BPD is a specific personality disorder, dimensional aspect of personality or personality organization (as theorized by Kernberg, 1984), or spectrum disorder (as theorized by Meissner, 1988). In the DSM-IV-TR (APA, 2000), text was added to the "course" section to point out that prognosis is good for many individuals diagnosed with BPD, though many clinicians believe it is poor.

No changes were made to the BPD criteria in the DSM-5 (APA, 2013) from the previous volume, DSM-IV-TR (APA, 2000).

ETIOLOGY

There are a myriad of theories as to the etiology of BPD, including biological and genetic factors, and psychological factors such as childhood abuse, family environment, separation and loss, and attachment disruption. Paris (1994, 1999) proposed that since no one factor can fully account for the development of BPD, an interaction of biological, psychological, and social risk factors is most probable. Several studies have been conducted that examine BPD within families confirm that BPD does "breed true" (Links, Steiner, & Huxley, 1988), meaning that BPD is more common in first-degree relatives than in controls (Belsky et al., 2012; Sansone & Sansone, 2009; Zanarini, Gunderson, Marino, & Schwartz, 1988). Results have shown that BPD individuals who have a relative with BPD are five times more likely to be diagnosed with the disorder (Gunderson, 1994). The conceptualization of BPD as an extreme presentation of temperament or associated traits such as impulsivity, neuroticism, affective instability, and interpersonal relationship disturbance has been found to show strong familial lineage and discrimination (Paris, 2003; Skodol et al., 2002; Zanarini et al., 2004).

Skodol and colleagues (2002) reported the heritability of specific borderline traits to produce a heritability co-efficient range between .44 and .53 for anxiousness, affective lability, submissiveness, insecure attachment, cognitive dysregulation, and identity problems. Several researchers have conducted studies examining trait emotional intelligence (the process of utilizing and understanding intrapersonal and interpersonal emotions) and BPD. Results consistently show that BPD symptomatology is associated with low trait emotional intelligence (Gardner & Qualter, 2009; Leible & Snell, 2004; Petrides, Pérez-González, & Furnham, 2007), and one study was able to accurately predict BPD diagnosis 95% of the time (Sinclair & Feigenbaum, 2012). Bornovalova, Hicks, Iacono, and McGue (2009) examined the heritability and course of BPD over the 10-year span from age 14 to 24. Their sample consisted of adolescent female twins from the Minnesota Twin Family Study (MTFS) that showed a decline in BPD traits from adolescence to adulthood, but little change from age 14 to 17. After age 17, the traits began to "decline significantly at each assessment point" (p. 1348). The authors also showed moderate heritability of BPD traits. This result is not in isolation, as Distel and colleagues (2008) studied BPD features in twins from three countries—the Netherlands, Belgium, and Australia—with a total sample of 5,496 twins. Results showed that across all the countries studied, females scored higher than males, younger adults scored higher than older adults on BPD features, and that genetic influence accounted for 42% of the variation in both genders.

A growing area of research has utilized neuroimaging to study the etiology of BPD. Findings have shown bilateral decreases in hippocampal and amygdalar volumes when compared to individuals without BPD (Hall, Olabi, Lawrie, & McIntosh, 2010). It has been found that individuals with BPD are hyperreactive to emotional stimuli, which manifests in heightened activation of the amygdala (Donegan et al., 2003). Using functional magnetic resonance imaging (fMRI) to study the brain response of BPD individuals when presented with emotional faces, researchers have consistently found that areas that process emotional stimuli, such as the amygdala, become activated in both control and BPD patients, but those with BPD show a greater activation in the middle and inferior temporal cortical areas; these are the areas that assist in the processing of facial features that are emotionally salient (Guitart-Masip et al., 2009).

Childhood abuse has been found to have a causal link with BPD (Herman, Perry, & Van der Kolk, 1989), but others have not found this result when examining physical abuse alone (Ogata, Silk, Goodrich, & Lohr, 1990). Using a sample of Chinese participants, Huang and colleagues (2012) found maternal physical abuse to be as strong a predictor of BPD as sexual abuse. The experience of physical and sexual abuse and parental neglect increased the risk for development of ten of the twelve personality disorders by four times compared to those who did not have such experiences (Johnson, Cohen, Brown, Smailes, & Bernstein, 1999). The more consistent finding is the link between BPD and specific childhood maltreatment in the form of sexual abuse, with prevalence rates in those who develop BPD to be between 36.5% to 67% (Elzy, 2011; Herman et al., 1989; McGowan, King, Frankenburg, Fitzmaurice, & Zanarini, 2012; Paris, 1994). Yen and colleagues (2002) found that 91.6% of 167 participants identified as meeting criteria for BPD disclosed specific sexual trauma, with 55.1% reporting physical force/unwanted sexual contact, 36.5% reporting rape, and 13.3% witnessing sexual abuse. In addition, the BPD individuals in the sample reported the highest rate of trauma exposure and highest rate of post traumatic stress disorder (PTSD), and earlier age of first traumatic event (Bradley, Jenei, & Westen, 2005). Due to the complexity of personality development it is rarely a linear one-to-one causal event. BPD is not immune to such a theory, as there are many factors such as social, genetic, and environmental, and multiple and repetitive instances, such as trauma, abandonment, etc., that lead to disordered personality (Bradley, Jenei, & Westen, 2005; Paris, 1997).

Studies have shown that several factors contribute to the degree of impairment related to BPD symptoms, such as severity of abuse, age of onset of abuse, and number and types of abuse (Silk, Lee, Hill, & Lohr, 1995; Yen et al., 2002; Zanarini et al., 2002). Studies have also shown that collective trauma, as opposed to a singular event, appears to have a greater relationship to the development of BPD (Ludolph et al., 1990; Weaver & Clum, 1993). Childhood sexual abuse is just one of the well-researched components of the etiology of BPD and one that will continue to be studied within the context of this personality typology.

The familial environment has been found to be a contributing factor in the development of BPD. Afifi and colleagues (2011) examined personality disorders within the context of childhood adversity, which included familial environment. Findings showed that individuals with BPD had the highest prevalence of physical, sexual, and emotional abuse, as well as physical and emotional neglect and general household dysfunction. The family environment makes it difficult to extrapolate abuse from the overall family environment in which the abuse takes place, which also tends to have familial chaos, disrupted attachments, multiple caregivers, parental neglect, alcohol and drug abuse, and affective instability (Dahl, 1985; Golomb et al., 1994; Gunderson & Phillips, 1991; Ogata et al., 1990).

Studies have consistently found that individuals with BPD grew up in severely dysfunctional family environments that featured neglect, conflict, hostility, chaotic unpredictability, and abnormal bonding with parents who provided a mix of neglect and over-protective responses (Frank & Paris, 1981; Giffin, 2008; Links, 1990; Soloff & Millward, 1983). Linehan (1993) writes about three types of invalidating families seen in her clinic: "chaotic, "perfect," and "typical." They are shown graphically below:

Chaotic Families	Perfect Families	Typical Families
• Problems with substance abuse • Financial problems • Parents absent much of the time • Little time/ attention given to child • Needs of the child are disregarded and invalidated	• Parents cannot tolerate negative emotional displays from their children • Express sympathy toward identified BPD child • Express invalidating attitudes toward BPD child	• Emphasis of cognitive control over emotions • Focus on achievement and mastery as criteria of success • Sharp boundaries between self and others

Types of Invalidating Families

Invalidating environments feed emotion dysregulation and vice versa to enhance the actions and reactions of the BPD individual (Linehan, 1993). Linehan (1993) describes two common errors. First, the expectation that the child can display different or more behaviors than he or she is capable of, followed by excessive punishment and insufficient responses in the form of maladaptive modeling, instruction, coaching, cheerleading, and reinforcement. The second error is the reinforcement of "extreme expressive behaviors" (p. 59), and the stifling of more moderate expressive behaviors that can be beneficial.

Parental separation and loss have been found to be precursors to the development of BPD (Bandelow et al., 2005; Links et al., 1988; Reich & Zanarini, 2001; Soloff & Millward, 1983). Bradley (1979) examined childhood separation in 14 children and adolescents diagnosed with BPD. Results showed that separation before age 5 had a higher frequency rate among those diagnosed with BPD than those deemed psychotic, non-psychotic, psychiatric and not psychiatrically referred in delinquent controls. Interestingly, there was no difference in the number of separations between ages 5 and 10 for BPD individuals and remaining groups.

There is an extensive amount of research conducted on BPD individuals and childhood histories that include long separations from, or permanent loss of, one or both parents. Additionally, BPD has discriminated from individuals with schizophrenia, depression, and other personality disorders (Bradley, 1979; Frank & Paris, 1981; Goldberg et al, 1986; Links et al., 1988; Soloff & Millward, 1983; Zanarini et al., 1988). Noting the prevalence of parental separation, loss, neglect, and other dysfunction present in BPD individuals' histories, questions arise about the BPD parent and how he or she interacts with the child. Hobson and colleagues (2009) examined how women with BPD interacted with their 12- to 18-month infants. Results showed that 85% of the BPD mothers showed disruptive affective communication with their infants as compared with mothers without mental health disorders.

Benjamin (1996) proposes a pathogenic hypothesis for the development of symptoms in the BPD individual which has four main features. First, the family environment is dominated by chaos. Crises are in the form of "terrible fights, affairs, abortions, infidelity, drunken acting-out, suicide attempts, murders, imprisonment, disowning, and illicit births" (p. 118). When calm does prevail, the BPD individual feels empty, bored, and lackluster. There is no sense of constancy; the BPD individual's world is in constant flux heavily peppered with chaos and instability. The second aspect is the traumatic abandonment experiences that included hours or days of being left alone without protection, companionship, or materials for positive activities. Benjamin (1996) gives the example of the BPD child being locked in a room alone while the parent is out on a date, being locked in a basement for alleged misbehavior, or being available for sexual or abusive religious rituals. This time alone becomes associated with the notion that the BPD individual is a bad person, as they are left alone or left with an abusive or neglectful "supervisor" or "caretaker." When sexual abuse is painful, the probability that the BPD individual will engage in self-mutilation is increased, due to pleasure and pain becoming confused. The abuse also teaches the BPD individual to shift from idealization to devaluation. The devaluation disrupts his or her ability to accurately test reality and make sound judgments, causing the individual with BPD to become confused and disoriented.

The third feature in Benjamin's (1996) hypothesis is that the physical or sexual abuse occurred when the BPD individual was unprotected and alone, and family ideals held that autonomy is bad and that dependence and compassionate misery with the family are good. Thus, the BPD individual learned while growing up that allegiance to the chaos and maladjustment meant pleasure and "peace." From this comes the tendency to self-sabotage as good things begin to happen, such as in school, a relationship, therapy, or a new job. More specifically, self-sabotage is derived from two possible sources: the internalization of the abuser, and a jealous parent or sibling who implements revenge or causes pain that is a recapitulation of earlier instances of abuse. The second premise is that the BPD individual needs to be sick in order to continue to be cared for; if he or she gets better in treatment, he or she will be "ejected" from treatment. The final pathogenic hypothesis is that BPD individuals learn that to gain love and concern from family or loved ones, they must experience misery, sickness, and debilitation. Familial abandonment was a genuine concern and caring and nurturance only came when the BPD individual was needy and miserable. Benjamin's (1996) four hypotheses for BPD development are illustrated below:

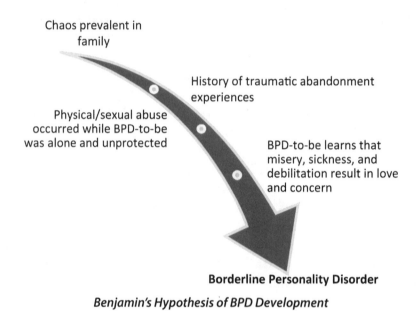

Benjamin's Hypothesis of BPD Development

PREVALENCE

According to the DSM-5 (APA, 2013), prevalence rates for BPD are estimated to be 1.6%, but potentially are as high as 5.9%. Within primary care settings it is estimated to be approximately 6%, 10% in outpatient mental health clinics, and approximately 20% in psychiatric patients. It is possible that BPD may decrease in prevalence in older age groups (APA, 2013). Within all personality disorders, BPD is proposed to range from 30% to 60%. Several research studies have found similar prevalence rates for BPD to be 1% to 2% in community samples, 10% in out-patient psychiatric clinics, and 20% for in-patient psychiatric environments (Gross et al., 2002; Lenzenweger, Loranger, Korfine, & Neff, 1997; Torgersen, Kringlen, & Cramer, 2001).

     Zanarini and colleagues (2011) assessed the prevalence of BPD in two samples: one composed of 6,330 11-year-old children in Bristol, England; and the other composed of 34,653 adults in the United States. The children were interviewed in the UK using the UK version of the Childhood Interview for DSM-IV Borderline personality disorder (UK-CI-BPD; Zanarini, Horwood, Waylen, & Wolke, 2004), and the adults were given the Wave 2 Alcohol Use Disorder and Associated Disabilities Interview Schedule – DSM-IV Version (AUDADIS-IV). The study revealed prevalence rates for symptoms associated with the DSM-IV BPD diagnosis in both samples to be similarly comprised of chronic emptiness, physically self-damaging acts, and stormy relationships. In children, there was a higher prevalence of feeling angry and moody; adults reported a higher prevalence of being paranoid/dissociated, having a serious identity disturbance, being impulsive, and making frantic efforts to avoid abandonment. Of the entire sample, 5.9% of adults and 3.2% of children met criteria for BPD based upon DSM-IV criteria. The utility of these findings are vast, as separation and similarity of symptoms provide clinicians key components to look for when conducting intake interviews or treatment.

Widiger and Weissman (1991) examined the epidemiology of BPD by conducting a meta-analysis illustrating that a preponderance (76%) of individuals diagnosed with BPD are female, with a gender ratio of 3:1. There is some speculation that the gender bias in BPD is based upon cultural factors. Historically, antisocial personality disorder (ASPD) is not typically seen in females. This may be related to the more intense social control placed on the behavior of females, but as societal attitudes have shifted and females gained a greater degree of self-expression, the prevalence of ASPD has increased in females (Akhtar, 1995). Overlap has been found between ASPD and BPD (Zanarini & Gunderson, 1997), and due to this overlap, when a male client presents with symptoms and meets criteria for BPD, he is more likely to be diagnosed with ASPD. Another aspect to consider is the tendency for self-mutilation in the BPD client that has been hypothesized to possibly be due to gender ideologies based in class-structured industrialized societies where the female body is seen as a commodity and females are seen as more emotional beings with greater relationship focus and dependency than males (Sargent, 2003). As Wright and Owen (2001) concluded, gender stereotypes affect females and the diagnosis of mental illness.

To examine the possibility of gender bias in the mental health community, Becker and Lamb (1994) sent a survey to social workers, psychologists, and psychiatrists to assign diagnoses to hypothetical scenarios where the client met criteria for either BPD or post traumatic stress disorder (PTSD). Half of the recipients received a male case and the other half a female case. Results illustrated a gender bias in that clinicians rated females higher for the applicability of BPD criteria than male clients, though both scenarios met criteria for BPD. It is critical for clinicians in every domain to be aware of the potential for gender bias when making a diagnosis.

ATTACHMENT

Bowlby's theory of attachment (1980, 1988, 1989) is directly applicable to the development and functioning of BPD. It has been found that there is a critical link between attachment and early separation or attachment distortion in the development of psychopathology in individuals of all ages (Mikulincer & Shaver, 2007). Agrawal and colleagues (2004) reviewed 13 studies that examined attachment and BPD or dimensional characteristics of BPD. Results showed that: "All 13 of the studies relating attachment to BPD concluded that there was a strong association with insecure forms of attachment" (p. 101). The authors further conclude that unresolved or fearful insecure attachment or other disorganized type in infancy or childhood may be an indicator of later development of BPD.

Researchers have found that distorted internal working models are likely to result in the inability to predict, understand, process, and adjust in response to the actions and reactions of significant others (Lyons-Ruth & Jacobvitz, 1999; Main, Kaplan, & Cassidy, 1985). Bowlby (1958) conceptualized internal working models to represent how the child or individual sees the world and others. It is the interruption of the development of coherent internal working models by the individual's caregiver through unpredictable, frightening, and/ or abusive behavior that has been found to underlie BPD. Levy and colleagues (2005) examined 99 individuals who were diagnosed with BPD and found that approximately 90% were grouped within avoidant, preoccupied, or fearful-preoccupied attachment types. The individuals who fell within the preoccupied pattern displayed more concern and behavioral response to real or imagined abandonments, the avoidant group tended to show higher scores on inappropriate anger, and the fearful-preoccupied showed higher ratings on identity disturbance. In another study, 90 adults (6 males and 84 females) diagnosed with BPD participated in transference-focused psychotherapy, dialectical behavior therapy, or modified psychodynamic supportive psychotherapy. At initial assessment, the secure attachment type was least prevalent—5%, with the other 95% falling into an insecure attachment pattern. Results showed that transference-focused psychotherapy produced a significant increase in secure attachment classification when compared to the other treatment approaches (Levy et al., 2006).

Individuals with BPD are notorious for having relationship dysfunction, and studies have consistently found an association between attachment and romantic relationship disturbance (Agrawal et al., 2004; Blatt & Levy, 2003; Hill et al., 2008). Hill and colleagues (2011) examined attachment, relationship dysfunction, and BPD symptoms in two samples, one was composed of a community sample of women and the other was a psychiatric sample with 75.4% being female. Results showed that insecure attachment, specifically preoccupied attachment, was related to romantic dysfunction and BPD in both samples. The therapeutic relationship is key to not only therapeutic outcome but to the BPD individual's life and perception of self.

A study that explored BPD and attachment to transitional objects, such as stuffed animals, was conducted by Hooley and Wilson-Murphy (2012) with a nonclinical sample of 80 adults (61 females and 19 males). Results showed the most intense attachment to transitional objects in BPD participants. In addition, those with intense attachments to transitional objects reported less parental care, caregivers who were more controlling, greater relationship anxiety, and more childhood trauma experiences. This particular finding is helpful for the clinician in that the exploration of transitional object attachment is likely to prove useful in identifying the connection to BPD symptoms and adverse early childhood experiences. The attachments to these transitional objects may be serving as substitution of attachment needs that were not met early on and illustrate the desire for connection and the emotional inability to obtain it.

DIAGNOSIS

The criteria most commonly used to diagnose BPD are the seven listed below in Table 1 from the DSM-5 (APA, 2013):

TABLE 1: DSM-5 DIAGNOSTIC CRITERIA FOR BORDERLINE PERSONALITY DISORDER
A. A pervasive pattern of instability of interpersonal relationships, self-image, and affects, and marked impulsivity beginning by early adulthood and present in a variety of contexts, as indicated by five (or more) of the following:
(1) Frantic efforts to avoid real or imagined abandonment. Note: Do not include suicidal or self-mutilating behavior covered in Criterion 5.
(2) A pattern of unstable and intense interpersonal relationships characterized by alternating between extremes of idealization and devaluation
(3) Identity disturbance: markedly and persistently unstable self-image or sense of self
(4) Impulsivity in at least two areas that are potentially self-damaging (e.g., spending, sex, substance abuse, reckless driving, binge eating). Note: Do not include suicidal or self-mutilating behavior covered in Criterion 5
(5) Recurrent suicidal behavior, gestures, or threats, or self-mutilating behavior
(6) Affective instability due to a marked reactivity of mood (e.g., intense episodic dysphoria, irritability, or anxiety usually lasting a few hours and only rarely more than a few days)
(7) Chronic feelings of emptiness
(8) Inappropriate, intense anger or difficulty controlling anger (e.g., frequent displays of temper, constant anger, recurrent physical fights)
(9) Transient, stress-related paranoid ideation or severe dissociative symptoms

Consistent with all of the criteria listed in the DSM, these are not hard and fast rules of diagnosis, but rather guidelines and criteria to making diagnoses, as individual and cultural differences will impact presentation and expression of BPD. The first criterion pertains to the BPD individual's hypersensitivity to being rejected or abandoned. These individuals often misread instances that would be seen by most as benign. For example, a woman feels rejected by her boyfriend because he shows up late for their anniversary date due to an emergency at work; this also tends to mean to her that he was with another woman. Due to the strong internal tendency to need another nearby to validate his or her sense of self, the BPD individual does not tolerate time alone well. Disagreement is often seen as an internalized rejection of who he or she is and a disallowance of being a part of another individual's life; he or she jumps to the conclusion that he or she will be alone forever and will never be loved. This belief and the feeling that he or she is being rejected or abandoned leads to acting-out in a frantic effort to avoid being rejected or abandoned.

Criterion two entails the pattern of unstable and intense interpersonal relationships that tend to vacillate between idealization and devaluation. The BPD individual "jumps all the way in" when new relationships emerge and feels a deep sense of connection that is not consistent with a standard beginning relationship. The date that ends in sexual interaction is followed by deep feelings of love and a belief that the act signaled enduring love and commitment with a "perfect person." At the end of the date, when he or she leaves to return home, the BPD individual is distraught and sees the other individual as tyrannical and "a user." This cycle continues until the intimate partner decides it is too much and breaks it off, which not only validates the internal view held by BPD individuals who all men or women, or both, are nothing but heartless losers. These tumultuous relationships include family and friends as well. The BPD mother places unreasonable visitation demands on the ex-boyfriend or ex-husband and his family. In friendships, relationships are again seen as deep and overly meaningful and the identified other is a "best friend" or an "only friend." Due to these unrealistic expectations and demands, the non-BPD friend distances himself or herself and the friendship ultimately ends, so the once-hero is now a user and despicable for having hurt the BPD individual in this manner.

The third criterion is related to the inconsistent manner in which the BPD individual sees himself or herself. As there is no solid sense of self or identity, the BPD individual often changes styles, attitude, social preferences, sexual preferences, and interests. Typically, these changes are an attempt to draw in a lost friend or lover, or identified other, even the therapist in some cases. The BPD individual who idealizes his or her therapist may make attempts to wear similar clothes or overly relate to any self-disclosure the therapist may engage in. In extreme cases, the BPD individual may even try to move into the therapist's neighborhood or apartment complex.

Criterion four pertains to the engagement in activities that are self-defeating or self-damaging; for example, the BPD individual who is sexually promiscuous and does not use protection because "it doesn't feel as good or the same," or engages in substance abuse, shopping sprees, or other behaviors to feel better about himself or herself. These behaviors tend to occur following a rejection or perceived abandonment episode, The BPD individual justifies this behavior by believing that he or she is deserving of new clothes, drinking heavily, or having sex with several partners in a very short time period. Typically, the BPD individual will find one or two self-damaging behaviors that fill or remove the void of rejection and abandonment, which helps the therapist better identify maladaptive patterns for change. This criterion is also one that typically causes the BPD individual to be misdiagnosed with bipolar disorder though an identifiable trigger is evident and other criteria are not met.

Criterion five is the one that is most associated with the BPD individual and not evident in the other personality disorders. The BPD individual engages in self-mutilation, para-suicidal and suicidal gestures, or makes threats to gain attention and keep others close to avoid loss of love or rejection. The threat of self-harm or engaging in cutting or like behaviors is typically reinforced by family, friends, and romantic partners as these behaviors cannot be ignored and thus gratify the need for a sense of importance, value, and safety. However, if they ever felt important or safe they would not be able to articulate it and would likely reject it as a foreign and threatening sensation. These behaviors should not be ignored and must be dealt with in treatment with a trained professional. Statements like, "you'll never do it," "you're always bluffing," and "go ahead, I dare you" can result in serious harm to self and even death.

The sixth criterion entails emotional lability and the tendency to overreact to situations that do not warrant it. The reaction is seemingly "out of the blue" and without purpose. The BPD individual may appear irrational, but in almost all cases there is a link to a triggering event. Typically, the BPD individual is resistant to being "talked down" or rationalized with, and this may further exacerbate his or her emotional reactivity. The sense of rejection and loss is followed by loneliness, even in the presence of others. However, those that tend to be nearby are the targets of intense anger, anxiety, and depression. Though the emotional expression is meant to relieve the loneliness and feelings of abandonment, the BPD individual only ends up distancing others, and causing the feared loneliness.

Criterion seven is related to the BPD individual's consistent feelings of emptiness. This feeling does not dissipate over time. It is typically related to a lack of sense of self, and if the BPD individual cannot define who he or she is, how can anyone else? Due to their lack of depth of interests, BPD individuals are easily bored and complain of an empty life with nothing that fascinates them.

The overblown reaction of the BPD individual pertains to criterion eight, when he or she responds to a seemingly insignificant issue with anger, physical fights, or tantrums. The response is an expression of the underlying pressure and stress the BPD individual experiences on a constant and daily basis, and this release is an effort to obtain connection to others, ensure that others care, or unconsciously to do to others what has been done to them. Sarcasm, intense anger, and physical aggressiveness are not uncommon, as well as the tendency to harm self or others during these florid periods. The final criterion entails the BPD individual's tendency to experience short-lived paranoid ideation or to dissociate as a response to extreme stress. The episode is typically related to a perceived loss or abandonment, but will remit upon the identified other's return.

Additional features of BPD in the DSM-5 (APA, 2013) include a pattern of self-undermining just prior to completing a goal; typically it is prior to obtaining a degree. This self-sabotaging can also be seen when the BPD individual has an affair close to his or her wedding or engagement. The BPD individual may feel more comfortable with a transitional object or a pet as opposed to interpersonal relationships. Recurrent job loss, inconsistent educational history, and broken marriages are common, as well as physical impairments and medical problems following self-mutilation or failed suicide attempts. Brief psychotic episodes are probable as a reaction to intense stress in the form of "hallucinations, body-image distortions, ideas of reference, and hypnagogic phenomena" (p. 665). Hypnagogic phenomena occur during periods of being "half-asleep" or between wakefulness and sleep and consist of visions, prophesies or premonitions, apparitions, and inspiration. They are not psychotic episodes, and they do not occur outside of a mid-wake-sleep period.

Millon and colleagues (Millon et al., 2004) proposed four subtypes of BPD. These four types can be seen in treatment and can dictate the course and areas of concern for the therapist. It is Millon's (2004) view that there are few pure personality prototypes but rather there are mixed variants of one major type with one or more secondary or subsidiary subtypes.

Discouraged (avoidant, melancholic, or dependent features) Submissive, loyal, feels vulnerable and in constant jeopardy; hopeless, helpless, powerless	Petulant (negativistic features) Impatient, restless, sullen, pessimistic; easily slighted and quickly disillusioned
Impulsive (histrionic or antisocial features) Capricious, superficial, frenetic, seductive; fears loss, becomes agitated, gloomy, and irritable; potentially suicidal	Self-Destructive (melancholic or masochistic features) Inward-turning, angry at self, deferential; increasingly high-strung and moody; possible suicide

Millon's Subtypes of BPD

Skodol and colleagues (2011) identified several personality traits and domains for inclusion in the DSM-5 proposed types and traits. They found the following 14 traits within four domains shown below:

Negative Emotionality	Antagonism	Disinhibition	Schizotypy
• Emotional lability • Self-harm • Separation insecurity • Submissiveness • Anxiousness • Low self-esteem • Depressivity • Suspiciousness	• Hostility • Aggression	• Impulsivity • Recklessness	• Dissociation proneness • Cognitive dysregulation

BPD Domains and Traits

Benjamin (1996) has proposed a connection between the BPD individual's interpersonal history and the symptoms listed in the DSM-IV-TR. The fear of abandonment (criterion 1) is derived from associations with past trauma. The strong family background of chaos accounts for the instability and intensity of interpersonal relationships (criterion 2) and affective instability due to reactivity of mood (criterion 6). The BPD individual's identity disturbance is the end result of internalization of objects that would attack him or her when no signs of differentiation or self-definition, and/or happiness were present (criterion 3). The BPD individual has internalized the abandonment so that he or she behaves recklessly, hurting himself or herself (criterion 4). Self-mutilation (criterion 5) is a recapitulation of the abuse and an attempt to assuage the internalized attacker. Past neglect is internalized and associated with boring times alone and danger that lead to feelings of emptiness (criterion 7). The classic BPD anger and difficulty controlling such anger (criterion 8) is triggered by perceived abandonment and is driven by the need to achieve nurturance from identified other(s). The final criterion of paranoia and severe dissociation (criterion 9) is associated with the experience that confirms that attacks will occur and the learned tendency to "tune out" the traumatic stress or previous physical, sexual, and/or emotional abuse. Benjamin and Wonderlich (1994) compared the social perceptions of 31 patients with BPD, 39 unipolar, and 13 bipolar patients. The study found that borderline patients were most likely to see maternal relationships as hostile and highly autonomous, as well as more likely to see current relationships as characterized by hostility. More specifically, "they viewed themselves as hostilely recoiled from staff and attacked by other patients" (p. 618).

Skodol and colleagues (2002) estimate that a client can be given a diagnosis of BPD through 151 different possible combinations of the nine criteria in the DSM-IV-TR (APA, 2000) based upon choosing five of the nine. It is important to recognize that two clients could be diagnosed with BPD but only share one symptom, which brings up critical clinical implications of the subtypes of BPD that are present (Bradley et al., 2007; Bradley et al., 2005; Digre, Reece, Johnson, & Thomas, 2009; Hallquist & Pilkonis, 2012; Millon et al., 2004). The categorical model may be too simplified to encapsulate a complex personality type like BPD. Most of the research that is done on BPD tends to use a dimensional framework (Miller, Morse, Nolf, Stepp, & Pilkonis, 2012; Widiger, 1995).

Differential Diagnosis

According to the DSM-5 (APA, 2013), BPD is frequently comorbid with depressive and bipolar disorders, and, if criteria are met, for both, both are diagnosed. Due to BPD presentation's likely mimicking depressive and bipolar disorder symptoms, the clinician is cautioned against giving a diagnosis of BPD based on cross-sectional presentation only. A history of patterned behavior at early onset and continual course must be present. Broken down by gender, men who are diagnosed with BPD are more likely to have an another comorbid diagnosis of substance abuse and intermittent explosive disorder, and women with BPD are more likely to be diagnosed with an eating disorder, depressive or bipolar disorder, anxiety disorder, or Post-traumatic stress disorder (Grant et al., 2008; Johnson et al., 2003; Tadić et al., 2009; Zanarini et al., 1998; Zlotnick, Rothschild, & Zimmerman, 2002).

In examining the comorbidity of BPD and bipolar disorder, it has been found that there is substantial overlap due to the inherent complexity of presentation and shared features (Deltito et al., 2001; MacKinnon & Pies, 2006). Goldberg and Garno (2009) conducted a study of 100 adults from the Bipolar Disorder Research Program of the Payne Whitney Clinic in New York. In 55% of the participants, onset of bipolar disorder was prior to age 19, onset of first depressive episode was before age 19 in 56%, and first manic or hypomanic episode in 44%. Findings revealed that early onset of bipolar disorder increased the probability of a BPD diagnosis. The authors controlled for severe childhood trauma and abuse.

As with all disorders, substance abuse must be assessed and the behavior must be distinguished from foundational to the personality versus due to the direct effect of the substance. In addition, personality change due to another medical condition must be ruled out if the behavior mimics BPD, but does not have a longstanding occurrence prior to the medical issue, such as in mild or major neurocognitive disorder due to traumatic brain injury. Developmental phase issues should be considered a qualifier for a diagnosis of personality disorder. Most teenagers will qualify for BPD at one point or another, but they do not actually possess the disordered personality of the BPD individual and should be diagnosed with the specific disorder, as long as it meets the criteria.

Individuals with BPD are typically confused or comorbid with several other personality disorders (APA, 2000; Trull, 2001; Widiger, 1995), and the clinician is required to distinguish and assess each disorder for accurate diagnosis. If an individual meets criteria for more than one personality disorder, it should be diagnosed along with BPD. Histrionic personality disorder (HPD) is most similar to BPD, sometimes called "BPD light." HPD individuals are typically characterized by attention seeking, manipulative behavior, and vacillating emotions, but the BPD individual tends to be destructive, have angry upheavals in relationships, and long-term feelings of emptiness and loneliness. Both BPD and schizotypal personality disorder (SZT) individuals exhibit paranoid ideas and delusions, but in BPD the symptoms are short-lived, a reaction to an interpersonal issue or crisis, and tend to respond to being "talked down." Individuals with both paranoid personality disorder (PPD) and narcissistic personality disorder (NPD) have a tendency to have angry reactions to minor stimuli, stable self-image with a reduced tendency for self-sabotage, impulsive behavior, and abandonment issues, than seen in the BPD individual. The individual diagnosed with ASPD is similarly manipulative, as is the BPD individual, but the ASPD individual engages in his or her behavior for profit or material gain, compared to the BPD individual who is manipulative to gain nurturance and caring. The BPD individual and the person diagnosed with dependent personality disorder (DPD) both possess heightened concern and fear of abandonment, but the BPD individual responds with rage, emptiness, and demands, whereas the HPD individual will increase capitulation and pacification and will desperately seek to replace the relationship to resume getting external caring and support.

ASSESSMENT

There are several methods to assess BPD, the most common being the unstructured clinical interview, followed by the structured clinical interview such as the Structured Clinical Interview for DSM-IV personality disorders (SCID-II; First et al., 1997) and the Structured Interview for DSM-IV Personality (SIDP-IV; Pfohl et al., 1997). Screening and self-report instruments available to the qualified clinician are very useful in providing accurate diagnosis of BPD. These instruments include the Personality Diagnostic Questionnaire-IV (PDQ-IV; Hyler, 1994), Wisconsin Personality Inventory (WISPI; Klein, Benjamin, Rosenfeld, & Treece, 1993; Smith, Klein, & Benjamin, 2003), Personality Assessment Inventory (PAI; Morey, 1991), and Schedule for Normal and Abnormal Personality (SNAP; Clark, 1993a). The Minnesota Multiphasic Personality Inventory, Second Edition (MMPI-2) and the Millon Multiaxial Clinical Inventory, Third Edition (MCMI) have been used most widely in research and clinical settings. When a BPD individual is given the MMPI-2, results are expected to show elevations on scales 2 (depression), 4 (psychothemia), and 8 (schizophrenia). This code type illustrates a tendency to feel depressed, dysphoric, hopeless, and have feelings of deprecation; BPD individuals do not seem to fit into their home environments (Graham, 2011). In addition, these individuals are typically seen as odd, nonconforming, and resentful of authority, with erratic behavior and impulse control issues. They fail to learn from past mistakes, may act out in asocial/antisocial ways, may be sexually deviant, harbor deep feelings of insecurity, and poor self-concept, have a strong need for attention, and seem as though they set themselves up for rejection and failure (Graham, 2011). Additionally there are elevations on scales 0 (social introversion) and K (correction); F (frequency) tends to be low (Graham, 2011).

On the MCMI, the BPD individual tends to show elevations on scales C (borderline), 8A (passive-aggressive), A (anxiety), H (somatoform), N (bipolar-manic), and D (dysthymia) as noted by Choca & Van Denburg (1997). Results are related to the individual's mood instability, self-mutilation, interpersonal difficulties, intense fear of abandonment, vacillation in the assessment of others, poorly defined self, feelings of emptiness, and disorganized thoughts along with anxiety, physical complaints, and chronic and long-lasting depressed mood.

The Rorschach has been used to explore the pathology of the BPD individual (Baity, Blais, Hilsenroth, Fowler, & Padawer, 2009) and found significant differences between clinical and nonclinical protocols. The Rorschach has been used successfully to distinguish between psychotic individuals, dissociative identity disorder (DID) individuals, and the BPD individual (Brand, Armstrong, Loewenstein, & McNary, 2009). The Thematic Apperception Test (TAT) has been used with BPD individuals and results typically show "primitive splitting" in narratives with characters as all bad or all good, separation anxiety themes, examples of extreme affect, and impulsive responses to get needs met (Bellak & Abrams, 1997).

CASE EXAMPLE – MALE

Luther is a 22-year-old white male who has been admitted to an in-patient facility after threatening to cut himself when his girlfriend would not allow him to move in with her. Luther has visible scars along his arms and neck. He has several tattoos on his body of various demonic figures and skulls. When he was admitted he screamed obscenities and threatened staff until he was sedated. The following morning, he asked for a pen to write an apology letter to his girlfriend whom, he stated, "he could not live without." The orderly told Luther he would get him a pen but it would take 10 minutes. Luther then looked on the floor and the wall until he found a loose hard piece of plastic he could use to cut himself. He proceeded to cut a seven-inch gash into his forearms and smear the blood on the wall and floor. When the orderly arrived he called an emergency and Luther fell to the ground closing his eyes. The other orderlies and a doctor ran into his room and began to treat his wounds. After his wounds were sutured, he was asked why he cut himself. Luther stated that "if you can't even bring me a pen, then how can you feed me; if you can't feed me, then I'm going to starve to death. I am not going to let you starve me to death."

CASE EXAMPLE – FEMALE

Paula just started spending time with Sharon who she met during a Zumba class. They have been going out dancing the last two nights and "cruising for guys." Paula just broke up with her "longtime" boyfriend, of one month, and was really excited to have met her "twin from another mother." One night Paula was at Sharon's house after a night of "cruising" and she moved to kiss her. Sharon recoiled and Paula ran out of the house crying and into her car. Paula sat in her car watching Sharon's house to see if she would come out to see what was wrong with her, but she never did, only proving no one really cared. Paula called the house approximately 30 times in 10 minutes, but Sharon never picked up. She left messages trying to explain and then began leaving increasingly angry and threatening messages, at one point stating how cruel Sharon was to lead her on like that. Paula then began punching her car window and kicking the floor, followed by grabbing a razor she keeps in the glove box and cutting her inner thigh. Paula was then able to relax and walked up to Sharon's door and began kicking the door. Sharon came to the door and saw the blood and called 9-1-1 immediately. She tended to the cuts until the ambulance came and took Paula to the hospital. When paramedics brought Paula into the emergency room, the attending physician said, "Hey Paula, another rough night?"

TREATMENT

It is well known throughout treatment circles that BPD is one of the most difficult conditions to treat. Starting in the 1950s and 1960s, modifications to psychoanalytic treatment were used to treat these complex cases and later, in the 1980s, a cognitive behavioral treatment emerged with a specific treatment regimen called dialectical behavior therapy (DBT; Linehan, 1993).

The psychodynamic approach has shown significant improvement in the treatment of BPD (Adler, 1981, 1989; Gabbard, 2010; Kernberg, 1984; Levy, Wasserman, Scott, & Yeomans, 2009). Utilizing this approach, the focus is on understanding BPD through the examination of skewed development and the manner in which the BPD individual experiences self and others, and regulates emotions and impulses (Bradley & Westen, 2005). Kernberg (1975) developed an approach that drew upon several psychoanalytic schools of thought including ego psychology and object relations, and together they address adaptive functioning, interpersonal relationships, and how the BPD individual sees himself or herself and others (Bradley et al., 2007). Kernberg's method utilizes the relationship as a central factor to progress through distorted ways of understanding interpersonal relationships, the value in aggression that is often projected onto others, and the defense mechanism of "splitting" that is often used. Therapists who utilize this method often confront aggression and manipulation, and assist clients in reaching a greater degree of balance in how they see themselves and others, with conflicts interpreted as blockades to love and work (see Bradley, et al., 2007).

Another popular psychodynamic approach is based upon the work of Kohut, (1977, 1984), which focuses on self-psychology that postulates that psychopathology is rooted in disrupted or unmet developmental needs and centers on identity and self-soothing (Bradley,

Conklin, & Westin, 2007). Kohut's (1984) goal was to move the strictly BPD individual into an "analyzable narcissistic personality," as long as the therapist can "stand the heat" of the inherent tumultuous and labile emotions that are likely to emerge at the start of this process. Kohut's method is less often used with more severe forms of BPD.

Cognitive-behavioral therapy (CBT) emphasizes observable behaviors and internal scripts and stresses the role of assumptions (Beck et al., 2004). An example of some typical internal scripts of the BPD individual is "I'll be alone forever"; "No one will be there for me"; "I'm a bad person"; "No one would love me if they really got to know me." The CBT therapist views these assumptions as important themes indicating fear of abandonment, exaggerated guilt, and determination to be unlovable (Pretzer, 1990). The assumption and cognitive characteristics are hypothesized to play a key role in the maintenance of BPD and should be targeted for treatment. The contradictory combination of an assumption of dependency that manifests in the belief that he or she is weak and incapable and others are strong and capable, paired with the paranoid assumption that others are untrustworthy and cruel drive the labile and extreme behavior seen in the BPD individual.

The CBT treatment approach must initially identify type and objective, such as whether therapy will be short-term and focus on the reduction of the most severe and problematic behaviors, or longer-term and emphasize intrapersonal and interpersonal relationships and utilize the therapeutic relationship to challenge childhood issues, especially those related to abuse and attachment concerns (Brown, Newman, Charlesworth, Crits-Christoph, & Beck, 2004; Gunderson, 1996; Linehan, Armstrong, Suarez, & Allmon, 1991). Several specific interventions outlined by Beck et al. (2004), utilizing a CBT modality, have been proposed for treating the BPD client and are listed below:

Benjamin (1996) describes her five categories of correct response with the BPD client as the therapist's assisting the client in learning about maladaptive patterns and their origins, making decisions to do things differently, and learning new patterns of seeing and responding to the world. The initial step in facilitating collaboration begins by building a therapeutic alliance and collaborating against "it." The "it" is the destructive patterns that the BPD individual has internalized. The therapist must be prepared to manage the inevitable disruption and prevented from falling into the role of proving to the BPD client that the therapist can "deliver" good services and a positive alternative future. Facilitating pattern recognition is the second step. The therapist utilizes techniques such as "dream analysis, free association, role plays, catharsis, 'regression in the service of the ego,' interpretation of transference, educational assignments, and more" (p. 135) to assist the BPD individual to learn about patterns without causing self-harm or harming others. The therapist must be careful in technique selection to make certain that it does not respond to primitive needs and to reality test with validation, recognizing that old experiences, such as abuse, were painful and traumatic. Blocking maladaptive patterns is the third step and includes the BPD individual's learning to "recognize regressive danger" when he or she perceives abandonment which ignites a series of destructive patterns. The therapist should anticipate regression when things are going well and this should be pointed out to the client as a previous pattern and provide evidence in a "reflective, concerned, tentative manner rather than as indictment" (p. 137).

The fourth step is strengthening the will to give up maladaptive patterns through developing dislike for abusive attachment figures or developing stronger attachment to an

Hierarchical Approach
- Life and death issues
- Behaviors that threaten the therapeutic relationship
- Self-damaging behaviors (e.g., self-mutilation)
- Schema work and trauma processing

Handling Crises
- Address negative beliefs about experiencing emotions that drive crises
- Therapist takes calm, accepting, soothing stance
- Empathic listening for feelings, validations, and interpretations
- Appropriately challenge punitive ideas and actions

Limit-Setting
- Do not permit behaviors that cross personal boundaries (i.e., stalking, threatening, etc.)
- Confront these behaviors when appropriate and client can handle the confrontation
- Be firm, use personal motives to explain it, discuss client's behavior and do not criticize
- Never assume client should have known behavior was inappropriate

Cognitive Techniques
- Unraveling Underlying Schemas - Utilize a journal to address feelings, thoughts, and behaviors; link underlying schemas or modes of thinking to client's history to illustrate schema development
- Tackling Dichotomous Thinking - Identify dichotomous thinking and harmful consequences, and teach client how to be aware of it; utilize a whiteboard to illustrate polarized thinking.
- Flashcards - Use the cards to aid memory of learned skills and counter pathogenic reasoning and activated schemas and modes to illustrate how emotions are derived from activation of the schema or mode of thinking.

Experiential Thinking
- Imaginal Rescripting and Historical Role Play - A current negative feeling is used as a bridge to a childhood memory that the client imagines with eyes closed; as the client engages in this behavior, the therapist enters the scene and intervenes, stopping the abuse or other difficult situation, rescuing the child, and asking what he or she needs
- Empty-Chair Technique - Past abusive or negative individuals can be representationally placed in an empty chair and the client can safely express feelings and thoughts about past occurrences
- Experiencing Emotions - The therapist works with the client to appropriately express emotions and not fear them, and emphasizes the ability to control feelings, even during difficult and confrontive moments.

Behavioral Techniques
- Role Plays - Therapist helps the client learn interpersonal skills, assertiveness, and feeling expression toward others
- Experimenting with New Behavior - Therapist asks the client to behave appropriately to the new schemas and learned strategies, which assists in integrating the new skills into a repertoire of new behaviors.

Cognitive Behavioral Therapy Interventions for BPD

individual who is more positive for the client. The client must commit to eliminating specific maladaptive behaviors, including self-mutilation, self-sabotage, and suicidal or homicidal acting-out. They must also work to remove the abusive attachment figure that has been internalized. Attachment to the therapist is counter productive. The therapist is seen as a vital "emotional cheerleader" who assists in developing positive love and work relationships. Strict limits on hospitalization are essential. The idea of a nurturant hospital stay is seen as regressive, but hospitalization may be necessary following the activation of a core issue. Hospitalization must be clearly discussed between therapist and client. It should be clarified that it does not represent treatment, but rather necessary intervention to avoid serious or fatal behaviors. The therapist should utilize encouragement and positive affirmations regarding client growth and development, recognizing that this can produce concern about treatment ending. The final stage entails facilitating new learning when the new behaviors are utilized in an effective manner to move forward in a healthy and constructive way. The critical step here is to assist the BPD client to accept and extend autonomy while remaining friendly, and it is here that traditional therapeutic techniques to enhance personal growth are effective.

Dialectical Behavior Therapy

Dialectical Behavior Therapy (DBT) is a therapeutic system developed by Marsha M. Linehan to treat BPD (Linehan, 1993). DBT aims to have the client view the therapist as an ally as the therapist attempts to accept and validate the BPD individual's emotions at any particular time, while subsequently indicating that some emotions and behaviors are maladaptive and that there are more personally profitable behaviors. Within DBT there is commitment to core conditions of acceptance and change through a dialectical process with three primary characteristics:

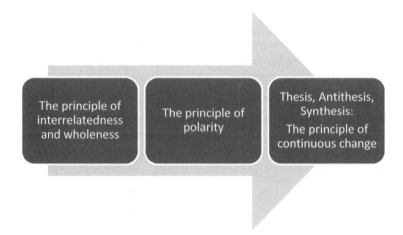

The principle of interrelatedness and wholeness

The principle of polarity

Thesis, Antithesis, Synthesis:
The principle of continuous change

Dialectical Behavior Therapy

The first characteristic is the principle of interrelatedness and wholeness that applies a systems perspective on reality that identity is relational. The second is the principle of polarity, which includes the understanding that reality is not static but compromised by opposing forces out of which synthesis is achieved. The final characteristic is the principle of continuous change which views change, or process, rather than structure or content, as a key component of life and that tension between opposing forces produces change. Based upon these characteristics, a collection of skills, which are largely based upon cognitive-behavioral and interpersonal components, are utilized for emotional self-regulation.

Basic assumptions of DBT include that the client is doing the best he or she can, wants to improve, needs to do better, work harder, and be motivated to change. Further assumptions include the fact that he or she must learn new behaviors in all areas of life, cannot fail, and that the lives of suicidal individuals are unbearable as they currently exist.

The DBT therapist makes every reasonable effort to conduct competent and effective therapy, obey standard ethical and professional guidelines; be available for weekly therapy sessions, phone consultations, and provide needed "therapy backup." The DBT therapist is also tasked with respecting the rights and integrity of the client while maintaining confidentiality, and obtaining consultation when needed. Within DBT there are five skills that are taught: mindfulness, interpersonal effectiveness, emotion regulation, distress tolerance, and self-management. DBT treatment length for an out-patient setting is not static, but depending upon individual treatment and skills training groups, it can last 13 to 14 months (Comtois et al., 2007).

Psychopharmacology

Pharmacotherapy tends to focus on the client's specific symptoms. Selective serotonin reuptake inhibitors (SSRIs), such as fluoxetine, can be used to lessen depressive symptoms and suicidal ideation and behaviors (Markovitz, Calabrese, Schulz, & Meltzer, 1991; Markovitz & Wagner, 1995). Rinne and colleagues (2002) utilized a double-blind, placebo-controlled randomized trial using an SSRI with 38 non-schizophrenic, non-bipolar female participants with BPD and found improvement in rapid mood shifts, but no significant improvement in impulsivity or aggression. Low doses of antipsychotics have been found to be effective for several symptoms, such as perceptual distortions, anger outbursts, suicidality, and mood instability in BPD individuals (Rocca, Marchiaro, Cocuzza, & Bogetto, 2002; Sadock & Sadock, 2007). Bogenschutz and Nurnberg (2004) explored the efficacy of the atypical antipsychotic, olanzapine, with 40 BPD patients (25 female and 15 male) and found that the medication improved scores on the Clinical Global Scale modified for BPD created by the authors over those taking placebo.

The classification system devised by Soloff (1998), and adopted by the American Psychiatric Association to create guidelines for the treatment of BPD (Oldham et al., 2002), illustrate that medication is incorporated into treatment to balance symptoms, which are hypothesized to be predicted based upon knowledge of drug effects in mental disorders. It is up to the clinician to determine whether the primary symptoms are related to issues with affect control, (e.g., lability of mood, inappropriate intense anger, chronic emptiness, dysphoria) and would warrant SSRIs or monoamine oxidase inhibitors (MAOIs) or impulsivity and aggression, which include sensation-seeking, no reflective delay, recurrent assaultiveness, impulsive binges, recurrent suicidal threats and behavior, which might benefit from mood stabilizers (e.g., lithium, carbamazepine, valproate, or SSRIs; or cognitive/perceptual disturbance) (suspiciousness, paranoid ideation, magical thinking, episodic distortions of reality, depersonalization) which might benefit from treatment with antipsychotics (i.e., olanzapine, clozapine, risperidone, etc.) and prescribe the appropriate medication to attenuate presenting symptoms. There are no medications to treat BPD, but medication can be used as ancillary treatment to control symptoms that thwart therapeutic efficacy and advancement.

FILM AND POPULAR MEDIA EXAMPLES

Fatal Attraction (1987) – Alex Forrest, played by Glenn Close

Girl, Interrupted (1999) – Susanna Kaysen (also writer of the book), played by Winona Ryder

Great Expectations (2012) – Miss Havisham, played by Helena Bonham Carter and others (also character in the book)

Play Misty for Me (1971) – Evelyn, played by Jessica Walter

Single White Female (1992) – Hedra Carlson, played by Jennifer Jason Leigh

Eternal Sunshine of Spotless Mind (2004) – Clementine Kruczynski, played by Kate Winslet

Blue Valentine (2010) – Dean, played by Ryan Gosling

Shame (2011) – Brandon, played by Michael Fassbender

Expired (2007) – Jay Caswell, played by Jason Patric

The Cable Guy (1996) – The Cable Guy, played by Jim Carrey

CHECKLIST: BORDERLINE PERSONALITY DISORDER

Below is a complete list to best identify and diagnose Borderline Personality Disorder. DSM-5 (APA, 2013) criteria are first, followed by discernible components, and lastly, associated features.

- ❑ A pervasive pattern of instability of interpersonal relationships, self-image, and affects, and marked impulsivity beginning by early adulthood and present in a variety of contexts*
- ❑ Frantic efforts to avoid real or imagined abandonment*
- ❑ A pattern of unstable and intense interpersonal relationships characterized by alternating between extremes of idealization and devaluation*
- ❑ Identity disturbance: markedly and persistently unstable self-image or sense of self*
- ❑ Impulsivity in at least two areas that are potentially self-damaging (e.g., spending, sex, substance abuse, reckless driving, binge eating)*
- ❑ Recurrent suicidal behavior, gestures, or threats, or self-mutilating behavior*
- ❑ Affective instability due to a marked reactivity of mood (e.g., intense episodic dysphoria, irritability, or anxiety usually lasting a few hours and only rarely more than a few days)
- ❑ Chronic feelings of emptiness*
- ❑ Inappropriate, intense anger or difficulty controlling anger (e.g., frequent displays of temper, constant anger, recurrent physical fights)*
- ❑ Transient, stress-related paranoid ideation or severe dissociative symptoms*
- ❑ Tendency to undermine self just prior to reaching a goal
- ❑ Psychotic-like symptoms prompted by continual and severe stress
- ❑ Intensive attachment to inanimate or transitional object, such as a stuffed animal
- ❑ Has experienced an "out-of-body" experience as a stress reaction
- ❑ Feels victimized
- ❑ May be overprotective and isolate others
- ❑ Evokes guilt and anxiety in others
- ❑ Those around him or her tend to emotionally sacrifice to keep BPD individual calm
- ❑ Harbors intense fear that is overtly displayed as hostility
- ❑ Seductive towards atypical figures and in atypical situations
- ❑ Demands loyalty, though shows little
- ❑ Intrusive and tendency to violate boundaries of others
- ❑ Mood lability with definable trigger

*distinguishing characteristics

THERAPIST CLIENT ACTIVITY

Use these probes to explore your BPD client's vacillating moods, tenuous inner-self, and cautious views of the world that are central to the pathology and enhance the socioeconomic dysfunction.

- When you feel alone or empty what is the first thing that comes to your mind?
- Do you see a need for change that is possible in your future?
- How could therapy help you achieve change?
- What has worked in therapy before and what has not?
- What is the most difficult urge you have and what thought or action precedes it?
- When was the last time you felt emotionally overwhelmed because someone you loved or needed might leave you, and what happened?
- How would you describe your relationships with friends and lovers?
- How does your view of yourself change from day to day?
- When was the last time you tried to hurt yourself to get someone to love you?
- What have you done in the past to prevent a loved one from leaving?
- What object are you closest to?
- What mood is the most difficult for you control?
- What do you find peaceful?
- When was the last time your anger got the best of you?
- When was the last time you engaged in a sex act and regretted it afterward, and what did you do?
- What does sex represent to you?
- What is the best way for you to connect to someone?
- What would it be like to have a strictly professional relationship with another that is intimate and caring?
- What would you change first in your life?

CLIENT QUESTIONNAIRE

The following questions are to be given to your client to help him or her identify past challenges and provide guidance for treatment.

What is your earliest recollection? (describe only as much as you feel comfortable with).

List three things that led up to your losing control, the last time you felt out of control:

Draw a picture of how you see yourself as a child and how you see yourself now:

Histrionic Personality Disorder

Histrionic personality disorder (HPD) describes an individual with a history of engaging in emotional and dramatic behavior in order to be the center of attention to get his or her needs met. HPD has an extensive history dating back four thousand years when it was designated "hysteria" (Veith, 1977). Hysteria is one of the earliest known disorders, and was written about and diagnosed as early as Freud's time (Freud, Breuer, & Luckhurst, 2004). Hysteria has represented many conditions over time including extreme stress reactions, specific conversion symptoms, somatization, and other aspects of the human condition up to and including HPD (Lazare, 1971; Pfohl, 1991). Today's conceptualization of HPD is most closely associated with Freud's writings on "hysterical neurosis" (Freud, 1984/1997) which would be classified as a somatic symptom disorder or a related disorder (e.g., illness anxiety disorder). *The Diagnostic and Statistical Manual, First Edition* (DSM-I; APA, 1952) does not list the diagnosis of HPD. However, it does present a similar symptom-based conceptualization titled "conversion hysteria" associated with dissociative reaction and conversion reaction, as well as "anxiety hysteria" associated with a phobic reaction that would fall into what we now consider to be a conversion disorder (functional neurological symptoms disorder). Within the DSM-I personality trait disturbances, "emotionally unstable personality" is most closely linked to today's HPD as this diagnosis includes excitable, undependable, and ineffective reaction to even minor stress, as well as relationship difficulties due to emotional attitudes that consist of strong and poorly controlled hostility, guilt, and anxiety.

In the DSM-II (APA, 1968) under "personality disorders and certain other non-psychotic mental disorders," the identifier histrionic personality disorder appeared parenthetically after "hysterical personality" with the following description: "These behavior patterns are characterized by excitability, emotional instability, over-reactivity, and self-dramatization. This self-dramatization is always attention-seeking and often seductive, whether or not that patient is aware of the purpose. These personalities are also immature, self-centered, often vain, and usually dependent on others."

The DSM-I and DSM-II received considerable criticism for poor psychometric properties (Nathan, 1998), particularly the poor reliability and validity (Blashfield & Flanagan, 1998; Kirk & Kutchins, 1994). Additional concerns were that the diagnostic descriptions were not detailed, leaving a lot of room for error, and had been written by a small number of academics rather than by using empirical studies. With the publication of the DSM-III (APA, 1980), the term "hysterical personality" was changed to "histrionic personality" to identify the behavioral pattern of its Latin root, *histrio,* meaning theatrical, and to lessen the association with hysteria (Spitzer, Williams, & Skodol, 1980). Due to overlap with borderline personality disorder (BPD), several changes were made in the next edition of the manual, DSM-III-R (APA, 1987; Pfohl, 1991). Other significant changes to HPD were made in the DSM-III-R, including removing criteria that were related to cravings for activity and excitement; irrational, angry outbursts, or tantrums; and inclinations toward manipulative suicide attempts (Pfohl, 1991). The DSM-III-R added two new criteria that connected HPD to its historical roots. These included criteria 2, inappropriately sexually seductive in appearance and behaviors; and criteria 8, excessively impressionistic speech that also lacks detail (Pfohl, 1991). Concerns arose regarding HPD criteria and validity, and consistency with clinical theory and practice (Blashfield & Davis, 1993; Bornstein, 1999a).

Blashfield and Breen (1989) conducted a study to examine the face validity of personality disorders in the DSM-III-R. Utilizing a sample of 29 psychiatrists and 32 psychologists who were asked to identify which criteria went with which personality disorder, the authors concluded that face validity was in need of revision because clinicians assigned correct diagnostic criteria to the correct personality disorder in only 66% of the cases. HPD (41%) had the lowest rate of correct assignment; its criteria were frequently identified as being associated with narcissistic personality disorder (NPD). Only three criteria for HPD were recognized by a majority of the sample. The authors concluded that "the DSM-III-R definition of histrionic does not match the definition for this category that is used by contemporary American clinicians [and] this category needs a major change in definition in DSM-IV" (p. 1,578).

In the DSM-IV (APA, 1994), the HPD criterion "is self-centered, actions being directed toward obtaining immediate satisfaction; has no tolerance for frustration of delayed gratification" was removed due to low specificity. In order to keep the number of criteria at 8, "considers relationships to be more intimate than they actually are" was added. Due to lack of distinction and overlap with other personality disorders, the criterion "constantly seeks or demands reassurance, approval, or praise" and was replaced with "is suggestible, that is, easily influenced by others or circumstances." The requirement of meeting four criteria out of eight in the DSM-III-R was increased to five out of eight in the DSM-IV. With these modifications in the DSM-IV, issues arose with psychodynamically-oriented clinicians who felt that the hysterical personality disorder was more accurate for the primitive, lower-functioning individuals who qualify for HPD within the DSM-IV (Gabbard, 1994a). Bakkevig and Karterud (2010) examined the construct validity of HPD within the DSM-IV using a sample of 2,289 patients from the Norwegian Network of Psychotherapeutic Day Hospitals and found a prevalence rate of 0.4% and high comorbidity with borderline personality disorder (BPD), narcissistic personality disorder (NPD), and dependent personality disorder (DPD) and broke into two discernible clusters: exhibitionistic and attention-seeking traits, and impressionistic traits, but the authors concluded poor construct validity for HPD. No text revisions were made to HPD within the DSM-IV-TR (APA, 2000).

No changes were made to the HPD criteria from the previous volume, DSM-IV-TR (APA, 2000) in the DSM-5 (APA, 2013).

ETIOLOGY

There is a paucity of research on the etiology of HPD, especially its heritability. Torgersen and colleagues (2008) examined the influence of genetic factors and genetic and environmental combined influence on Cluster B personality disorders, the cluster that houses HPD. The authors utilized a sample of 1,386 Norwegian twin pairs and found estimated heritability to be 31% for HPD and concluded that there is a high rate of comorbidity within cluster B that is derived from genetic and environmental influence. The popular view of the etiology of HPD tends to focus on developmental and cultural aspects. The cultural view is utilized with caution. The DSM-5 (APA, 2013) specifically addresses this issue, by requesting that before clinicians make a final diagnosis of HPD, cultural behavior and presentation of the related traits be explored and aberrant expression be present. HPD has been found to be diagnosed less frequently in cultures that discourage obvious sexual expression, such as Asian and Middle Eastern cultures, and more frequently in Hispanic and Latin American cultures due to the view of sexual expression (Padilla, 1995; Trull & Widiger, 2003). There are no empirical studies that directly explore this issue (Blagov, Fowler, & Lilienfeld, 2007).

The developmental view postulates that the HPD adult experienced strong needs for attention that were erratically met by caregivers (Kraus & Reynolds, 2001). Baker, Capron, and Azorlosa (1996) examined the family environment of HPD and DPD individuals and a control group (whose members did not meet criteria for a personality disorder) and found that those who met HPD criteria had high control and high intellectual-cultural orientation on the Millon Multiaxial Clinical Inventory (MCMI; Millon, Davis, & Millon, 1997). When compared to the DPD group, HPD individuals, but not the control group, presented with high achievement orientation.

Millon (2011) places HPD within the SPH Spectrum: sociable style, pleasuring type, and histrionic disorder. He identifies a pathogenic developmental hypothesis that includes heredity, infantile reaction patterns, neurological characteristics, and physicochemical characteristics.

Heritability is seen as related to family traits that allude to physiological commonalities, but cannot be attributed solely to heredity due to the contributions of learning and experience aspect to development. Infantile reaction patterns in HPD entail a high degree of alertness and emotional responsiveness as seen in infancy and early childhood, but continue into adulthood regardless of social influence to lessen these core traits. Neurological and physicochemical characteristics in the HPD individual entail the high emotional responsiveness seen in their "neutrally dense and abundantly branched limbic region" (p. 364) and "low threshold for reticular activation" (p. 364), as well as highly responsive sympathetic arousal and adrenal reactivity. Millon admits that this is speculation and not based upon empirical findings. The HPD individual has an experiential history that includes being highly stimulation-seeking as an infant and having that behavior reinforced by external forces, which in turn cause him or her to rely on externally based rewards. Parental control by conditional or inconsistent reward is another assumption made by Millon (2011) in that children with minimal punishments and a plethora of rewards will develop an intense and emotionally uncertain outlook when relating to others and actively look externally for rewards instead of internally. Due to inconsistent recognition of success in childhood, the individual develops a self-view of inadequacy and looks to others for confirmation of what is good.

Benjamin (1996) proposes a pathogenic hypothesis for the development of HPD through four main developmental experiences. The first feature entails the HPD individual's being loved for his or her good looks and ability to entertain others; the individual's self-concept is derived from how attractive, pleasant, and entertaining he or she could be. The second experience is that the HPD individual is responded to by an "adoring daddy who dotes on his daughter, flirtatiously and admiringly doing anything and everything for her" (p. 171), for example. Here the HPD individual learns that physical attractiveness and charm are functional and can be used to meet his or her needs with important others. The third aspect pertains to the unpredictability of the HPD individual's household due to parental instability, possibly related to substance abuse. The familial chaos is dramatic and "interesting" (p. 172), not primitive and life-threatening as in the case of the BPD family of origin. Due to previous theatrical upbringing and having to act in a sufficient manner to keep familial peace, the HPD individual continues this pattern of acting "as-if" surface relationships are deeper than they really are. In the final experience, the HPD individual is the type that receives nurturing and caring for being ill and learns to take the sick role to elicit warmth and control as the family rewarded the sickness. If the HPD individual adopts this role, somatization disorder is a possible comorbid condition. Either the coquettish or the sickly role for the HPD individual will determine the functioning with the family of origin and how the family responded to him or her. With an attractive child there is a greater likelihood for the more prototypic HPD pattern, whereas, a physically weak and sensitive child is at a greater likelihood to develop the sickly pattern. Benjamin's (1996) pathogenic hypothesis is shown below:

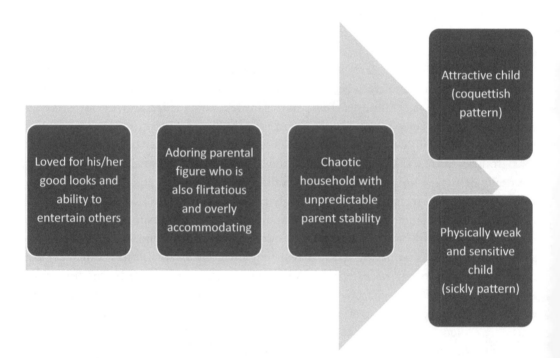

Benjamin's Hypothesis of the Development of Histrionic Personality Disorder

PREVALENCE

The DSM-5 (APA, 2013) lists the National Epidemiologic Survey on Alcohol and Related Conditions (NESARC) prevalence rate for HPD at 1.84%. Bakkevig and Karterud (2010) examined the construct validity of HPD and, in doing so, compiled a segmented list of prevalence rates from studies ranging from 1989 to 2007. Results showed HPD prevalence rates within community samples to be between 0.0% and 3.2%, whereas in psychiatric samples HPD ranged between 1.0% and 6.0%. Due to the date ranges, various editions of the DSM were utilized which could account for fluctuation in HPD prevalence, as well as gender biases and gender distribution. (The latter was not addressed by the authors, but results showed a 71% female composition within their sample).

A source of concern and debate has been the disproportionate rate of females being diagnosed with HPD which has been attributed to the criteria being indicative of behaviors and traits typically seen in stereotyped feminine behavior (Bornstein, 1999a; Sprock, Blashfield, & Smith, 1990; Widiger, 1998). The DSM-5 notes that the sex ratio between males and females in regard to HPD may be an artifact of a higher number of females in clinical settings, biased clinical assessments, or biased diagnostic criteria (First, France, & Pincus, 2004). The DSM-IV-TR addresses the sex ratio concern and notes that: "A man with this disorder may dress or behave in a manner often identified as "macho" and may seek to be the center of attention by bragging about athletic skills, whereas a woman, may choose for example very feminine clothes and talk about how much she impressed her dance instructor" (p. 712). This statement was omitted from the DSM-5 (APA, 2013) and new information was added stating that although HPD is diagnosed more often in females, "the sex ratio is not significantly different from the sex ratio of females within the respective clinical setting. In contrast, some studies using structured assessments report similar prevalence rates among males and females" (p. 668).

ATTACHMENT

Individuals with HPD fall in the broad category of disorders that include awareness of distress, poor emotional control, and expression of symptomatology aimed at the self (Rosenstein & Horowitz, 1996). HPD individuals typically fall in the preoccupied attachment style which includes holding a mental representation of others as positive causing them to approach others, and a view of self as negative causing them to feel vulnerable, particularly to rejection (Bartholomew, Kwong, & Hart, 2001). Individuals with a preoccupied attachment style have an intensive need to relate to others, actively seek relationships, but are highly sensitive to interpersonal stress and tend to react with a desire to attach to others, which can be so intense as to cause friends or partners to withdraw.

The preoccupied attachment style fits the HPD individual as someone who seeks a high level of intimacy, approval, and responsiveness from identified others and values intimacy to the extent that he or she can become overly clingy. Additionally, high levels of worry, impulsivity, and emotional expressiveness is often seen in the HPD individual's relationships.

DIAGNOSIS

The most commonly used criteria to diagnose HPD are the eight listed below in Table 1 from the DSM-5 (APA, 2013):

TABLE 1: DSM-5 DIAGNOSTIC CRITERIA FOR HISTRIONIC PERSONALITY DISORDER
A. A pervasive pattern of excessive emotionality and attention-seeking, beginning by early adulthood and present in a variety of contexts, as indicated by five (or more) of the following: (1) Is uncomfortable in situations in which he or she is not the center of attention (2) Interaction with others is often characterized by inappropriate sexually seductive or provocative behavior (3) Displays rapidly shifting and shallow expression of emotions (4) Consistently uses physical appearance to draw attention to self (5) Has a style of speech that is excessively impressionistic and lacking in detail (6) Shows self-dramatization, theatricality, and exaggerated expression of emotion (7) Is suggestible, i.e., easily influenced by others or circumstances (8) Considers relationships to be more intimate than they actually are

Reprinted with permission from the *Diagnostic and Statistical Manual of Mental Disorders, Fifth Edition*, (Copyright ©2013). American Psychiatric Association. All Rights Reserved.

Consistent with all of the criteria listed in the DSM, these are not hard and fast rules of diagnosis but guidelines and criteria to help make diagnoses, as individual and cultural differences will impact presentation and expression of the HPD. The first criterion pertains to the HPD individual's exhibiting behavioral patterns that draw attention to him or her due to a sense of entitlement—that they deserve to be noticed and are distressed if they are not. When the appropriate amount of attention is not given, he or she feels unappreciated and will engage in behaviors that will place him or her in the "spotlight."

Criterion two entails sexually seductive and provocative behavior to draw attention that may be directed toward an identified sexual partner or may be within a social or work setting. The HPD individual may direct his or her sexual energy toward someone who is in a committed relationship with another and within settings that may promote conflict or confrontation. The HPD male may act inappropriately or provocatively to gain the attention of another's wife or significant other and be affectionate at inappropriate times and in front of others.

The third criterion addresses the HPD individual's tendency to vacillate in emotional expression due to attempting to gain attention from new arrivals or changes within the environment that may be present to lessen the focus on him or her. The emotional expression tends to be shallow and fake, especially during a time in which genuine emotional expression is required. Criterion four is related to inappropriate clothing worn by both male and female HPD individuals in an effort to gain attention and be noticed. These types of clothing are worn in inappropriate settings, such as at the office, children's birthday parties, or funerals. Plastic surgery may be considered so as to look as perfect as possible.

Criterion five pertains to the HPD individual's tendency to use speech that is attention-getting, such as using a seductive tone, but minimal as to actual content or relaying of information. The sixth criterion entails the use of theatrical behavior to gain the "spotlight" and be noticed.

These individuals manage their environments through the use of dramatic behavior to gain attention, get needs met, or express agitation and frustration. This type of behavior may lead others to become agitated and create distance from the HPD individual which tends to cause stress, leading the HPD individual to increase dramatic antics to gain attention that only continues the cycle of behavior and relational distance. The seventh criterion pertains to the HPD individual's being highly suggestible, particularly by someone who is attractive. They are particularly likely to engage in showy or risky behaviors if and when suggested by an attractive figure.

Criterion eight is the tendency to misinterpret relationships as closer than they actually are. Early in relationships, the HPD individual feels that he or she is in love or that he or she is "best friends" with a mere acquaintance. If the identified other has a social status that further promotes the HPD individual's getting noticed, the relationship is seen as even closer and more valuable than in actuality it is.

Additional features listed in the DSM-5 (APA, 2013) include difficulty in romantic and sexual relationships due to emotional intimacy that is often flat or transparent. The HPD individual often acts out a particular role within a relationships (e.g., "hero," "princess," "sage"), and typically is not conscious of doing so. Control is sought through emotional manipulation and seductiveness, while simultaneously displaying dependency on the identified other as well. Same-sex friendships tend to be unsuccessful due to the HPD individual's sexually charged behavior that threatens these relationships. The HPD individual is likely to lose friendships and close relationships due to the constant seeking of attention. When not the center of attention they are likely to become depressed. HPD individuals are often sensation seekers and are easily bored with routine, as well as intolerant and easily agitated when they need to delay gratification and when their actions do not bear immediate fruit for them in their need to garner attention. There tends to be little follow-through on tasks that were accepted or begun with great enthusiasm. This holds true for relationships as well. The HPD individual's new relationships get more attention than older, less novel ones. The DSM-5 (APA, 2013) notes that the actual rate of suicide among individuals with HPD is not known, but there is an increased probability for para suicidal behaviors to gain attention and coerce caregiving.

Millon and colleagues (Millon et al., 2004) proposed six subtypes of HPD. These six types can be seen in treatment and can dictate course and areas of concern for the therapist. It is Millon's (2004) view that there are few pure personality prototypes and that instead, there are mixed variants of one major type with one or more secondary or subsidiary subtypes. The following figure shows Millon's (2004) six histrionic subtypes.

Benjamin (1996) identifies connections between the HPD individual's interpersonal history and the symptoms identified in the DSM. The need to be the center of attention (criterion 1), engaging in seductive behaviors (criterion 2), intensive focus on physical appearance (criterion 4), and the need to feel closer in friendships and romantic relationships than he or she actually is (criterion 8), is related to the HPD individual's seeing himself or herself as the entertainer or "showpiece" with a need to be seen as attractive and to receive adulation for his or her entertainment value. This assumed role further explains the exaggerated expression and theatrical behavioral patterns (criterion 6), and shallow expression and vacillating moods (criterion 3). The HPD individual's impressionistic speech and the deficiency of detail (criterion 5) can be attributed to the inability to maintain focus and competence as a way of

Millon's Histrionic Personality Subtypes

Appeasing (dependent features)	Vivacious (narcissistic features)	Tempestuous (negativistic features)	Disingenuous (antisocial features)	Theatrical (variant of "pure" pattern)	Infantile (borderline features)
Seeks to placate, mend, and repair troubles; moderates tempers by capitulating; sacrifices self for commendation	Vigorous, charming, flippant, impulsive; seeks momentary cheerfulness and playful adventures	Impulsive, out of control; moody complaints, sulking; stormy, impassioned, easily wrought-up; periodically inflamed, turbulent	Underhanded, plotting, crafty, false-hearted; egocentric, insincere, deceitful, and calculating	Affected, mannered postures are striking; markets self-appearance; simulates desirable/dramatic poses	Labile, high-strung, volatile emotions; chidlike hysteria and nascent pouting; fastens to and clutches at another; is overly attached to an identified other

Millon's Histrionic Subtypes

being perceived as attractive. The HPD individual is suggestible to the statements of others. He or she tends to present as incapable of cultivating nurturance, and this incompetence is intended to derive caring from others (criterion 7).

Differential Diagnosis

The DSM-5 (APA, 2000) notes that HPD is comorbid with somatic symptoms and related disorders, conversion disorder (functional neurological symptoms disorder), and major depressive disorder. There is a paucity of studies that examine HPD and depression and anxiety. Many studies examine cluster B disorders, but due to the overlap between HPD and BPD specifically, it is difficult to tease out HPD individuals from those with BPD and other cluster B disorders (Crawford, Cohen, & Brook, 2001). However, clinical experience will illustrate the strong link between HPD and depression and anxiety when needs for attention and affection are not met, resulting in an exacerbation of symptomatology (see Benjamin, 1996). The link between HPD and somatization disorder was explored by Stern and colleagues (1993) utilizing a sample of 25 females, with 72% meeting criteria for somatization disorder. Results illustrated that individuals with HPD in this sample were significantly more likely than controls to have somatization disorder. Another study that examined the comorbidity of personality disorders with somatization disorder found that HPD was significantly associated with somatization disorder, as well as seven other personality disorders (Bornstein & Gold, 2008).

Conversion disorder (functional neurological symptom disorder) comorbid with HPD has been found in many studies (Lempert, Dieterich, Huppert, & Brandt, 1990; Saxe, Van der Kolk, Berkowitz, & Chinman, 1993; Shearer, 1994). Binzer and Eisemann (1998) examined personality traits and motor conversion disorder using 30 inpatients diagnosed with conversion disorder with motor symptoms and found that five females and no males met criteria for HPD. Conversion and HPD had the highest prevalence compared to the remaining personality disorders diagnosed.

The greatest degree of overlap within cluster B is between HPD and BPD individuals as both possess a tendency to be attention-seeking, manipulative, and vacillating in their emotions. However, the BPD individual is more likely to have a self-destructive and angry disruption in close relationships, as well as longstanding emptiness and disrupted identity. Antisocial personality disorder (ASPD) and HPD share the common tendency to be impulsive, without depth, sensation-seeking, irresponsible, seductive, and manipulative, but the HPD individual is manipulative to gain nurturance and caring while the ASPD individual manipulates others to gain profit, power, or other material gratification. Narcissistic personality disorder (NPD) and HPD both desire attention and praise from others, but the NPD individual who does this to confirm his or her superior status, as opposed to the HPD individual who will transition into a dependent or fragile state in order to gain attention and affection. Both NPD and HPD individuals will distort and expand intimacy in relationships. However, the NPD individual does this to affirm unique or special status or to be linked to the wealth of their friends. Dependent personality disorder (DPD) and HPD individuals both share dependency needs related to others' praise and caring, but the DPD individual does this without the magnified emotional aspects.

It is important with HPD, as with all mental health disorders that the clinician be certain that HPD is differentiated from anything associated with a another medical condition (e.g., mild or major neurocognitive disorder due to traumatic brain injury) or debilitating substance use.

ASSESSMENT

Currently, there are no assessments specifically designed for HPD (Blagov et al., 2007), but there are several that can be used to assess traits related to HPD. The Structured Clinical Interview for DSM-IV personality disorders (SCID-II; First et al., 1997) has one item related to each HPD criterion based upon the DSM-IV. The assessments most commonly used to assist in the diagnosis and treatment of HPD are the Minnesota Multiphasic Personality Inventory, Second Edition (MMPI-2), Millon Clinical Multiaxial Inventory, Third Edition (MCMI), the Rorschach Psychodiagnostic Test, and the Thematic Apperception Test (TAT). While these tests are commonly used, there are many others available.

When using the MMPI-2 with the HPD individual, a typical profile would be the 2-3/3-2 (Sperry, 2003). According to Graham (2011), the 2-3 code type illustrates an individual who tends not to experience disabling anxiety, but may report feeling anxious or tense along with sleep disturbances. In addition, sadness and depression is typically reported as well as suicidal ideations. These individuals may lack interest or not participate in their events and have difficulty getting started on tasks and following through. Somatic complaints are likely, as well as harboring feelings of inadequacy while focusing on achievement and power. This code type is seen more often in women than men. The HPD individual may also produce elevations of the 3-4/4-3 or 4-9/9-4 code type (Graham, 2011).

On the MCMI, the HPD individual is likely to produce elevations on scale 4 (histrionic) and H (somatization), while scale 1 (schizoid) and scale 2 (avoidant) are low (Sperry, 2003). These results illustrate a tendency to be dramatic with a low tolerance for boredom, as well as possessing a strong need for dependency, and being loud, demanding, and attention-seeking. In addition, the HPD individual sees himself or herself as outgoing, egocentric, extroverted, and flirtatious. Elevations on scale H tend to be due to the attention-seeking component of taking the sick role.

Blais and Baity (2006) provide a comprehensive review of the Rorschach and HPD, and information derived from using it as an assessment method. When using the Rorschach with HPD, a low number of results is typical, as well as low W (whole), M (human movement), C (pure color), and Y, YF, or T (shading) responses, with an infrequent potential for a "blood" response (Sperry, 2003). The HPD individual will tend to provide TAT responses that are themed in dependency and control, with the possibility for personalized stories that are themed with sexual or aggressive perceptions (Sperry, 2003).

CASE EXAMPLE – MALE

Adonis, real name Steve Jackson, entered treatment at the Minnesota Wellness Center due to depression. He asked for a female therapist, saying he had previous success with female therapists in the past. When Adonis shows up for his first session, he is dressed in a tight black shirt with Gold's Gym written across the front and tight workout pants. When the therapist tries to get to his depression, Adonis goes into long stories about his sexual conquests and his workout schedule. He makes several attempts to ask about her dating life as she is not wearing a wedding ring and there are no pictures in the office of her with men or family—only one picture of her in a running outfit. Adonis continues to try and talk about fitness and the healthy lifestyle that helps him stay "in such great shape." This continues until the third session, when the therapist tells Adonis that she received his EAP request due to poor work performance and reported depression. Adonis appears initially embarrassed and attempts to minimize his depression, but tells her that he was having problems at work due to a change in dress code and a new boss who was competing with him and wanted to make him look bad. Adonis tells the therapist that he is hoping to sleep with his boss's wife as "the ultimate stick it to him. That'll show him who the better man is." The therapist asks Adonis about his family and he becomes quiet and pensive and tells her that his sister is a physicist at MIT, like both of his parents, and that he was going to medical school until he was expelled for steroid use and selling to other students on campus. He received one year felony probation for the offense. He then took his recent job at the medical supply company, but has been having continued problems due to his new boss. His old boss was a female and he had a sexual relationship with her until her promotion and relocation. As therapy progresses, Adonis discusses his history of poor relationships, his mother's alcohol addiction, and his father's "perfect life" that gave him everything he always needed. Adonis found that he could shine in both academics and bodybuilding, so he focused on those two things until his recent expulsion. Therapy continued to progress for one year, and while Adonis continued to base his self-worth on his appearance, he was able to have more genuine relationships with others and allow others the "spotlight for a minute or so."

CASE EXAMPLE – FEMALE

Tiffany is a 32-year-old female who entered therapy as follow-up out-patient treatment due to a three-day hospitalization after she was brought in by her boyfriend for reported suicidal ideation. Tiffany reported that she was recently let go from her job at a video game development company after a meeting where she opened her blouse too much and made a sexually inappropriate comment regarding group sex. Tiffany said that without her job she feels alone and insignificant. Her boyfriend of two weeks is her soul mate and he understands "the way I am" and that the job is within an industry that is very incestuous— losing a job at one company is like losing a job at all of them. As the therapist gathered past information, Tiffany revealed that she has a history of sexually provocative behavior and sexual relationships with many of her co-workers. She sees herself as life of the party, and recalled one instance where she took her shirt off at the company Christmas party to get the attention of a new male co-worker. As the therapeutic relationship deepened, and Tiffany's depression attenuated, she made a sexual advance towards her therapist. When this was rebuffed and immediately discussed in treatment, Tiffany reported a history of sexual abuse by her brother, which was ignored by her parents as her family was always seen as "the good 'ol American family." Tiffany was able to get another job at a different, much smaller, electronic development company, but the challenge remained for her to stay within appropriate office behavior. Her relationship with her soul mate lasted one more week and Tiffany continues to have short-lived but intense relationships.

TREATMENT

Long-term psychotherapy is beneficial to the HPD individual and likely to be cost-effective by minimizing detrimental economic outcomes related to the disorder (Quality Assurance Project, 1991, as cited by Blagov et al., 2007). Within today's climate it is difficult to provide long-term mental health treatment for a personality disorder. Callaghan and colleagues (2003) provided single-subject data on utilizing a functional psychoanalytic psychotherapy approach with an individual who evidenced both histrionic and narcissistic features. The sessions were tracked and rated. Results showed statistically significant in-session and out-of-session improvements. The client was able to develop and maintain meaningful relationships and, at the conclusion of treatment, did not meet criteria for a personality disorder with histrionic and narcissistic features.

Gabbard (1994) gives a good prognosis for high-functioning individuals with HPD utilizing a psychoanalytic approach, as the therapeutic relationship is easily developed and the patient views the therapist as a helping source. Lower-functioning HPD individuals would benefit best from a treatment approach designed for BPD individuals (Gabbard, 1994). Glickauf-Hughes and Wells (1997) describe treatment goals for the hysterical personality, which is similar to HPD, using an object-relations approach, and delineate clear goals for treatment. The therapist works to develop appropriate self-initiative assertion, and independent actions, and to help the client distinguish between the need for sex and his or her need for affection and comfort. The therapist also helps the client express his or her needs clearly and concisely as opposed to circuitous communication patterns. Due to the relatively intact ego function of the HPD individual, the therapist should focus on integrating thoughts and feelings, thinking before acting, and noticing needs and motivations.

A variety of specific cognitive-behavioral therapy (CBT) techniques are beneficial with an HPD client, including identifying and challenging automatic thoughts, activity scheduling, and relaxation training (Beck et al., 2004). Beck and colleagues (2004) recommend working to change the client's interpersonal behavior and thought style, incorporating changes to attain short-term goals, and addressing underlying assumptions such as, "I am inadequate and unable to handle life on my own" and, "it is necessary to be loved—by everyone, all the time," to solidify treatment gains. When working with any client, developing a collaborative strategy is crucial to therapeutic and long-term success. The HPD client can be challenging as emotional issues and theatrical behavior can interfere with treatment, but if dealt with directly, and the issues are resolved, therapeutic progress can be resumed. The therapist needs to remain steadfast, consistent, and fluid in approach until the HPD individual can accept and understand a mode of functioning that is foreign to him or her. Early in treatment, it is common for the HPD client to see the therapist as an all-knowing savior figure. This must be challenged and removed, as it prevents the client from becoming an active participant in treatment.

Specific interventions proposed by Beck and colleagues (2004) include teaching the HPD individual to focus on one issue at a time, which can be done though setting a session agenda. This can lessen the probability of the HPD client's spending most of the session theatrically relaying dramatic stories. The HPD client tends not to remain in treatment very long due to boredom and the need to move on to more exciting interactions. To maintain the HPD client in treatment it is important to keep the goals interesting and meaningful to encourage intrinsic motivation, as well as provide both short-term and long-term benefits. The HPD individual is likely to set broad and vague goals, but treatment goals need to be specific and concrete and within the client's appropriate level of functioning. Do not set goals that are too high-functioning if dealing with a primitive-process HPD client.

The interventions chosen must clearly and directly address the HPD client's particular presenting problem and goal. An example is shown graphically below (data derived from Beck et al., 2004):

Directly assessing and orienting goals to the HPD individual's assumptions prevents therapeutic derailment and encourages the continuation of the process. Using a technique such as this teaches the HPD client a skill to monitor and pinpoint specific thoughts that are

"I must make them notice and like me"

Strong focus on response of others; inattention to own thoughts and feelings

Little skill in handling own emotions and lack of clear sense of identity.

HPD Cognitive Problem and Goal Process

attributed to behavioral manifestations. Written homework assignments will typically be seen as boring, so extra time needs to be dedicated to addressing this issue. Including a smartphone (theirs, not yours) or tablet application to do this may add some excitement, as well as clearly illustrating the benefit of doing the homework.

Having the HPD individual make a list of the advantages and disadvantages of specific behaviors, thoughts, and consequences can be valuable for encouraging coping skills and self-monitoring (Beck et al., 2004). Beck and colleagues (2004) recommend using this tool early in treatment and as soon as the HPD client resists focusing on an agreed-upon topic.

Benjamin (1996) utilizes an interpersonal approach to treatment and applies her five categories of correct responses to the HPD client. The first is to facilitate collaboration, which can be difficult as "a female therapist with a female HPD has the challenge of getting a viable therapy contract with a person who takes a dim view of the therapist's competence" (p. 184). The contract is with the HPD client's observing ego, and the "enemy" is the destructive behavioral patterns. The therapist in this case should communicate support that is warm and accepting in a competent manner; if this is fruitful, then therapy should progress. If there is a male therapist and female HPD, the task is easier initially due to the HPD individual's having a natural gravitation towards male figures as warm and accepting. Regardless of gender, a collaborative relationship to combat "it" must be achieved. "It" represents the part of the individual who promotes maladaptive functioning. The therapist is to use his or her knowledge of the HPD individual's basic behavioral patterns and typical wishes to establish and build a therapeutic alliance. Facilitating pattern recognition is the second step and it is critical for the HPD client to address inherent beliefs that powerful others that take care of essential needs, such as money, housing, and problem solving, because the HPD individual is so likeable and desirable. This step may be stymied by the HPD individual's tendency to lose focus, not think clearly, and vacillate when things become difficult. The HPD's centrally held view that if he or she becomes skilled and proficient in caring for himself or herself, so no one else will provide caring for them, must be addressed. It is also important to address the removal of the "scattered cognitive style" (p. 185), which the HPD individual will not be thrilled to address as it is so deeply rooted in his self-view and how she believes she is seen by others.

The third correct response entails blocking maladaptive patterns and this is where the therapist must direct the client's attention to probable destructive acting-out to fulfill underlying wishes and fears. The HPD individual is not fully informed of his or her patterns and motivating forces; rather, the therapist supportively questions the client by using gentle challenging techniques to protect the client from his or her past and causing a protective reaction that brings about those maladaptive patterns. The central goal is to increase options and awareness within the therapeutic setting. The blocking of maladaptive patterns is accomplished by the therapist's reviewing options to assist the HPD individual to fully understand his or her life choices. Next, the therapist assists the HPD client to incorporate constructive change to develop the will to do things differently. This task is better facilitated if there are examples that connect past problems to current ones and assist the HPD client to make the decision to give up the goals and wishes that encourage this pattern. The final step is where most popular therapeutic techniques from a wide variety of modalities are appropriately included into treatment as the critical foundation has been laid for change, and the client is a willing participant to do so.

Psychopharmacology

Histrionic personality disorder has not been examined in controlled pharmacological trials (Koenigsberg et al., 2002). Medication can be used as an adjunct to treat specific trait manifestation that becomes evident, such as antidepressants for depression and somatic complaints, anti-anxiety medications for anxiety, and antipsychotics for derealization and illusions (Sadock & Sadock, 2007).

FILM AND POPULAR MEDIA EXAMPLES

Who Framed Roger Rabbit (1988) – Jessica Rabbit, voiced by Kathleen Turner

Austin Powers Movies (1997, 1999, 2002) – Austin Powers, played by Mike Myers

Gone with the Wind (1939) – Scarlett O'Hara, played by Vivien Leigh

A Streetcar Named Desire (1951) – Blanche DuBois, played by Vivien Leigh

What About Bob (1991) – Bob New York: John Wiley & Sons, played by Bill Murray

CHECKLIST: HISTRIONIC PERSONALITY DISORDER

Below is a complete list to best identify and diagnose Histrionic Personality Disorder. DSM-5 (APA, 2013) criteria are first, followed by discernible components, and lastly, associated features.

- ❏ A pervasive pattern of excessive emotionality and attention-seeking, beginning by early adulthood and present in a variety of contexts*
- ❏ Is uncomfortable in situations in which he or she is not the center of attention*
- ❏ Interaction with others is often characterized by inappropriate sexually seductive or provocative behavior*
- ❏ Displays rapidly shifting and shallow expression of emotions*
- ❏ Consistently uses physical appearance to draw attention to self*
- ❏ Has a style of speech that is excessively impressionistic and lacking in detail*
- ❏ Shows self-dramatization, theatricality, and exaggerated expression of emotion*
- ❏ Is suggestible (i.e., easily influenced by others or circumstances)*
- ❏ Considers relationships to be more intimate than they actually are*
- ❏ Has difficulty with emotional intimacy in romantic or sexual relationships
- ❏ Tends to act out a relationship role, such as "princess" or "hero"
- ❏ Has a tendency to control significant others via emotional manipulation or seductiveness while appearing dependent on them
- ❏ Impaired same-sex friendships due to sexually provocative/threatening style that may impede such relationships
- ❏ Friendships have dissolved due to constant demands for attention
- ❏ Extensive history of novelty and sensation-seeking and difficulty sticking to a routine
- ❏ Difficulty delaying gratification, and when he or she must, becomes frustrated or engages in behaviors to meet immediate needs
- ❏ Interest wanes quickly for projects he or she initially approaches with much verve
- ❏ Sacrifices long-term relationships for the excitement of new ones
- ❏ Seeks to placate and appease others
- ❏ Sacrifices self for condemnation to obtain nurturance
- ❏ Flippant, cheerful, and seeks playful adventures
- ❏ Stormy, impassioned, out-of-control behavior
- ❏ Behavior that is underhanded and double-dealing
- ❏ Volatile in emotional expression, demanding, and overwrought

*distinguishing characteristics

THERAPIST CLIENT ACTIVITY

Use these probes to explore your HPD client's vacillating moods, need for attention and caretaking, and surface-focused views of the world that are central to the pathology and enhance the socioeconomic dysfunction.

> ➢ What would it be like to feel unnoticed or invisible to others?
> ➢ How do you see therapy as helpful for you?
> ➢ Have you ever lost a relationship due to poor behavior on your part?
> ➢ What relationships in your life do you wish were better?
> ➢ Do you think therapy can be helpful for you?
> ➢ Do you think you can work with a man/woman (therapist's opposite gender) better, if so why?
> ➢ What do you wish were different growing up?
> ➢ What role do you think you played in your family growing up?
> ➢ How do you see yourself in comparison to your siblings or other relatives your age?
> ➢ How do you define success in your life?
> ➢ Have you ever had a sexual encounter you regretted afterwards; what caused you to regret it?
> ➢ What holds your attention longest, and why do you think that is?
> ➢ What do you typically find to be boring?
> ➢ Have you ever lost a job due to your behavior and can you tell me what happened?
> ➢ If you have to wait for something how do you feel?
> ➢ Who in your life is empathetic towards you and how does that make you feel?
> ➢ Have you ever been promoted or received special treatment for something that is special about you and can you tell me what it is?
> ➢ What is it that makes you unique and how do you let others know about this trait or skill?

CLIENT QUESTIONNAIRE

The following questions are to be given to your client to help him or her identify past challenges and provide guidance for treatment.

What is your earliest recollection? (Describe only as much as you feel comfortable with.)

List three things that led up to your behaving in way that was later found to be detrimental.

Draw a picture of how you see yourself and how you think the world sees you:

List three goals for treatment you want met within the next 2-4 weeks:

List three long-term goals you would like to achieve through treatment:

Narcissistic Personality Disorder

Narcissistic personality disorder (NPD) describes an individual with an underlying fragile ego who displays an overconfident, often cocky, and aristocratic style. The term narcissism is rooted in the Greek mythological figure of Narcissus, who rejected the advances of the nymph Echo and, as punishment, fell in love with his own reflection in a pool of water. As Narcissus pined away, gazing at his own reflection, he changed into a flower that bears his name, the narcissus (Graves, 1993). The story has been retold countless times. The first psychoanalytic paper to address vanity and narcissism was published by Otto Rank in 1911 (Millon et al., 2004). In 1914, Freud (1914/1957) published *On Narcissism: An Introduction* that addressed the repression of any information or emotion that lessens the individual's sense of self, as well as the dimensional aspect of narcissism from a balanced self-concept to one of grandiosity as a defense mechanism. Freud never viewed narcissism as a personality disorder but rather as a personality type (Levy, Reynoso, Wasserman, & Clarkin, 2007).

Kernberg (1967) used the term "narcissistic personality structure," and later (Kernberg, 1970) furthered his description to include clinical characteristics and foundational components including overt behavior that can distinguish between normal and pathological narcissism. Kohut (1968) was the first to use the term "narcissistic personality disorder," which he used to describe long-term characterological functioning. Both Kernberg (1967) and Kohut (1968) were interested in narcissism and its treatment. They disagreed regarding the etiology of NPD but agreed on its expression, especially for individuals who possessed a healthier form of the disorder.

Narcissistic personality disorder was not included in the first two editions of the *Diagnostic and Statistical Manual* (DSM), but made its first appearance in the DSM-III (APA, 1980). The criterion set included the following: grandiose sense of self-importance or uniqueness; preoccupation with fantasies of success, power, brilliance, beauty, or ideal love; exhibitionism; indifference, rage, shame, humiliation, or emptiness in response to criticism or defeat; feelings of entitlement; interpersonal exploitativeness; over-idealization and devaluation of others; and lack of empathy. The definition in the DSM-III was derived from writings prior to 1978 that were considered by a committee of psychiatrists and psychologists who reached a consensus on various aspects of the disorder. No empirical studies were included (Levy et al., 2007). The DSM-III-R (APA, 1987) added feelings of envy and the belief that one's problems are unique, and deleted the criterion of the alternation between feelings of idealization and devaluation was deleted due to overlap with borderline personality disorder (BPD; Widiger et al., 1988).

Ronningstam and Gunderson (1990) attempted to provide an empirical basis to improve the criterion set for NPD and were able to successfully distinguish individuals with NPD from those with other personality disorders and/or individuals with other psychiatric disorders. The authors found that the most distinguishing criterion was grandiosity, defined as a belief in his or her uniqueness and superiority with an unrealistic overvaluation of his or her own abilities, and grandiose fantasies. Grandiosity can also be seen as a central and defining aspect of NPD. In the DSM-IV (APA, 1994), the criterion pertaining to the reaction to criticism with feelings of rage, shame, or humiliation was deleted, and the criterion related to preoccupation with feelings of envy was revised to include attributing envy of the NPD individual to others. Additionally, a new criterion emerged that addressed arrogant, haughty behaviors or attitudes (Ronningstam & Gunderson, 1990). Linde and Clark (1998) assigned disordered symptom criteria from the DSM-IV to a national sample of psychiatrists and psychologists and asked them to identify the disorder to which the criteria belonged. Results showed significant incorrect assignment of the NPD criterion, "is interpersonally exploitive," to antisocial personality disorder (ASPD) 70% of the time, but the NPD criterion "grandiosity and lack of empathy" was appropriately assigned 97% of the time, leading the authors to identify this as a NPD core concept, tantamount to the conclusion drawn by Ronningstam & Gunderson (1990). There were no text changes made from the DSM-IV (APA, 1994) to the DSM-IV-TR (APA, 2000), or to the criteria in the DSM-5 (APA, 2013).

ETIOLOGY

Kernberg (1975, 1984, 1992) postulates that narcissism develops out of parental rejection, devaluation, and an emotionally invalidating environment filled with parental inconsistencies in regard to their children, or that parents interact with their children to meet the parents' own needs. Due to rejecting parental figures, the child withdraws and creates a pathological self-grandiosity that includes the following aspects:

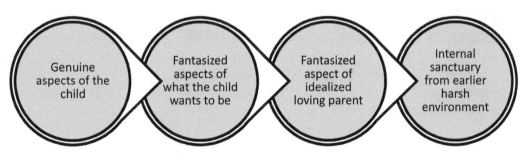

Pathological Grandiosity in the NPD Individual

The negative aspects of the self are denied and supplanted by the grandiose aspect to form the foundation for the narcissistic personality to develop. The splitting of the self becomes a critical aspect of the NPD individual and is evident in emptiness, continuous desire for admiration and thrills, as well as self-disgrace.

Kohut (1966, 1971, 1972, 1979, 2011) wrote extensively on narcissism and its treatment and postulated that NPD is derived from arrested development due to inevitable maternal shortcomings. Initially the child rejects the narcissistic imbalance, only to later develop an ego-centered self-image to regain his or her narcissism. The grandiose self is encouraged, mirrored, and solidified through maternal behaviors reflective of the child's primitive grandiosity. The NPD further develops out of a disrupted normal developmental path, and primitive grandiosity is left unchecked if the idealized parent's (typically the mother's) responses are inadequate.

Millon (2011) identifies several areas of influence derived from social learning therapy that shape the development of narcissistic traits. Little attention is given to the biogenic aspect of narcissistic development, "where the existence of distinctive bio-physical traits seem lacking, conjectures would have usually weak ground" (p. 412). Thus, the focus is on experiential history. He addresses the issue of parental overvaluation and indulgence that teaches the child that if they wish it, they deserve it, without providing any reciprocation, as well as being deserving of special privileges just for being or through minimal effort. Due to the continued acquiescence and indulgence of the parents, the child expects similar treatment from others and utilizes presumptuous and demanding strategies to evoke positive reactions when his or her parents are unavailable to do so. This learning creates a tendency to take others for granted and to take advantage of them for self-benefit.

Capron (2004) examined four parental types and their effect on the development of narcissism among 200 undergraduates (with equal gender distribution) and found that, overall, the parenting style of over-indulgence was highly associated with the narcissistic traits of entitlement, authority, exhibitionism, and exploitativeness; and the parenting style of over-permissiveness was associated with the narcissistic trait of entitlement only. Over-domineering and over-protecting parental styles were not associated with narcissistic traits. Broken down by gender, results are shown below:

Females

Over-indulgence	Over-domineering	Over-protecting	Over-permissiveness
• Entitlement • Authority • Exhibitionism • Exploitativeness	• Entitlement • Exhibitionism	• Entitlement • Self-Sufficiency • Vanity	• Exploitativeness

Males

Over-indulgence	Over-domineering	Over-protecting	Over-permissiveness
• Entitlement • Self-Sufficiency • Exhibitionism	• Entitlement • Exhibitionism • Exploitativeness	• No significant findings	• No Significant findings

Development of Narcissistic Traits

These results lend credence to Millon's (2011) assertion that parental style can encourage narcissism within children.

A second area of focus by Millon (2011) is the only child or first-born, who tends to be viewed as special by his or her parents, is fawned over, has few if any restrictions, and is limited in understanding the value of sharing compared to a child who has siblings. Eyring and Sobelman (1996) found no significant relationship between narcissism and birth order, but other researchers found a significant relationship (Curtis & Cowell, 1993). This opens many questions as to how narcissism is assessed, the degree of narcissism present, and countless other familial variables that may help in identifying a connection between birth order and narcissism.

Benjamin (1996) proposed three main features related to the development of NPD. The NPD individual grew up with a parent who was selfless, and love and adoration were not contingent upon anything. The child has no notions regarding the parent's separate feelings and needs and so the child learns that the parent is there solely to delight in his or her presence. Due to this understanding, the NPD individual fails to learn that other people have feelings, needs, and concerns of their own. As the NPD-to-be child develops, he or she fails to learn critical lessons about natural consequences or vulnerabilities, and is enveloped within himself or herself. The second main feature entails the parent approaching the child in a "deferential and nurturant" manner that encourages arrogance and the expectation that he or she is entitled to this treatment from everyone; if the NPD-to-be child fails to receive such treatment, he or she is shocked and potentially angered. The final developmental feature is the "ever-present threat of a fall from grace" (p. 146). Due to the rare instance of the NPD-to-be child being extraordinary, being merely average in skill or ability creates disappointment for the parent, which in turn, devastates the child. The internalized view of perfection is accompanied by extreme stress, and failure is linked to shame and removal of caring. The internal workings of the NPD individual are best described as follows: "Since the narcissist's self-concept stems from internalization of unrealistic adoration, the substitution of disappointment or criticism for love is devastating. The NPD is demolished, empty, and terribly alone. He or she can 'dish it out,' but is not equipped to 'take it'"(Benjamin, 1996, p. 147).

PREVALENCE

The DSM-5 (APA, 2013) lists NPD prevalence "based on DSM-IV definitions" (APA, 2013, p. 671) between 0% and 6.2% in community samples. The DSM-5 (APA, 2013) goes on to report that 50% to 75% of individuals diagnosed with NPD are male. Stinson and colleagues (2008) found a lifetime prevalence rate of 6.2% in those diagnosed with NPD, and further gender breakdown showed that 7.7% of these were male and 4.8% were female. Crawford and colleagues (2005), using the Structured Clinical Interview for DSM-IV Personality Disorders (SCID-II; First, Gibbon, Spitzer, Benjamin, & Williams, 1997) found that the prevalence of NPD in a community sample was 5th, with 2.2%, behind avoidant personality disorder (AVD, 6.4%), paranoid personality disorder (PPD, 5.1%), obsessive-compulsive personality disorder (OCPD, 4.7%), and borderline personality disorder (BPD, 3.9%). It has been estimated that the prevalence of NPD has more than doubled in the United States in the last two decades and that 1 in 16 individuals have some components of significant NPD traits (Twenge & Campbell, 2009).

Within a clinical sample, NPD was found to have a prevalence rate of 2%. This sample was not only unique as a result of the NPD being in treatment, which is very rare, but what brought the NPD individual there in the first place. These issues included loneliness, distress, poor social functioning, inability of others to meet their needs, divorce, unemployment, and subsequent depression (Miller, Campbell, & Pilkonis, 2007; Ronningstam, 2011; Zimmerman, Rothschild & Chelminski, 2005).

ATTACHMENT

Based upon Kohut's (1971, 1977, 1984) writings, it can be hypothesized that attachment security sets the foundation and development of "healthy narcissism," as it permits the individual to create a bonded, well-integrated, and consistent sense of self (Mikulincer & Shaver, 2007). Beyond the concept of "healthy narcissism", the more typical manifestation is the pathological forms that have been found to be related to overt and covert forms. Overt narcissism, characterized by a successful, high achieving, and intimidating personality style, has been found to be associated with avoidance as well as self-appraisal and refusal to acknowledge weaknesses (Gabbard, 1998; Mikulincer & Shaver, 2007; Wink, 1991). Covert narcissism, characterized by the use of indirect methods to gain attention, has been associated with attachment anxiety and hypersensitivity to attention or evaluation by others while holding firmly to unrealistic expectations and a sense of entitlement (Hendin & Cheek, 1997; Mikulincer & Shaver, 2007; Wink, 1991).

Dickinson and Pincus (2003) examined grandiose and vulnerable styles of narcissism and found that those individuals who met criteria for the grandiose type tended to be classified as having a more secure or dismissing attachment style, illustrating a stance of positive self-appraisal as well as a denial of interpersonal distress. The vulnerable narcissistic style tended to be represented as having a fearful or preoccupied attachment style, which indicates a negative self-appraisal that causes them not to say positive things about themselves, experience interpersonal distress, and have a tendency to avoid relationships. Evidence for vulnerable or covert narcissism was substantiated in two other studies conducted by Otway and Vignoles (2006), and Smolewska and Dion (2005).

Sperry (2003) postulates that NPD is associated with a negative view of others and a view of self that fluctuates from positive to negative, matching a fearful-dismissing style. As they see themselves as unique and special, NPD individuals recognize the need others serve and appreciate that they can potentially be harmed by them.

DIAGNOSIS

The most commonly used criteria to diagnose NPD are the seven listed below in Table 1 from the DSM-5 (APA, 2013):

TABLE 1: DSM-5 DIAGNOSTIC CRITERIA FOR NARCISSISTIC PERSONALITY DISORDER
A. A pervasive pattern of grandiosity (in fantasy or behavior), need for admiration, and lack of empathy, beginning by early adulthood and present in a variety of contexts, as indicated by five (or more) of the following: (1) Has a grandiose sense of self-importance (e.g., exaggerates achievements and talents, expects to be recognized as superior without commensurate achievements) (2) Is preoccupied with fantasies of unlimited success, power, brilliance, beauty, or ideal love (3) Believes that he or she is "special" and unique and can only be understood by, or should associate with, other special or high-status people (or institutions) (4) Requires excessive admiration (5) Has a sense of entitlement, i.e., unreasonable expectations of especially favorable treatment or automatic compliance with his or her expectations (6) Is interpersonally exploitative, i.e., takes advantage of others to achieve his or her own ends (7) Lacks empathy: is unwilling to recognize or identify with the feelings and needs of others (8) Is often envious of others or believes others are envious of him or her (9) Shows arrogant, haughty behavior or attitudes

Consistent with all of the criteria listed in the DSM, these are not hard and fast rules of diagnosis but rather guidelines and criteria to make diagnoses, as individual and cultural differences will impact the presentation and expression of the NPD. The first criterion is related to the individual's tendency to take pride in him- or herself and tell others about various achievements while enhancing details to make him or her look good, and the tendency to expect others to treat him or her in manner consist with a level of attainment that has not actually been earned. Criterion two pertains to the tendency to be deeply absorbed in thoughts regarding his or her own power, success, intelligence, good looks, or status as a consummate lover. Though the level of perception is equal to the level of distorted reality, he or she is not psychotic or delusional to the degree of a thought disorder.

The third criterion includes the NPD individual's firm belief that he or she is distinctive in some way and can only connect to others that hold that same status, and demand that others see him or her and thus respond in kind. Within this criterion, the NPD individual will attempt to associate with others they perceive as high-status and unique, such as those who are wealthy or those who put forth the appearance of skill and excellence. The need for continual and boundless adoration is described in criterion four. These individuals never get enough compliments, recognition, or praise, and if others fail to meet these needs he or she will deride or belittle them. Personal failure that reflects less than perfect performance is met with excuses and blaming of others for the lack of success. There is never ownership of misdeeds or less than stellar functioning as this would not merit the level of admiration and recognition he or she feels deserving of.

That the NPD individual possesses a sense of entitlement that is tantamount to that of royalty or celebrity is reflected in criterion five. This can be seen, for example, when the NPD individual is kept waiting and is immediately enraged as expectations and needs are not sufficiently being met by others, due to their not noticing "who they are dealing with." Within this criterion, he or she tends to treat others as lower social-status creatures that are there simply to serve him or her. This can include significant others who must be very attractive at all times, and waiters, waitresses, valets, retail workers, etc. The sixth criterion pertains to the "snake in the grass" tendency to use others to meet his or her needs without any compunction for "doing what had to be done." This extends to all, even relatives, friends, co-workers, etc. The NPD individual will not make a distinction if it will advance his or her needs and expectations. The seventh criterion pertains to the lack of understanding or empathy for others, with these qualities being clouded by egocentricity and unique and special status. The NPD individual's needs, emotional, financial, sexual, or otherwise, are central. Empathy is not evinced for relatives, friends, co-workers, or any others as, in the mind of the NPD individual, they will not merit understanding and do not hold the same status as the NPD individual, and thus they are not deserving of it. Criterion eight relates to bidirectional envy. This is the envy she has for others who hold a particular status or possessions she does not, and the envy that he assumes others have for him due to his unique status, power, skills, or other features. The tendency for NPD individuals to display arrogant behaviors and attitudes in which they talk down to others or "walk with their nose in the air" is related to criterion nine. He or she exhibits a behavioral style that communicates to others that he or she is unique, special, attractive, and deserving of such treatment.

The DSM-5 (APA, 2013) indicates additional features for NPD. Due to vulnerable self-esteem, the NPD individual is highly sensitive to "injury" as a result of negative appraisal or defeat. The NPD individual tends to internalize feedback or the illustration that he or she did not do something just right, and as a result he or she tends to feel empty or hollow. The narcissistic rage can be seen as a reaction to protect his or her ego defenses and counterattack those who caused the wound. Relationships with the NPD individual tend to be hampered due to entitlement issues, the need for constant admiration, and neglect of others' feelings, beliefs, and views. His or her performance is thwarted as a result of the inability to take feedback, but in some cases these individuals are able to attain high levels of achievement. Vocational performance can be lowered due to the tendency not to take risks out of fear of failure, especially if the possibility is highly visible failure. Withdrawing socially, depressed mood, and dysthymic or major depressive disorder can be the result of continual feelings of shame, failure, or inner self-ridicule.

It is Millon's (2004) view that there are few pure personality prototypes and that, instead, there are mixed variants of one major type with one or more secondary or subsidiary subtypes. Millon and colleagues (2004) have identified four subtypes of NPD, which are shown below:

Unprincipled (antisocial features) Malformed conscience, immoral, fraudulent, deceptive, dominating, and vindictive	**Elitist** (variant of "pure" pattern) Holds sense of empowerment and entitlement due to "special" childhood status and pseudo-achievement; seeks favored and good life; attains special status and advantage via association
Amorous (histrionic features) Sexually seductive, enticing; uninterested in genuine intimacy; intensive pleasure-seeker; pathological lying and cheating	**Compensatory** (negativistic, avoidant features) Attempts to counter or remove feelings of inferiority and lack of self-esteem; compensates for weaknesses by creating illusion of superiority; self-worth is produced from self-enhancement

Millon's Four Subtypes of NPD

Benjamin (1996) proposes a link between the NPD individual's interpersonal history and the manifestation of the DSM criteria. She identifies the "total NPD" as the individual who meets all of the criteria listed in the DSM. Several of the criteria are derived from the unconditional love and adoration the NPD child experienced. For example, the expanded view of self-importance (criterion 1), preoccupation with fantasies of unlimited success (criterion 2), need to be linked to individuals who are seen as special (criterion 3), need for continuous attention and veneration (criterion 4), and the presence of haughty behaviors and views (criterion 9). Due to the selflessness that ran concurrently with the exaltation, empathy fails to develop (criterion 7). Submissive nurturance tends to breed exploitation (criterion 6) and a sense of entitlement (criterion 5) within the NPD individual. The stress of meeting the expectation to be perfect makes him or her sensitive to anything that might undermine that image and as a result, envy (criterion 8) and egotistical (criterion 9) behaviors are produced.

Narcissistic Personality Subtypes

In addition to the subtypes reported previously by Millon (2004), Russ and colleagues (2008) examined the NPD construct and found three viable subtypes. The grandiose/malignant subtype engages in the exploitation of others while not considering the impact or welfare of those they take advantage of. Their grandiosity is central to their personality structure, as opposed to a means of compensating for weak self-esteem and vulnerability. The fragile narcissist subtype possesses combined feelings of grandiosity and inadequacy, illustrating a vacillating concept of self that runs to extremes of superiority and inferiority. His or her grandiosity is a defensive mechanism produced under threat. The final subtype is the high-functioning/exhibitionistic individual who is grandiose, competitive, and attention-seeking as well as sexually seductive or provocative, while possessing strengths such as eloquence, high energy or interpersonal skills, and achievement-orientation.

Gabbard (1989) identified two subtypes seen in treatment: the oblivious narcissistic and hypervigilant narcissist. The oblivious narcissist is grandiose, arrogant, and resilient in order to gain attention and envy, and he or she is unaware of the impact upon others. On the other hand, the hypervigilant narcissist is easily hurt, highly sensitive to emotional slights with ashamed attempts to counteract devaluation by seeing others as biased and abusive, and attuned to his or her impact upon others. It is rare, though possible, for these subtypes to present in a pure form, but it is more likely for a mixture of the two to be present.

Differential Diagnosis

Individuals with NPD can sometimes be confused with those who are experiencing a manic or hypomanic episode due to the presence of grandiosity. However, those with manic or hypomanic episodes experience these symptoms in conjunction with mood changes and functional impairments. NPD should also be distinguished from substance use, as stimulants and other drugs can mimic NPD symptoms, such as an inflated self-view and drawing attention to oneself.

There is considerable overlap between NPD and other personality disorders (Becker, Grilo, Edell, & McGlashan, 2000; Gunderson, Ronningstam, & Smith, 1991; Morey, 1988), most commonly with the other cluster B disorders (antisocial, histrionic, and borderline). The key to discriminating NPD from other cluster B disorders is grandiosity, which is also the crucial factor in identifying this disorder (Allnutt & Links, 1996; Ronningstam & Gunderson, 1990; Sperry, 2003). The DSM-5 (APA, 2013) goes on to list many distinguishing factors. NPD can be distinguished from borderline personality disorder (BPD) by the presence of stable self-image, lack of destructiveness, impulsiveness, and fear of abandonment. The histrionic personality disorder (HPD) individual tends not to display the intensive pride in achievements, restricted emotional expressiveness, and disregard for others' feelings, thoughts, and beliefs that are seen in the NPD individual. For the NPD individual, attention is to gain admiration and perceived envy, whereas the HPD individual seeks attention to be noticed and recognized. The NPD individual and the antisocial personality disorder (ASPD) individual share many similar traits, such as hardheadedness, smooth-talking, lacking in depth, exploitive, and failure to relate emotionally to others. The NPD and ASPD individual can be distinguished by the former's drive to gain admiration and envy from others. The NPD individual is unlikely to have a previous diagnosis of conduct disorder. NPD has considerable overlap with obsessive-compulsive personality disorder (OCPD) as both are driven for perfection and see others as incompetent, but the NPD individual is at a greater likelihood of seeing himself or herself as actually achieving perfection.

Within cluster A, schizotypal personality disorder (SZT) and paranoid personality disorder (PPD) share similar traits with NPD in that individuals with all three of these disorders fear possible imperfections or having their weaknesses revealed. However, PPD and SZT individuals are often seen as odd and the NPD individual can adapt more efficiently when necessary or to his or her perceived betterment.

ASSESSMENT

There are several methods that can be used to assess NPD including self-report measures and structured interviews, but self-report measures have been found to be the most appropriate to determine the dimensional aspect or the identification of those who may be probable to be diagnosed with NPD (Levy et al., 2007). The following charts list NPD assessments and are divided by self-report measures and structured interviews:

Self-Report Measures for Narcissistic Personality Disorder	
Millon Clinical Multiaxial Inventory (MCMI)	Millon et al., 1997
Personality Diagnostic Questionnaire-4 (PDQ-4+)	Hyler, 1994
Personality Assessment Inventory (PAI)	Morey, 2007
Schedule of Nonadaptive and Adaptive Personality (SNAP)	Clark, 1993b
The Wisconsin Personality Disorders Inventory-IV (WIPSI-IV)	Klein et al., 1993
Narcissistic Personality Inventory (NPI)	Raskin & Hall, 1979

Structured Interviews for Narcissistic Personality Disorder	
Structured Interview for DSM-IV Personality (SIDP-IV)	Pfohl et al., 1997
Structured Interview for DSM-IV Personality Disorders (SCID-II)	First et al., 1997
Diagnostic Interview for Personality Disorders (DIPD)	Zanarini et al., 1987

The most commonly used assessment methods continue to be the Minnesota Multiphasic Personality Inventory, Second Edition (MMPI-2), Millon Clinical Multiaxial Inventory (MCMI), Thematic Apperception Test (TAT), and the Rorschach (Levy et al., 2007; Sperry, 2003). Utilizing Graham's (2011) method of interpretation of the MMPI-2, the 4-9/9-4 code type is most likely to be evident with the NPD individual. This code type illustrates a tendency to be narcissistic, disregarding others and societal values, impulsivity, difficulty with delaying gratification, poor judgment related to his or her actions and failure to learn from past mistakes. On the MCMI, the NPD individual is likely to display elevations on scale 5 (narcissistic), as well as 4 (histrionic), 6A (antisocial), and 6B (sadistic). Individuals with a scale elevation on 5 are likely to possess an exaggerated sense of self-importance, be highly sensitive to criticism, believe that conventional rules to not apply to them, be arrogant and haughty, and lack empathy. Elevations on the remaining scales indicate a dramatic, colorful style, low tolerance for boredom, an individual who is egocentric and exhibitionistic, attention-seeking, duplicitous, vicious, provocative while hostile and combative, antagonistic, authoritarian, and socially intolerant.

On the TAT, the NPD individual typically shows avoidance and lack of meaning in content; anxiety-provoking cards may elicit a superficial story of avoidance or may be filled with surprising or indecent content (Bellak & Abrams, 1997). The Rorschach results, for NPD individuals, tend to show a high number of C (pure color) and CF (color form) answers, while making texture responses (T, TF, or FT), and NPD individuals are unlikely to respond to shading (Y, YF, FY) directly (Meyer & Deitsch, 1996).

CASE EXAMPLE – MALE

Jesse is a 34-year-old white male who lives at home with his parents and was brought into treatment due to continual loss of employment, failing out of college, and difficulty achieving his "true potential." He is currently unemployed, and has minimal social contact aside from his running blog and Facebook friends. Jesse recently lost his job at the Burger Barn due to his "telling my manager exactly what I think of him." His longest period of employment was eight months at a gym where he was the lead personal trainer and was let go due to an altercation with a man he was training who "just wouldn't follow my direction, another idiot in a sea of idiots." Jesse attends a local community college due his low SAT scores. He and his family view the test as culturally biased to explain his results and poor grades in high school. While at community college, he would often argue with professors and then offend them by telling them that if they were really educated they would be working at Harvard or Yale. Jesse continues to discuss how he has grand ideas that he is sure will solidify his name in history, alongside Thomas Edison, Benjamin Franklin, Bill Gates, and Steve Jobs. When asked for greater detail, he tends to divert to other topics. Jesse recalled his last relationship, with Molly, whom he got pregnant, but they no longer speak due to his not wishing to burden himself with her "trifling issues." She should be thankful he shared his "seed" with her, but he knows she will just "mess the kid up with her stupidity." Sessions were limited due to Jesse's refusing to come back when the therapist attempted to point out how a change in his behavior or view might make life easier for him. His parents called the out-patient clinic administrator to try and get the therapist fired, due to her trying to make Jesse "depressed with lies."

CASE EXAMPLE – FEMALE

Dr. Conrad earned her doctorate in physics from Stanford University and has started treatment after being told that she is unlikely to get tenure. She has been working at Yale University for several years and during her evaluation meeting she was informed that due to poor teacher evaluations, not having enough on-campus time, and too few publications, her tenure is at risk. She is reluctant to start treatment as she believes the therapist is not "smart enough" to understand her issues and "most certainly you cannot understand physics." Dr. Conrad would not permit the therapist to call her Lisa, her first name, and felt that recognition of her degree and its value was important. Dr. Conrad said that she has been feeling empty since her meeting with the chair of the department, but she feels she knows what this is really about. Dr. Conrad refuses to attend department meetings at 8:00 a.m. on Fridays, and has been demanding that the meetings be held on Wednesdays at 11:00 a.m., as they make more sense and fit into her teaching schedule, and "no one wants a Wednesday off." Dr. Conrad is rarely included in department socials, as she tends only discuss how her research and hypotheses make more sense and are more provable than the research and hypotheses of "those I have to share the department with." She also stated that at the department meetings she constantly has to explain to "the others" the basics of her research "because they're just too dumb to get it." Lastly, Dr. Conrad explains how the chair—she refuses to use his name and recognize his title—wants to sleep with her, but he is "older than dirt and was probably here when the first ivy grew." She reported that she does think about the benefits of sleeping with him, but cannot see something so special (sexual contact with her) being shared with someone like him. Treatment lasted for six sessions, until Dr. Conrad was offered and accepted a professorship at Stanford, "where the beautiful and smart people go."

TREATMENT

The majority of information available on the treatment of NPD is based upon clinical encounters and theoretical approaches (Levy et al., 2007). Kernberg (2009) indicates that treatment is dependent upon the severity of the pathology and the combination of symptoms. One of the key issues when treating the NPD client is the inability to develop a suitable relationship where the client is connected to the therapist. The NPD individual sees the basis of the therapeutic relationship as a dependent one, where he or she is dependent upon the therapist. The NPD individual is averse to dependency and will fight against it in an effort to control the session and course of treatment. The NPD client takes to "self-analysis" (p. 106) as opposed to engaging in the relationship to grow and enhance his or her life experience. Kernberg (2009) goes on to describe the NPD client's view of the therapist and the relationship. The therapist is viewed as a "vending machine" through which relevant data is imparted, but that information is internalized by the NPD individual as his or her own developed insight and conclusion. The therapist is routinely blamed for the NPD individual's disappointments in treatment due to the quality and accuracy of interpretations; this also causes continuing sessions to be much like an ongoing "first session." The NPD individual is highly suspicious and competitive with the therapist or, conversely, idealizes him or her. However, this has the potential to quickly disintegrate into loathing and contempt (Kernberg, 2009).

Beck and colleagues (2004) identify the core beliefs of the NPD individual as feelings of inferiority or unimportance which are activated when he or she is confronted with a threat to self-esteem. As with all cognitive-behavioral treatment (CBT), the springboard to effective treatment is the collaborative relationship. In identifying a treatment approach, Beck and colleagues (2004) note that the therapist must be mindful of the negative feelings and opinions of the NPD client that may be evoked though his or her critiquing or praising the therapist. The therapist should identify and praise the NPD client's strengths and utilize successive approximations to help him or her feel comfortable as expectations are met, which in turn keeps the client involved in treatment. Beck and colleagues (2004) identify key target areas to guide treatment, such as improving mastery and gaining insight into the meaning of success, enhancing boundary awareness and others' perspectives, and improving beliefs about self-worth, emotions, and viable alternatives. There are several tools that can be utilized to guide treatment by identifying key target areas. Creating a problem list, agenda and motivation for treatment need to be addressed as ambivalence is likely to be present. Identifying the positives and negatives of using treatment to attain the goal and how many different people utilize therapy to their betterment (e.g., celebrities) can encourage participation. Due to the NPD individual's drive toward goal attainment as a means to clarify self-worth, the therapist should anticipate that previous failed attempts at "mastery experiences" (p. 260) are likely to trigger those core beliefs of inferiority and unimportance. These beliefs can be addressed, and possibly challenged, if the therapeutic relationship is strong enough, and the NPD client can be brought to see that pontificating about what should be and what has been lost is detrimental to what could be accomplished by attempts at more reasonable or reachable goals.

Beck and colleagues (2004) identify a critical aspect of treatment with the NPD individual which is to develop improved interpersonal skills, although this attempt is likely to offend these patients. Interpersonal skills are gained through teaching the rudimentary social skills of "listening, empathizing, caring, and accepting influence from the feelings of others that are lacking in the NPD" (p. 262). Physical, sexual, social, and emotional boundaries, and attention to self and others, can be learned through modeling and shaping techniques in treatment as the NPD attends to the therapist. Maladaptive beliefs regarding himself or herself and the associated emotions must be addressed in treatment. A typical distorted belief is that the NPD client's happiness and state of well-being are the responsibility of the therapist and dependent upon that person's skill. This can be challenged by the therapist through the use of empathic support and validation, followed by illustrating that this view inherently attaches any adverse emotion to the client's self-esteem. The testing of maladaptive beliefs and enhancing of functional beliefs allows the therapist and NPD client to gain understanding about how the generalized and black-and-white thinking, may appear beneficial in the short term, but is ultimately detrimental in the long term. Once the NPD client is willing to see issues and circumstances in this manner, more functional beliefs can be incorporated to allow for a balanced view of situations and assessment of self. Benjamin (1996) identifies treatment strategies when working with NPD individuals using her five correct responses. She notes that "the effect of interventions is assessed in terms of the actual impact on the patient, not in terms of the therapist's intention" (p. 156). When the NPD individual becomes enraged, withdraws, or acts grandiose in response to an intervention, an error has been made and an alteration is necessary. The key and central component when working with the NPD individual is facilitating collaboration. This can be best achieved through empathy, and the therapist should serve as an object for the NPD client to internalize and see as an extension of the self. Through the therapist's empathic stance, soothing, and affirmation, the NPD individual can learn self-regulation and potentially internalize an empathic understanding of himself or herself. The therapist is to model faults and acceptance of those faults, and focus on building tolerance to them. These slight reminders that the therapist is not perfect and that he or she can accept those faults and errors can enable the NPD individual to do the same.

Facilitating pattern recognition entails challenging the NPD client in a careful and supportive manner. If this fails, the NPD individual will respond with defenses that lock the treatment due to grandiosity, rage, or judgment. It is the therapist's responsibility to determine which empathic statements promote change or cause retreat. Empathic responses should focus on the entire clinical picture and be couched in supportive and thoughtful response. With the NPD individual, blocking maladaptive patterns pertains to him or her recognizing and thwarting typical response patterns, such as grandiosity, rage, and envy of others. These patterns should be identified by clear data from past experiences, and the client must be willing to acknowledge that past experiences stalled progress or personal benefit. Blocking these patterns is much like a dance where each partner permits the other to lead at various times, while both move to the same music. In this case the music is the lessening of negative patterns and enhancing interpersonal and intrapersonal skills. While strengthening the determination to give up maladaptive patterns of relating, sexual components come into play with the NPD individual, specifically the Klute syndrome. The Klute syndrome "suggests that patients cannot change in therapy if they repeatedly have orgasms while conjuring images having the interpersonal dimensionality of the disorder" (p. 161). An example would be climaxing while fantasizing about aggressive control or being admired. The therapist works with the client to identify a fantasy that is sexually arousing without components that enhance NPD pathology. Details of previous fantasies are not needed, but for the new one it is necessary to make certain that the prior components are not present and that it is not just a different form of early learned experiences. Once the new fantasy is deemed appropriate, the client is asked to incorporate it during orgasm. Resistance is expected, as "people do not wish to sacrifice sexual pleasure for the possibility that the switch in fantasy would help them change their interpersonal patterns for the better" (p. 162). Klute syndrome treatment is very powerful and Benjamin (1996) notes the importance of warning the client not to make any significant life decisions without discussing them in detail in therapy first. Facilitating new learning is the point at which many mainstream techniques can be employed, as the NPD pathology that would have derailed the treatment is removed or lessened to a point where such techniques have efficacy. Treatment techniques to be employed at this stage may include social skills, marital therapy and role play.

Psychopharmacology

There have been no known controlled pharmacological trials that have focused on NPD (Koenigsberg et al., 2007). Sadock and Sadock (2007) indicate that lithium has been used to deter mood swings. A further consideration is that the NPD individual has a low tolerance for side effects but is prone to depression, so selective serotonin reuptake inhibitors (SSRIs) may be beneficial.

FILM AND POPULAR MEDIA EXAMPLES

Basic Instinct (1992) – Catherine Tramell, played by Sharon Stone

There Will Be Blood (2007) – Daniel Plainview, played by Daniel Day-Lewis

Sunset Boulevard (1950, movie) – Norma Desmond, played by Gloria Swanson

Wall Street (1987) – Gordon Gekko, played by Michael Douglas

Wall Street: Money Never Sleeps (2010) – Gordon Gekko, played by Michael Douglas

The Office (2005-present) – Michael Scott, played by Steve Carell

House (2004-2012) – Gregory House, M.D., played by Hugh Laurie

Checklist: Narcissistic Personality Disorder

Below is a complete list to best identify and diagnose Narcissistic Personality Disorder. DSM-5 (APA, 2013) criteria are first, followed by discernible components, and lastly, associated features.

- ❑ A pervasive pattern of grandiosity (in fantasy or behavior), need for admiration, and lack of empathy, beginning by early adulthood and present in a variety of contexts*
- ❑ Has a grandiose sense of self-importance (e.g., exaggerates achievements and talents, expects to be recognized as superior without commensurate achievements)*
- ❑ Is preoccupied with fantasies of unlimited success, power, brilliance, beauty, or ideal love*
- ❑ Believes that he or she is "special" and unique and can only be understood by, or should associate with, other special or high-status people (or institutions)*
- ❑ Requires excessive admiration*
- ❑ Has a sense of entitlement (i.e., unreasonable expectations of especially favorable treatment or automatic compliance with his or her expectations)*
- ❑ Is interpersonally exploitative (i.e., takes advantage of others to achieve his or her own ends)*
- ❑ Lacks empathy: is unwilling to recognize or identify with the feelings and needs of others
- ❑ Is often envious of others or believes others are envious of him or her*
- ❑ Shows arrogant, haughty behavior or attitudes*
- ❑ Is fraudulent, exploitative, deceptive, and unscrupulous to enhance presentation or status
- ❑ Erotic and exhibitionistic to fulfill his or her own needs of grandiosity or sense of self
- ❑ Easily humiliated following criticism
- ❑ Reacts to feedback or criticism with rage
- ❑ Individual sense of entitlement and grandiosity interferes with interpersonal relationships
- ❑ Reluctance to take risks due to fragile sense of self

*distinguishing characteristics

THERAPIST CLIENT ACTIVITY

Use these probes to explore your NPD client's grandiosity, fragile ego, sense of entitlement and lack of empathy which are central to the pathology and enhance the socioeconomic dysfunction.

- ➢ What do you feel you are most capable of?
- ➢ What holds you back from your full potential?
- ➢ Can you describe an instance where you were held back from doing your best?
- ➢ Is there someone or something in your life that is a significant deterrent to your "being all you can be"?
- ➢ Can you describe how it feels when you may miss your exact goal?
- ➢ Can you describe the best part of being in a relationship with someone else?
- ➢ What are some of the great accomplishments you have had in your life?
- ➢ Can you describe a dream you have on a continual basis?
- ➢ Can you describe an instance where you felt bad about not meeting a goal?
- ➢ Do you find it difficult to find other people like yourself?
- ➢ Who do you feel you can connect with best?
- ➢ How do you feel when your friends and co-workers praise you for a job well done?
- ➢ Can you tell me about an instance when you received negative feedback at work or school?
- ➢ In what way are you special and unique and deserving of special treatment?
- ➢ What do you do when you do not get the treatment you feel you deserve?
- ➢ What tactics do you employ most often to get others to do what you want them to do?
- ➢ What is it like for you when someone else tells you about his or her issues or problems?
- ➢ Can you identify other people who have what you want or deserve?
- ➢ What are you willing to do to get what you deserve and want?

CLIENT QUESTIONNAIRE

The following questions are to be given to your client to help him or her identify past challenges and provide guidance for treatment.

What is your earliest recollection? Describe only as much as you feel comfortable with.

List three things that have helped you to achieve your goals in the past:

Can you list the three people who you trust most and why?

Can you list three things that make you angry or "set you off" most often and what goes through your mind right after that occurs?

If you were your therapist, what are three things you would make sure to cover during the course of treatment?

Avoidant Personality Disorder

Avoidant personality disorder (AVD) describes an individual with an intense fear of others, shyness, and sensitivity to rejection. Bleuler (1911/1987) originally wrote about his patients who exhibited signs of avoidant patterns and removed themselves from the outside world due to intense shyness and great fear of experiencing emotional arousal. Kretschmer (1925) later wrote about polar opposites who on one end was the schizoid-like personality (anaesthetic) and on the other a close match to the avoidant-like personality (hyperaesthetic). The avoidant-like personality will go to great lengths to avoid or remove outside stimulation. There has been extensive writing regarding AVD characteristics without identifying the disorder until Millon (1969) designated the disorder in individuals who presented with active aversion to social relationships.

Avoidant personality disorder did not appear in the *Diagnostic and Statistical Manual of Mental Disorders* (DSM) until the third edition (DSM-III; APA, 1980) and then it focused largely on excessive social withdrawal, hypersensitivity to rejection, reticence to engage in interpersonal relationships without certainty of success and acceptance, low self-esteem, and emotions that include sadness, tension, anger, and loneliness. In the DSM-III-R (APA, 1987), AVD's criteria were modified to address theoretical change and move toward a more psychoanalytic representation of a phobic style and provide greater distinction from the other disorders within cluster C (dependent and obsessive-compulsive). Low self-esteem and desire for acceptance was removed and several criteria such as "fear of being embarrassed by blushing" and "fear of saying something inappropriate" were added to bring a greater focus on social avoidance. The DSM-IV (APA, 1994) modeled the ICD-10 (World Health Organization, 1993) criteria for AVD emphasizing interpersonal concerns that are central to the disorder: (1) avoidance of activities out of fear of embarrassment and rejection, (2) reluctance to engage with others unless certain of acceptance, (3) disinclination to connect intimately unless it is deemed safe and the individual will not be rejected or criticized, (4) and though he or she may want to relate, the individual does not do so out of fear of disapproval or mockery. Two criteria centered on self-image issues: (1) feelings of inadequacy and low self-esteem and (2) the belief that he or she is socially incompetent and unattractive or inferior to others. A descriptor addresses the degree of embarrassment as being so great as to cause the individual to not take risks or try new things. The DSM-IV-TR (APA, 2000) made no text changes to AVD. There are no changes to criteria in the DSM-5 (APA, 2013) for AVD.

ETIOLOGY

Millon (2011) proposed three factors—biogenic, experiential, and self-perpetuating—that work in conjunction to create a particular personality style that are specific to each individual in quantity and degree of experience.

Biogenic Factors	**Heredity** - Genetic factors related to affective disharmony, interpersonal aversiveness, social apprehensiveness, and withdrawal.
	Infant Reaction Patterns - Infants that display hyperirritability, crankiness, tension, and withdrawal behavior can cause parental rejection or deprecation that encourages anxiety and withdrawal in the infant and later the adult.
	Slow or Irregular Maturation - Thwarted or discontinuous development in sensory, sensorimotor, or cognitive functioning may limit the child's ability to cope with the normal developmental challenges that arise. Parents may react aberrantly to the child's atypical development and as a result the child develops anxiety, withdrawal, social alienation, and low self-regard.
	Limbic Region Imbalances – Dense or excessively branched neural substrate in the areas of the brain that are thought to cause aversive behavior.
Experiential History	**Parental Rejection and Deprecation** - Infants handled in a cold and harsh manner by their parents during critical attachment stages experience feelings of tension and insecurity; scorning, ridiculing, and criticizing the child during the autonomy stage distort feelings of self-competence. Roots of self-deprecation start in the sensorimotor-autonomy stage and solidify in later stages, causing the child to see himself or herself as weak, unattractive, and deserving of ridicule.
	Peer Group Alienation - Individuals tend to experience rejection, isolation, or ridicule within social peer settings, as well as experiences that lessen self-competence and self-esteem due to failing to prove themselves in a wide variety of settings such as academic, social, and physical environments.
Self-Perpetuating Process	**Active Social Detachment** - The individual assumes that early life experiences will continue lifelong so he or she tends to limit participation in a variety of experiences, perpetuating the self-view of ineptitude by failing to engage in new experiences that may promote self-competence and growth.
	Suspicious and Fearful Behaviors/Emotional and Perceptual Hypersensitivity - A presentation of reluctance and suspiciousness evoke interpersonal responses in others that lead to more humiliating and degrading experiences; even the smallest disregard and frustration is focused upon and seen as validation of inadequacy, failure, and lack of interest from others, and this causes the very issues the individual is attempting to avoid.
	Intentional Interference - The individual tends to block, remove, tear down, or distort his or her thoughts and views to remove the self from relationships and protect the self, as reality is seen through unclear, intrusive, and conflicting emotions that cause him or her to fail to attend to the genuine environment and to learn new ways of relating or handling difficult issues.

Millon's General Contributors to Personality Style

Millon's (2011) various views of the etiology of AVD encompass each aspect of the individual's life and have been supported by other researchers. Johnson, Brent, Connolly, and Bridge (1995) examined the validity of personality disorder diagnoses in 66 adolescents and their first-degree relatives and found that those with relatives with AVD had an increased prevalence of avoidant and cluster A (paranoid, schizoid, and schizotypal) personality disorders. Tillfors and colleagues (2001) found that having a family member with social phobia and AVD puts the individual at a two to three times greater risk of developing these disorders.

Childhood experiences and interactions with parents or caregivers have been found to put an individual at an increased risk for AVD, as he or she tends to see caregivers as shaming, guilt-arousing, and less tolerant than those who do not develop this personality disorder (Stravynski, Elie, & Franche, 1989). Negative childhood experiences, as assessed using childhood narratives, temperament, and expectations have been linked to the development of AVD, as were negative childhood memories, sensory processing sensitivity, and pessimistic expectations (Meyer & Carver, 2000).

Cognitive factors have also been found to be associated with the development of AVD. Carr & Francis (2010) examined early maladaptive schemas as they related to early childhood experiences and the development of AVD and found that an overprotective mother that utilized subjugation and emotional inhibition created a significant pathway to AVD. Results further illustrated that a family environment that lacked outside interaction was related to the cognitive schemas of unavailability and unpredictability of interpersonal relationships, and a desire to discount one's own needs and emotions for others was related to AVD symptomatology.

Benjamin (1996) proposes a pathogenic hypothesis for the development of AVD symptoms. The developmental pathway for the AVD individual was nurturant, social bonding was provided, and the solid foundation of a secure base for attachment was present, which produces the desire for social contact. As a child, the AVD individual was highly controlled by parents or caregivers in order to create a dynamic and memorable social presentation. Outside opinions, beyond those of family members, were deemed very important and impression management was critical. The family, as well as the individual, was very embarrassed if faults or irregularities were noticed outside the family. Due to this intense focus on others and their opinions, the AVD individual is driven to social connection but stifled with fear of disgrace and shame. When the AVD individual experienced humiliation or embarrassment it was typically linked to exclusion and forced autonomy. When the family would go on pleasurable excursions, the AVD individual would be left alone. As an adult, the AVD individual withdraws socially to prevent a recapitulation of earlier abandonment and exclusion experiences. Though the AVD was rejected and derided, family was still seen as a central source of support and loyalty was an inherent value. Outsiders were seen as highly likely to reject the AVD-to-be and hurt or harm him or her in some way.

PREVALENCE

The DSM-5 (APA, 2013) lists the National Epidemiologic Survey and Alcohol and Related Conditions (NESARC) prevalence rate for AVD at approximately 2.4%. Grant and colleagues (2008), using the National Epidemiologic Survey on Alcohol and Related

Conditions (NESARC), found that females were at a significantly greater risk to develop AVD; Native Americans were 1.6 times more likely to meet criteria for AVD as compared to Caucasians. Individuals with less than a high school education were 2.7-times more likely to have AVD, 2.2-times for those with only a high school degree, and 1.7-times greater among individuals with "some college" as compared to those with at least a four-year college degree. Widowed/divorced/separated and never married individuals were approximately 1.6 to 1.9 times more likely to meet criteria for AVD compared to individuals who were married or cohabitating.

Prevalence rates have varied greatly for AVD depending upon context and assessment instrument used. Samuels and colleagues (2002) found a prevalence rate of 1.8% using the International personality disorder Examination (IPDE; Loranger, Susman, Oldham, & Russakoff, 1987) in a sample of 742 subjects between the ages 34 and 94, from Baltimore, Maryland. However, Lenzenweger and colleagues (2007) found a prevalence of 5.2% using the same instrument with a sample of 5,692 participants from the National Comorbidity Survey Replication (NCS-R). Using the Structured Clinical Interview for DSM-IV Axis II Personality Disorders (SCID-II), Crawford and colleagues (2005) found a prevalence rate of 6.4% for AVD in 644 participants from a sample first assessed in 1975 and then spanning the next 25 years.

ATTACHMENT

Individuals with AVD are likely to possess features of fearful attachment as they seek close relationships. They fear disapproval and rejection, and employ a behavioral strategy to avoid relationships (Bartholomew et al., 2001; Sheldon & West, 1990). The negative view of self and others in the AVD individual likely derived from childhood and further substantiates the fearful attachment pattern (Meyer & Carver, 2000; Stravynski et al., 1989). Meyer and colleagues (2004) examined attachment patterns in borderline, avoidant, and schizotypal individuals using a non-clinical sample of college students who rated emotionally neutral faces on various appraisal dimensions. The authors found that both borderline and avoidant personality-disordered individuals associated with anxious attachment and tended to appraise emotionally neutral faces more negatively. Attachment styles were more efficient at identifying information processing biases when compared to personality disorder symptoms. These results further substantiated that AVD individuals possess a fearful-avoidant attachment pattern.

DIAGNOSIS

The criteria most commonly used to diagnose AVD are the seven listed below in Table 1 from the DSM-5 (APA, 2013):

Consistent with all of the criteria listed in the DSM, these are not hard and fast rules of diagnosis but guidelines and criteria to make diagnoses, as individual and cultural differences will impact presentation and expression of the AVD. The first criterion pertains to the AVD individual's tendency to avoid employment opportunities and gatherings due to intense stress derived from negative evaluation by those around him or her. These individuals do best in

TABLE 1: DSM-5 DIAGNOSTIC CRITERIA FOR AVOIDANT PERSONALITY DISORDER

A. A pervasive pattern of social inhibition, feelings of inadequacy, and hypersensitivity to negative evaluation, beginning in early adulthood and present in a variety of contexts, as indicated by four (or more) of the following:

(1) Avoids occupational activities that involve significant interpersonal contact, because of fears of criticism, disapproval, or rejection

(2) Is unwilling to get involved with people unless certain of being liked

(3) Shows restraint within intimate relationships because of the fear of being shamed or ridiculed

(4) Is preoccupied with being criticized or rejected in social situations

(5) Is inhibited in new interpersonal situations because of feelings of inadequacy

(6) Views self as socially inept, personally unappealing, or inferior to others

(7) Is unusually reluctant to take personal risk or to engage in any new activities because they may prove embarrassing

solitary jobs, but tend to experience loneliness while in such positions. Criterion two is related to his or her slow-to-warm-up tendency due to the fear of not being accepted, and, accordingly, is highly focused on familial relationships or long-term relationships that have proven to be safe. The third criterion of resistance to connect out of fear of being embarrassed or humiliated causes the AVD individual to maintain more casual relationships and prevent intimacy from building. The loose connections with others tend to dissolve over time, leaving the AVD individual feeling lonely, abandoned, and justified in his or her view of being deficient. If the relationship does progress to an intimate level, the individual with AVD is likely to engage in distancing behaviors, which tends to cause the intimate partner to feel disconnected and hence leave the relationship, again justifying the AVD individual's self-view as malfunctioned and inept.

The intense preoccupation with being judged negatively and derided leading to embarrassment is the fourth criterion. The AVD individual holds an incredible amount of anxiety and stress inside as he or she attempts to balance relationships and impression management at all times. Within social situations, as the number of individuals increases so does the level of stress and fear. Though compelled to interact and attach socially, fear is ultimately overriding and the AVD individual declines most, if not all invitations to go out with co-workers and friends, or attend large family gatherings. Due to the continual refusal to participate, other people stop offering. This only causes the AVD individual to feel validated in his or her negative self-assessment. The fifth criterion entails the AVD individual's withdrawing in situations that require social interaction as it could potentially provide evidence that he or she is social inept. Due to intense anxiety, he or she tends to respond with one-word answers or avoid situations where frivolity or intense interpersonal relating is required. Again, the AVD individual seems uninterested in connecting with others, while internally shaming and ridiculing himself or herself for not meeting underlying social desires. The individuals they do interact with tend to remove themselves from the AVD individual, which only validates their feelings of inadequacy. Criterion six pertains to a view of self as defunct, inept, and as a continual "dud" in life. Due to the intense nature of this view, he or she creates situations that continually validate it. Even the slightest deviation from expectations causes severe internal derision, shame, and ridicule. It is unlikely, in typical interactions, that the AVD individual would reveal his or her negative views of self, which adds unique challenges for the therapist. The final and seventh criterion is related to the avoidance of new experiences due to fear of failure or embarrassment and revealing to others just how impaired he or she is. Though new experiences could provide for learning and counter evidence that the AVD individual is inept, he adamantly avoids these experiences out of fear of being "found out," that he is, in all actuality, a failure in life.

The DSM-5 (APA, 2013) lists several additional features associated with AVD. The AVD individual's tendency to be hypervigilant with regard to others' movements and expressions and intense, fearful and tense presentation may cause others to deride him or her, validating a negative view of self. He or she is extremely concerned about blushing or showing an emotional response. Others tend to see the AVD individual as "shy" and desolate. Due to their limited social support systems, these individuals do not have a source of external assistance in times of stress and crisis. Fantasies may center upon idealized relationships and affection and acceptance.

Millon and colleagues (Millon et al., 2004) proposed four subtypes of AVD. These four types can be seen in treatment and can dictate the course of treatment and areas of concern for the therapist. It is Millon's (2004) view that there are few pure personality prototypes and that, instead, there are mixed variants of one major type with one or more secondary or subsidiary subtypes.

Phobic (dependent features)	Conflicted (negativistic features)
General apprehensiveness; concerns and anxiety shown in relation to adverse and specific objects or circumstances	Self-dislike and ridicule; fears both independence and dependence; confused, tormented, and embittered; unresolvable angst
Hypersensitive (paranoid features)	Self-Deserting (melancholic features)
Intensely suspicious; varies as to panicked, terrified, edgy, and shy; thin-skinned, high-strung, ill-tempered, and childlike	Fragmented self-awareness; discards painful images and memories; deflects indefensible thoughts and impulses; ejects the self (suicidal)

Millon's Four Proposed Subtypes of AVD

Benjamin (1996) has proposed a connection between the AVD individual's interpersonal history and the symptoms listed in the DSM-IV-TR. She indicates that each of the criteria in the DSM pertain to the AVD individual's tendency to avoid "expected humiliation and rejection" (p. 293–294) in social situations (criterion 1, 3, 4, and 5), employment settings (criterion 1), and new and old activities (criterion 7) without certainty of being accepted and liked (criterion 2) due to seeing himself or herself as socially inept (criterion 6).

Differential Diagnosis

One of the greatest areas of overlap and diagnostic concern with AVD is with social anxiety disorder (SAD, social phobia). In regard to the research conducted on AVD, making a singular distinction between it and SAD has garnered the most attention (Herbert, 2007). Researchers have not reached a firm conclusion as to the distinction between the two constructs. While some see it as a variation within social anxiety and avoidance (Cox, 2009; LaFreniere, 2009), others view them as similar but separate issues (Bögels et al., 2010). Cox and colleagues (2011) explored this issue examining how AVD impacts generalized social anxiety disorder (GSAD) using a longitudinal sample from the National Epidemiologic Survey on Alcohol and Related Conditions (NESARC). They found that 55.8% of the sample that met criteria for GSAD also met criteria for AVD, and AVD was found to influence the course of GSAD. The tendency has been to find that individuals with AVD are more severely impaired than individuals with SAD alone, although from a theoretical standpoint there is no qualitative difference (Herbert, 2007). Even the DSM-5 (APA, 2013) notes that social anxiety disorder (social phobia), generalized type shares so much in common with AVD that they may be slight variations of the same disorder. In addition, avoidance is included in both agoraphobia and AVD, and both of these disorders often occur together.

Lenzenweger and colleagues (2007) found the following comorbidity rates between AVD and other personality disorders:

AVD	Percentage
Paranoid	70
Schizoid	55
Schizotypal	53
Antisocial	5
Borderline	54
Dependent	70
Obsessive-Compulsive	63

As can be seen by the chart above, AVD has significant comorbidity with other personality disorders, aside from antisocial personality disorder (ASPD). AVD is in cluster C with dependent personality disorder (DPD) and obsessive-compulsive personality disorder (OCPD) and they share much in common, such as anxiety and fear. Both AVD and OCPD have been found to be prevalent in individuals with binge-eating disorder (BED). Becker, Masheb, White, & Grilo

(2010) found that in their sample of 347 participants diagnosed with BED, 23% met criteria for AVD and 19% met criteria for OCPD. These results are explained as intense anxiety concerns regarding shape and weight reaching the level of personality pathology. Paranoid personality disorder (PPD) and AVD individuals both tend to be reluctant to confide in others, but the AVD individual does this out of fear of embarrassment as opposed to fearing the other person's harmful intent (APA, 2000).

According to the DSM-5 (APA, 2013), avoidance of anxiety-provoking stimuli can be seen in both AVD individuals and those with panic disorder and agoraphobia and may occur simultaneously, although it is diagnosed separately in the DSM-5. However, the avoidance in the latter tends to occur following a panic attack and vacillates based upon frequency and intensity of panic. Those with AVD will have a stable course of avoidance, no clear trigger, and an early onset. AVD and dependent personality disorder (DPD) share the tendency to feel inadequate, hypersensitive to criticism, and to need comfort from another, but the DPD individual is focused on being taken care of, as opposed to the AVD individual who is motivated by avoiding humiliation and rejection. Schizoid personality disorder (SPD) and schizotypal personality disorder (SZT) individuals share the tendency to socially isolate themselves as in AVD, but the AVD individual desires relationships and connection with others and without them feels lonely, whereas SPD and SZT individuals do not and prefer social isolation.

Assessment

The most common method of assessment for personality disorders is the clinical interview which has many variations. The Structured Interview for DSM-IV Personality (SIDP-IV; Pfohl et al., 1997) is a comprehensive semi-structured diagnostic interview for the assessment of all DSM-IV Axis II disorders. The Structured Clinical Interview for DSM-IV Axis II Personality Disorders (SCID-II; First et al., 1997) is a well-known and easy-to-use instrument.

An objective self-report measure, such as the Minnesota Multiphasic Personality Inventory, Second Edition (MMPI-2), when given to an individual with AVD, is likely to produce a 2-7/7-2 code type, with possible elevations on scale 0 (social introversion) and low scores on scale 9 (hypomania) (Graham, 2011; Millon, 2011; Sperry, 2003). The 2-7/7-2 code type indicates an individual who is tense, anxious, and high-strung, and is vulnerable to real or imagined threat. These individuals tend to anticipate problems before they actually occur and become easily distressed in reaction to minor stressors. Obsessive thoughts, compulsions, and somatic complaints are also likely, as well as eating disorder symptoms and a global pessimistic and hopeless view of the world. Elevations on scale 0 indicate a tendency to be introverted socially, insecure and uncomfortable in social situations, reserved, and more comfortable when alone or with family or a few close friends. Low scores on scale 9 are indicative of individuals who are introverted, have a stoic demeanor, and lack in self-confidence.

On the Millon Multiaxial Clinical Inventory (MCMI; Millon et al., 1997), the AVD individual is likely to produce elevations on 2A (avoidant), 2B (depressive), 8B (masochistic), and A (anxiety disorder). Individuals who exhibit these elevations are likely to desire social involvement, but be reluctant to engage, hypervigilant to surroundings, over-reactive to minor stressors as well as preoccupied with intrusive, fearful, and disruptive thoughts, feel alone, and isolated, and possess feelings of worthlessness, inadequacy, and guilt. In addition, they place themselves in the victim role, self-sacrifice with others, and feel they deserve to be shamed and humbled.

Projective measures, such as the Thematic Apperception Test (TAT) and the Rorschach, have been used with AVD individuals and produced valid results (Millon, 2011). On the TAT, results from AVD individuals are likely to illustrate anxiety and rejection themes with variability in length of story, with some personal content related to painful past experience being short and quickly dismissed, and content related to safer topics, such as family and some personal aspects of self, being of greater length. The Rorschach is likely to illustrate inclinations to distance themselves as they attend to minor details, and present suspiciousness and hesitation in the content and location of responses. Movement responses are likely to illustrate still or protective distancing behaviors. Frequent popular responses are likely, and those who are severely avoidant tend to include animal figures that are weak or inadequate and likely to be killed or hurt.

CASE EXAMPLE – FEMALE

Sally is brought into treatment by her parents due to her "hibernating in her room, all day, all year round." Sally is a 32-year-old female who is a high school graduate and has only been employed by her father with his Internet sales business. Sally sits in the therapist's room with her head down and makes no eye contact, unless asked to look at the therapist specifically. "We cannot get grandchildren with her in her room all day," her mother bellows. After her parents leave, Sally begins to rub her hands together and sweat can be seen building up on her hands. After much coercion, Sally states that no one will ever love her, except her family. She feels constantly alone, is a failure in all her relationships (though she has never had any), and the one thing that makes her feel better is her Apple computer. As sessions continue, Sally reveals that she often fantasizes about the people who buy from her father and how one day she meets a man with long blonde hair and an athletic build who "sweeps me away and we live on an island just he and I." Sally mentions having only one friend while in high school. She had known her since kindergarten and they were very close, but the friend went off to college and is now married with two kids: "She doesn't want to talk to me. I'm alone and I have nothing to share. She stopped writing me about eight years ago." Sally eventually mentions that she never responded to any of her friend's attempts to communicate as she thought she would just burden her with her "sorry life." Sally reports several instances when her parents tried to set her up with a man they met at synagogue or "even the grocery store." She typically refuses to get out of her room as she is sure she will trip down the stairs upon seeing him, and say something "idiotic or buffoon-like, or even worse he may just see me and turn and walk away." Sally attends approximately 40 sessions with little therapeutic movement. Topics eventually center upon how Sally feels the therapist is only seeing her because she pities her and Sally agrees, "I'm pitiful."

CASE EXAMPLE – MALE

Warren is a 45-year-old male who has worked at Industry-Tech for the last 12 years. His co-workers call him the Lurker, as he tends to lurk but not engage anyone. Warren is often seen looking over the top of his cubical watching the other office workers during office parties and birthday party gatherings, but he has never shown up at a Christmas party or New Year's Eve party. Warren lives alone, in a one-bedroom apartment, and spends considerable time on the Internet playing multiplayer role-playing games, such as World of Warcraft (WoW). There was a party for local WoW players, and Warren was determined to go and meet some of the people he had been pillaging cyber-space with for years. Warren bought new clothes, got his hair cut, and put on some new cologne. As he approached the bar he began telling himself, "you're just gonna mess this up," "no one wants to know you," and "what stupid thing are you going to do today to embarrass yourself?" As he stood outside in the 40-degree weather, people were going past him, a few bumping him accidentally, and he stepped back, overcome with anxiety. He could feel his face blushing and tripped backwards over a snow pile. No one in the bar actually noticed, though Warren imagined everyone in there laughing at him and talking about "how stupid" and "what a klutz" he is. As he lay there in the snow, frozen for only seconds but what felt like hours, a small blue mitten was extended to help him. Margery helped Warren up and she started talking with him. Though Warren provided little to no detail, she continued to talk and eventually coaxed him into the bar. Two years later they were married. Though Margery complains that Warren only likes to watch others, is "too hard on himself," is "deathly afraid of everyone," and stays in his cyber-world, they are happy.

TREATMENT

There have been few studies that explored the impact of treatment on AVD (Alden, Laposa, Taylor, & Ryder, 2002). When working with the AVD individual it is not uncommon for the therapist to develop counter transference issues with him or her. It is inherent in the pathology of the AVD individual to possess counter-therapeutic aspects which may appear as though he or she is thwarting the progress of treatment (Millon et al., 2000). The therapist may feel the client is not trying, being resistant, or feels the case is hopeless. However, treatment has been found to be efficacious in these individuals (Crits-Christoph & Barber, 2002).

Alden (1989) conducted the only known controlled randomized study of AVD using 76 men and women who met DSM-III criteria for the disorder. Individuals were assigned to one of three different treatment conditions or a wait-list control group. Results found that those within the treatment groups reported a decrease in "social reticence, less interference due to social anxiety, and greater satisfaction with social activities than did untreated subjects" (p. 762). In a study comparing short-term dynamic treatment with cognitive therapy for individuals with cluster C disorders, Svartberg and colleagues (2004) found that 62% met criteria for AVD. Both dynamic and cognitive therapy showed positive results during treatment and at the two-year follow-up. Borge and colleagues (2010) conducted a study that utilized 87 participants from Norway who were seeking treatment for social phobia and were randomly placed into two treatment groups: cognitive therapy or interpersonal therapy. Of the 87 participants, 57% were found to meet criteria for AVD. Results showed that personality scores were reduced from pre-treatment to one-year follow-up. AVD individuals who were prescribed anxiolytics at pre-treatment experienced greater treatment impact. It was shown that interventions designed to specifically treat non-personality disordered conditions can attenuate personality disorder conditions.

Beck and colleagues (2004) delineate a treatment approach when working with AVD clients. The foundational aspect of collaboration is addressed and two obstructions are noted: (1) fear of rejection and (2) mistrust of others' expressions of caring. The therapist is advised to test and identify these thoughts to form a viable collaborative relationship which, it is hoped, will generalize to relationships with others. It is important to be cognizant of the client's self-talk. Beck and colleagues (2004) provide examples such as "You must think I didn't do the homework well," and "you must be disgusted with me when I cry like this" (p. 304). Maintaining a rating on how much the client believes the therapist's feedback is beneficial, as this can be done at several stages of treatment to gauge the cohesiveness of the therapeutic relationship. Due to the AVD client's tendency to hide things that may be deemed embarrassing or possibly cause the therapist to not like the client, the therapist is advised to ask if the AVD client is afraid to reveal something or is holding back for fear of being negatively evaluated.

Specific cognitive interventions are noted by Beck and colleagues (2004) when working with the AVD client. Standard cognitive techniques have been found to be useful with the AVD client, but special interventions are also listed to assist the AVD client in surmounting the cognitive and emotional avoidant issues that lessen the impact of standard methods (Beck et al., 2004; Cummings, Hayes, Newman, & Beck, 2011). Diagramming avoidance patterns and characteristics, particularly in response to negative or adverse emotions, can assist the AVD individual in gaining insight into how his or her avoidance functions and how to intercede to break the cycle. Listing and rank-ordering dysfunctional beliefs about the outcome of experiencing negative emotions can assist the AVD client in building tolerance for such emotions.

Individuals with AVD typically have significant deficits in social skills (Herbert, 2007). Beck and colleagues (2004) recommend utilizing skill-training exercises that identify social cues with evaluations that are based in reality and not on negative cognitive assumptions. These skills can be incorporated into therapy sessions, as well as given as homework. The process of identifying and testing maladaptive beliefs helps the AVD client identify and confirm or deny the root of his or her avoidant tendencies, and can be outlined through several steps: (1) therapist and client develop insight into the roots of the negative beliefs and recognizing how they were once functional; (2) identifying new beliefs to counter the old negative ones that he or she wishes were accurate; (3) testing these new beliefs through experiments, guided observation, and role-plays of previous "schema-related incidents" (p. 312); and (4) encouraging the client to notice and remember information about himself or herself and the social experience that enhances and validates the new, more attractive beliefs.

Benjamin (1996) outlines her five categories of correct response when working with the AVD client and begins with facilitating collaboration, but this can be challenging due to the AVD individual's tendency to hide aspects of himself and content germane to treatment in order to protect himself and avoid being negatively evaluated by the therapist. The therapist will have to pass a "safety test" and, if successful will likely develop a strong and intensive therapeutic relationship. The AVD individual is likely to respond well to empathy and warm support, which must be delivered in a clear manner without the slightest indication of judgment or rejection. As the therapist shows acceptance, the AVD individual internalizes a sense of acceptance for herself. When gathering past data, the AVD individual may feel as though she is being disloyal or untrue to those individuals, but this is best countered by continual empathy and warm support.

The second category is to facilitate pattern recognition through teaching the AVD individual the impact of the avoidant patterns so that he or she will develop a desire and will to change. Couples therapy can serve as an excellent environment to learn about avoidant patterns and to increase motivation to facilitate change. These relationships are likely to possess significant triangulation to provide needed intimacy while also interpersonal distance. Benjamin (1996) provides the following example: "a single AVD may be 'the third wheel' of a marital couple and become secretly sexually involved with one member of the couple" (p. 302). Couples therapy can focus on believed rejection by the identified partner where the therapist makes suggestions that bring the rejecting partner closer to the AVD individual. Assertiveness training can be beneficial at this stage to assist the AVD individual in learning how to disclose and communicate effectively to get his or her needs met. The next category is blocking maladaptive patterns and to block any humiliation from the partner to provide a safe environment for the AVD individual to learn new patterns of functioning. The AVD individual must be willing to give up triangulated relationships and have more direct and authentic interactions. The therapist should illustrate how those types of relationships solidify the position of avoidance and perpetuate pathology. If the AVD individual is not in a relationship, helping him or her to find one is encouraged.

Strengthening the will to relinquish maladaptive patterns is likely to be the most difficult to implement and work through with the AVD client according to Benjamin (1996). The need for a safety net of withdrawing from social interaction and the intense fear of being out in the open and engaging with others is difficult for AVD individuals to change, as it is a large part of how they see and interact with the world. The AVD individual requires more than cognitive understanding that these baseline behaviors provide protection, and that he or she has the ability to leave the "safety zone" of withdrawal and reclusiveness to internalize new patterns of interacting.

To facilitate new learning, Benjamin's (1996) final step, the therapist intervenes and prevents self-deprecating thoughts and behaviors. Group therapy can be an excellent arena in which to do this. The AVD individual is permitted to be the group figure that is a bit removed until he or she feels comfortable engaging. Individual therapy is utilized to provide the secure foundation and the new skills that can be honed within the group setting. The goal of group therapy for the AVD client is to gain insight and understanding into the premise that flaws are accepted by the group. When the AVD client understands this, new social development can begin.

Psychopharmacology

Sadock and Sadock (2007) note several pharmacological approaches to treating symptoms, particularly anxiety and depression, associated with AVD. Atenolol (Tenormin), a β-adrenergic receptor antagonist, has been used to treat "autonomic nervous system hyperactivity, which tends to be high in patients with avoidant personality disorder, especially when they approach feared situations" (p. 813). SSRIs can be effective to manage rejection sensitivity, and medication that impacts dopamine can be used to encourage "novelty-seeking behavior," but the patient must be informed of and prepared for the experience that may result (Sadock & Sadock, 2007).

FILM AND POPULAR MEDIA EXAMPLES

Zelig (1983) – Leonard Zelig, played by Woody Allen

Adaptation (2002) – Charlie Kaufman, played by Nicholas Cage

CHECKLIST: AVOIDANT PERSONALITY DISORDER

Below is a complete list to best identify and diagnose Avoidant Personality Disorder. DSM-5 (APA, 2013) criteria are first, followed by discernible components, and lastly, associated features.

- ❑ A widespread pattern of inhibition around people, feeling inadequate and being very sensitive to being evaluated negatively, since early adulthood and occurring in a range of situations*
- ❑ Avoids occupational activities that involve significant interpersonal contact because of fears of criticism, disapproval, or rejection*
- ❑ Is unwilling to get involved with people unless certain of being liked*
- ❑ Shows restraint within intimate relationships because of the fear of being shamed or ridiculed*
- ❑ Is preoccupied with being criticized or rejected in social situations*
- ❑ Is inhibited in new interpersonal situations because of feelings of inadequacy*
- ❑ Views self as socially inept, personally unappealing, or inferior to others*
- ❑ Is unusually reluctant to take personal risk or to engage in any new activities because they may prove embarrassing*
- ❑ Hypervigilant with regard to actions and expressions of others
- ❑ Has been ridiculed and teased due to fearful and anxious demeanor
- ❑ Highly concerned about psychological reactions to embarrassment (i.e., blushing)
- ❑ Others would describe him or her as shy, anxious, timid, and asocial
- ❑ Limited social support network
- ❑ Possesses fantasies of idealized relationships
- ❑ Occupational difficulties due to avoidance issues

*distinguishing characteristics

THERAPIST CLIENT ACTIVITY

Use these probes to explore your AVD client's avoidance of others due to fear of rejection, poor self-concept, and fantasies of an idealized relationship that are central to the pathology and enhance the socioeconomic dysfunction.

- ➢ Do you find it hard to tell others about how you feel or what you think?
- ➢ Do you think others are particularly harsh in judging you?
- ➢ Who in your life has been the most critical?
- ➢ Tell me about a relationship you had that you valued most.
- ➢ Under what conditions are you most relaxed?
- ➢ When was the last time you went out of your way to avoid a work task due to too many people?
- ➢ Whom do you admire most and what qualities do you share and what qualities do you feel you are missing?
- ➢ Can you agree to tell me if I say something that hurts your feelings or makes you feel like I don't want you here?
- ➢ Have you ever avoided promotion or occupational advancement due to its requiring more interpersonal contact?
- ➢ Who was the last person you met and what was that like for you?
- ➢ What personal information do you keep to yourself and what do you think would happen if you told someone else?
- ➢ How do you feel when there are 5, 10, or even 15 people in the same room as you?
- ➢ What was school like for you and did you have close friends?
- ➢ Can you describe to me what it is like when you first meet someone?
- ➢ What is a comfortable level of risk for you?
- ➢ Whom do you connect best with in your family?
- ➢ Which is greater—loneliness, desire to be close to others, or fear of losing someone you once loved? Can you describe why and how it feels?

CLIENT QUESTIONNAIRE

The following questions are to be given to your client to help him or her identify past challenges and provide guidance for treatment.

What is your earliest recollection? Describe only as much as you feel comfortable with.

List three things you want to get out of therapy: List three things that motivate you to change:

Will you draw me a picture of yourself as at age 10 and now?

Dependent Personality Disorder

Dependent personality disorder (DPD) is characterized by the extreme need to be needed and finding value in self through the caring and pleasing of others. DPD was originally called asthenic personality disorder and first appeared in 1945 in a United States Department of War technical bulletin and then later in the *Diagnostic and Statistical Manual of Mental Disorder, First Edition* (DSM-I; APA, 1952). It was a subtype of passive-aggressive personality, labeled passive-dependent type and described as "characterized by helplessness, indecisiveness, and a tendency to cling to others as a dependent child to a supporting parent" (APA, 1952, p. 37). Beginning in the 1950s there have been upwards of 600 published articles on the dynamics and etiology of dependent personality traits. DPD was not included in the DSM-II (APA, 1968; Hirschfeld, Shea, & Weise, 1991) but did reemerge in the DSM-III (APA, 1980). The conceptualization of DPD in DSM-I was weighted towards psychodynamic theory, though the DSM in later editions has attempted to remain removed from any one theoretical orientation (Bornstein, 1993).

In the DSM-III, DPD was promoted to a full diagnostic category that included three broad, overlapping symptoms that have been judged to be "grossly inadequate" (Widiger & Bornstein, 2001). The three symptoms included (1) passivity in interpersonal relationships, (2) willingness to subordinate ones needs to those of others, and (3) a lack of self-confidence (Bornstein, 2007). The criteria were expanded in the DSM-III-R (APA, 1987) to include submissiveness and fears of separation, and this altered those who received the diagnosis (Widiger et al., 1988; Widiger & Bornstein, 2001). In a study examining face validity, 73% of the criteria for DPD were found to be correctly assigned and was rated the third highest, followed by paranoid personality disorder (PPD) and obsessive-compulsive personality disorder (OCPD) criteria (Blashfield & Breen, 1989).

A continual issue was that most individuals who met criteria for DPD also meet criteria for other personality disorders, especially borderline, histrionic, and avoidant (Stuart et al., 1998; Widiger & Rogers, 1989). It was found that 48% of individuals diagnosed with DPD met DSM-III-R criteria for borderline personality disorder (BPD) and 57% met DSM-III-R criteria for avoidant personality disorder (AVD; Widiger & Trull, 1998). The item that produced the greatest degree of concern and added to the overlap was the criterion related to being easily hurt by criticism or disapproval. This criterion was present in more than 70% of BPD individuals and 70% of the APD individuals (Widiger & Trull, 1998). The second most problematic criterion was related to feeling devastated or helpless when a close relationship ended as it was also highly rated by individuals with BPD (Widiger & Bornstein, 2001).

The criteria have remained largely unchanged since the DSM-III-R. The majority of studies on dependency have focused on the impact on interpersonal and health issues of excessive dependency. Clinical researchers have focused on the comorbidity of DPD and other psychological disorders, as well as how dependent traits are related to treatment outcome (Bornstein, 2007). Dependency research has been propelled by a consensus on the core features of a dependent personality (Birtchnell, 1988; Pincus & Gurtman, 1995). The core features are listed below (Bornstein, 2005a):

Core Features of DPD

A central aspect of this four-factor model is that dependent individuals exhibit a wider range of behavior than previously believed as they have a tendency to be passive and compliant, ingratiating themselves with identified caregivers by displaying a weak demeanor. In other situations they are capable of displaying assertive behaviors and potentially eliciting aggressive behaviors to attempt to ensure that a key relationship is secure and that in turn he or she is not abandoned (Bornstein, 2005a). The only change to DPD in the DSM-IV-TR (APA, 2000) was the removal of text that referenced gender association that suggested gender difference is largely artifactual. No changes were made to the criteria for DPD in the DSM-5 (APA, 2013).

ETIOLOGY

With the exception of Passive-Aggressive personality disorder (PAPD), evidence has been found for a heritable component of DPD and all Cluster C disorders (Torgersen et al., 2000). Prevalence rates for DPD in 129 dizygotic and 92 monozygotic twin pairs reveal that approximately 30% of the variance in DPD symptoms are genetically influenced (Torgersen et al., 2000). Utilizing a sample of 2,230 female twins, O'Neill and Kendler (1998) found a modest and stable genetic influence and a large and moderately stable environmental component in interpersonal dependency. DPD is not a simple linear construct but is influenced by both heritability and environmental forces. No studies have conclusively identified what inherited factors are associated with DPD (Bornstein, 2007), but the formation of DPD may be a composite of common personality traits that have become aberrant and maladaptive within larger constructs of neuroticism and agreeableness (Mongrain, 1993; Zuroff, 1994). More recent research revised this view and found high agreeableness not heavily weighted; low conscientiousness (paired with high neuroticism) is a better fit for DPD within the five-factor model (Miller & Lynam, 2008).

Four potent environmental factors have been found to influence the development of DPD: culture, parenting, illness, and abuse. Culture in the United States and Great Britain is based upon individualism and autonomous function, whereas countless other cultures throughout the world place value on collectivism and emphasize group cohesiveness and interpersonal connection. Collectivistic cultures, such as those seen in China and India, often do not subscribe to a dependent personality and see independent functioning as dysfunctional (Bornstein, 2005a). Chen, Nettles, and Chen (2009) contend that in regard to DPD, the DSM is culturally skewed toward an Americanized cultural view of beliefs, values, and assumptions, and postulate that Confucianism and Chinese rationalism illustrate that a varied self is not inherent in all human beings and necessary for a healthy existence, and that dependence and submission are appropriate and expected to fulfill social obligation, as opposed to being an indication of personality make-up.

Overprotective and/or authoritarian parenting has been found to be associated with DPD in later life, (Bornstein, 1993; Bornstein & Malka, 2009). Head, Baker, and Williamson (1991) examined three groups of participants: from an eating disorders program, an outpatient program for adult children of alcoholics, and a control group. Results illustrated that low cohesion (interfamilial commitment, support, and help among family members), low independence (assertiveness, self-sufficiency; extent to which family members make their own decisions), and low intellectual-cultural orientation (degree to which emphasis is placed on political, social, intellectual, and cultural activities) are common in families of origin of individuals who develop DPD. In addition, families of the DPD group showed low expressiveness (openness and directness in action and expression of feelings is encouraged within the family) and high control (family life is run by rules and procedures). This study lent credence to Millon's (2011) theory of DPD development that includes a history of overprotectiveness, limited stimulation, and provincialism resulting in the development of independence.

Millon (2011) identifies three self-perpetuating processes that promote pathological dependency from seemingly authentic affection and caring experienced in childhood: (1) Self-deprecation includes the actual and believed incompetence related to an individual's talents and abilities; by continually announcing these deficits, whereby convincing himself or herself and others of such deficits, he or she only deepens the self-image of incompetence. (2) Avoidance of adult activities is rooted in the DPD individual's tendency to be hesitant and fearful of activities that may foster mature and independent functioning. The restrictions he or she places are intended to lessen short-term embarrassments and anxieties related to failure, as well as lessen the probability that the DPD individual will acquire the skills necessary for independent functioning, resulting in continued dependence on others. (3) Clinging social behaviors entail the DPD individual's tendency to appease others and be contrite for his or her incompetence. The need for affection and a guarantee that he or she will not be abandoned becomes so continual as to tire and distance those the DPD individual is dependent upon.

A serious illness in early life has been found to increase the probability of developing DPD due to the contribution of a helpless self-concept and the tendency of serious illness to evoke overprotective parenting (Hoare, 1984; Parker & Lipscombe, 1980). Dependency in individuals who experienced childhood sexual abuse was explored by Hill, Gold, & Bornstein (2000) who examined 24 male and 85 female participants who were seeking outpatient treatment for problems related to childhood sexual abuse. Abuse was incurred from a parent or stepparent in 39.4%, another family member in 28.4%, and a non-family member in 32.1% with age of onset of abuse before age 5 in 49.5%, 6 to 12 years of age in 42.2%, and 13 to less than 18 years of age in 8.3%. Results showed that females who incurred childhood sexual abuse had higher dependency scores than non-childhood sexual abuse psychiatric patients, community adults, and college students. For men, the results were less consistent but evidenced "a similar overall pattern" (p. 82) and the author hypothesized that this is due to men's reluctance to acknowledge thoughts and feelings of dependence on self-reports as reported in previous research by Bornstein, Rossner, Hill, and Stepanian (1994).

Benjamin (1996) proposes four features that compose her pathogenic hypothesis to account for the DPD individual's symptoms as outlined in the DSM. The first feature is that the DPD individual experienced a natural developmental sequence that possessed "warm caring and intense attention" (p. 223). The baby learned appropriate bonding and that others would provide for his or her needs. Benjamin postulates that the DPD individual masters the early developmental trust stages well. This trust continues into adulthood for the DPD individual as illustrated by trusting a chosen dominant significant other individual. As the DPD individual moves into the next developmental stage he or she continues to require nurturing beyond what is appropriate. Here the DPD individual does not wean and the parents insulate the child from autonomous exploration and independent learning and skill development. Benjamin (1996) proposed two reasons for the failure to wean: (1) the parent enjoys the intimacy with the dependent child and refuses to give it up; (2) the parent subscribes to the "empty tank" theory, which postulates that "if a child is given enough attention and nurturance, all will be well" (p. 223) and that if any frustration is present, it is subsequent to neurotic behaviors. By incorporating this theory, the parent believes in taking care of every need the child has immediately, completely, and consistently. Due to providing this extreme level of nurturance and encapsulation, the child is not helped or protected, but rather demeaned and degraded.

The third feature in the pathogenic hypothesis for the DPD individual is that he or she is mocked by peers for inadequacy and is teased, which becomes internalized and a significant part of how the DPD individual sees himself or herself. The final feature is the outcome of intense parental control, which leaves the DPD individual with limited options other than to capitulate. An alternate pathway proposed by Benjamin (1996), aside from intensive and extreme protection, is that the family is hostile and over-controlling, leading the DPD individual to a position of submission. However, intensive control within the family can be present and not develop into DPD if it is intermixed with other messages. Benjamin's (1996) pathogenic hypothesis is shown below:

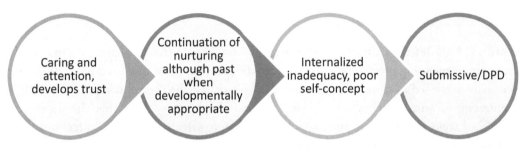

Pathogenic Process of DPD

PREVALENCE

The DSM-5 (APA, 2013) lists the National Epidemiologic Survey and Alcohol and Related Conditions (NESARC) prevalence rate for DPD at 0.49%. It further reports prevalence from the National Comorbidity Survey Replication (NCS-R; Lenzenweger, Lane, Loranger, & Kessler, 2007) for DPD to be 0.6%. However, greater clarification is needed. DPD has been found within in-patient settings to be between 15% and 25% (Oldham et al.,1995) and has been found to range between 0% and 10% in out-patient settings (Bornstein, 1997; Klein, 2003; Poldrugo & Forti, 1988). The frequency of DPD in out-patient settings is considerably lower than other personality disorders, such as borderline, histrionic, narcissistic, avoidant, and obsessive-compulsive personality disorders.

Morey (1988) utilized a sample of 291 patients who were identified by their treating clinicians as having a personality disorder and found a prevalence rate of 22.3% for DPD, but with substantial diagnostic overlap with borderline personality disorder (50.8%) and avoidant personality disorder (49.2%). The least overlap was with antisocial personality disorder (3.1%).

The high prevalence of DPD within in-patient settings may be due to "motivated hospitalization" or "institutional dependency" where they are placed or check themselves in to gain nurturance and care from authority figures (Booth, 1986; Greenberg & Bornstein, 1989). In examining dependency and hospital stay, it was found that the level of dependency did predict length of hospital stay for women but not men (Greenberg & Bornstein, 1989). The gender difference in DPD has been well founded with 11% of women and 8% of men diagnosed with DPD (Bornstein, 2005a). It has been found that a woman is 40% more likely to be diagnosed with DPD than a man due to men's tendency to minimize their self-reported dependency traits, attitudes, and behaviors when compared to women which skews gender differences when assessing dependency using self-report measures (Bornstein, 1995; Bornstein et al., 1994).

It is important to consider the influence of culture when examining DPD prevalence. Though there is limited cross-cultural data, findings do report a higher base rate of DPD in China and Japan when compared to North America or Western Europe (Behrens, 2004; Chen et al., 2009; Johnson, 1993). Prevalence rates and DPD diagnosis have been found to vary across cultures due to differential value being placed on independence and dependency-related behaviors (Alarcón, Foulks, & Vakkur, 1998).

ATTACHMENT

Bowlby (1977) described attachment behavior as any form of behavior that results in a person attaining or retaining proximity to some other differentiated and preferred individual, who is usually perceived as stronger and/or wiser. Dependency, the central component of DPD, is intertwined with attachment behavior as described by Bowlby in that the dependent individual seeks a strong and more secure individual to which to connect to feel protected and safe. Bornstein (1993) conceptualizes dependency as a function of an individual's working model of self and others, which intersects with the very roots of attachment theory (Ainsworth & Bowlby,1991).

Dependent personality disorder may be viewed through the lens of attachment theory as an interaction of an anxious, fearful temperament with an insecure attachment to a capricious and fluctuating parental figure (McGuffin & Thapar, 1992). The parent, when seen as a secure base, may provide DPD individuals with the reassurance and security they are unable to create for themselves (Rothbart & Ahadi, 1994), leading to a more pathological dependency. Sroufe, Fox, and Pancake (1983) examined infant-caregiver relations and later over-dependency to identify the roots of dependency and attachment utilizing a sample of 40 children between the ages of 47 and 60 months. Results clearly illustrated that securely attached infants showed less emotional dependence on preschool teachers, as rated by teacher rankings, ratings, and descriptions. Children that were identified as anxiously attached as infants—those that were highly passive or preoccupied with the mother and crying and contact-seeking, even before the mother had separated— were overly dependent on the preschool teachers at school age. It is clear that attachment and dependency have deep roots in early development and the later DPD individual is no different.

Dependency continues into later life as DPD has been found to be highly associated with the anxiety dimension underlying attachment styles. Brennan and Shaver (1998) utilized a college sample to examine the relationship between Bartholomew's (1990) four attachment styles (secure, dismissive-avoidant, anxious-preoccupied, and fearful-avoidant) and personality disorders. Results showed that the preoccupied group had the highest mean DPD score, second to the fearful group. This result is consistent with the anxiety dimension underlying attachment styles, more specifically, with the preoccupied style, which tends to exhibit high anxiety and low avoidance (Brennan, Clark, & Shaver, 1998).

Millon (2011) classified DPD within the deferential-attached-dependent (DAD) personality: the DAD spectrum. Within this spectrum, dependent pathology develops out of learning that feeling good, secure, and confident necessitates the passive reliance on the good will of others. For the DAD spectrum individual, strong bonding is present with the need for interpersonal support and attention. If or when he is deprived of this "social affection and nurturance" (p. 272), he is likely to experience significant discomfort, sadness, and anxiety in response.

The DPD client tends to be highly extrinsically oriented in self-definition, as he or she has developed an inner view of self as unworthy and a positive evaluative style of others which places him or her within the preoccupied attachment style.

DIAGNOSIS

The most commonly used criteria to diagnose DPD are the seven listed below in Table 1 from the DSM-5 (APA, 2013):

TABLE 1: DSM-5 DIAGNOSTIC CRITERIA FOR DEPENDENT PERSONALITY DISORDER
A. A pervasive and excessive need to be taken care of that leads to submissive and clinging behavior and fears of separation, beginning by early adulthood and present in a variety of contexts, as indicated by five (or more) of the following: (1) Has difficulty making everyday decisions without an excessive amount of advice and reassurance from others (2) Needs others to assume responsibility for most major areas of his or her life (3) Has difficulty expressing disagreement with others because of fear of loss of support or approval *Note:* Do not include realistic fears of retribution (4) Has difficulty initiating projects or doing things on his or her own (because of a lack of self-confidence in judgment or abilities rather than a lack of motivation or energy) (5) Goes to excessive lengths to obtain nurturance and support from others, to the point of volunteering to do things that are unpleasant (6) Feels uncomfortable or helpless when alone because of exaggerated fears of being unable to care for himself or herself (7) Urgently seeks another relationship as a source of care and support when a close relationship ends (8) Is unrealistically preoccupied with fears of being left to take care of himself or herself

Consistent with all of the criteria listed in the DSM, these are not hard and fast rules of diagnosis but guidelines and criteria to make diagnoses, as individual and cultural differences will impact presentation and expression of DPD. Criterion 1 entails difficulty with routine decisions in the absence of an inordinate amount of external advice and reassurance that can include even the most basic of decisions, such as what clothes to wear or what food to eat. This inability is derived from feelings of inadequacy and indecisiveness, which may result in criticism or nurturance. The second criterion pertains to deflecting responsibility onto others for areas of major concern in the DPD individual's life. This is perpetuated by fear of an inability to perform competently, and the belief that nurturance and caring will provide answers and soothing. Criterion three includes problems associated with voicing disagreement out of fear of loss of support or approval. The DPD individual is submissive and supplies passive agreement, as she views her opinions as wrong, insufficient, and inferior. Instances where an identified caregiver is in disagreement with others is the only time a DPD individual would provide counter opinion to a group of others or a non-care giver so as to make certain that the perceived nurturance will continue. The fourth criterion pertains to difficulty beginning projects or completing tasks autonomously, due to low self-confidence in her ability to complete the project well. The DPD individual tends to withdraw from projects at school or work that would mean he is the sole participant in the project or responsible for its completion. The DPD individual may participate if not in a position of responsibility, but participation would be minimal out of the belief he or she has little to contribute.

Criterion five is related to the extensive lengths the DPD individual will go to in order to receive nurturance and support from others. This can include participation in activities that are unpleasant. The need for nurturance and support shrouds the DPD individual's typical behavior or belief in what is right or wrong, even if it includes participation in illegal or immoral activities. The tendency for the DPD individual to feel dissonant or helpless when alone due to extreme fears of an inability to care for himself or herself is criterion six. The DPD individual possesses a pervasive sense of helplessness and tends to develop paranoia associated with being alone. DPD individuals also tend to feel incapable of sustaining himself or herself. It is common for the DPD individual to live with his or her parents well into adulthood, unless a dominant and perceived caregiver is obtained due to the inherent issues of criterion six. The seventh criterion entails the desperate search for another relationship that can provide care and support when a significant relationship ends. It is in this situation that the DPD individual will attach to another to foster a relationship prematurely instead of letting it develop normally. He or she is driven by intense anxiety to find the nurturant relationship that will provide the perceived equilibrium of safety and security. The eighth and final criterion pertains to preoccupation with fears of abandonment and having to provide for himself or herself. The DPD individual creates a vicious cycle by seeking constant reassurance that the other will not leave, which creates frustration in the idealized partner, who eventually leaves, as this fear is never quelled. The loss of the identified caregiver only provides further proof of the DPD individual's inadequacy, incompetence, and unlovability that can only be attenuated through another relationship as he or she is not capable of prosperous independent living.

Gude and colleagues (2006) examined the criteria associated with DPD in the DSM-IV (APA, 1994) using a sample comprising 1,078 patients treated in the Norwegian Network of Psychotherapeutic Day Hospitals from 1996 to 2000. The sample was composed of 81% of individuals who met criteria for one or more personality disorders and 11.3% of patients met criteria for DPD. These results brought into question the presence of a core component of DPD, which the authors state is not likely to exist and note also that DPD is based too heavily on a bi-dimensional model of incompetence and dysfunctional attachment.

Bornstein (2011) concedes that research on DPD and dependency has found high levels of anxiety and separation concerns, but the issue of submissiveness is context-dependent, as in some cases DPD individuals are assertive or even aggressive when particular relationships are threatened.

Millon and colleagues (2004) proposed five subtypes of DPD, shown here:

Disquieted (avoidant features) restlessly anxious, feels dread and apprehension, lonely unless near supportive figures	Selfless (masochistic features) merges with and immerses into another and willingly gives up one's own identity
Immature (variant of "pure" pattern) childlike, unsophisticated; inexperienced and gullible; incapable of assuming adult responsibilities	Accomodating (histrionic features) compliant, obliging, agreeable; blocks disturbing emotions; adopts a submissive as well as inferior role

Ineffectual
(schizoid features)

unproductive, incompetent;
seeks quiet life; refuses to deal
with difficulties; untroubled by
inadequacies

Five Proposed Subtypes of DPD

Differential Diagnosis

Ng and Bornstein (2005) conducted a meta-analysis examining 53 studies to determine the comorbidity between DPD and anxiety disorders. The authors found that DPD was significantly comorbid with panic disorder with and without agoraphobia (in DSM-5 these conditions are separated into two distinct categories), social anxiety disorder (social phobia), post-traumatic stress disorder, and obsessive-compulsive personality disorder.

Lenzenweger and colleagues (2007) reported findings consistent with the DSM-IV-TR (APA, 2000) in regard to DPD and comorbidity with other personality disorders, such as borderline personality disorder (BPD) and avoidant personality disorder (AVD). Lenzenweger and colleagues (2007) did not show a significant relationship between histrionic personality disorder (HPD) and DPD due to no one in the sample meeting criteria for this disorder. The authors showed a positive relationship between DPD and obsessive-compulsive personality disorder (OCPD). BPD and DPD both share a fear of abandonment, but the BPD individual reacts with emotional emptiness, rage, and demands, as opposed to the DPD individual who becomes more submissive, has a greater drive to satisfy the identified other, and desperately seeks another relationship that will provide perceived caring and support. In addition, instability and emotional turmoil are characteristic in BPD relationships, but typically absent in the relationships of the DPD individual.

Individuals with AVD and DPD share the tendency to feel inadequate and overly-sensitive to criticism, as well as a need for reassurance, but the AVD individual possesses intense fears of humiliation and rejection so that he or she will withdraw until certain of inclusion within an environment that is deemed safe. The DPD individual is relationship-seeking and will expend considerable effort to maintain relationships to perceived caregivers. HPD and DPD individuals share a strong need for reassurance and approval and the tendency to appear childlike and immature. The HPD individual is not likely to be self-effacing and submissive, but will behave in a manner that is excessive in presentation and hyper-social with intensive demands for attention, whereas the DPD individual will not. Both DPD and OCPD individuals possess a base fearful and anxious style, while the management and interaction style within their environment tends to vary greatly. Fossati and colleagues (2006) found support for the cluster C domain, which houses both OCPD and DPD, due to common factors, but also discernible criteria from the other two clusters, A and B.

Other considerations regarding differential diagnosis with DPD are personality change due to another medical condition in which DPD-like traits become present following a medical issue that affects the central nervous system and substance abuse that elicits behavior similar to that seen in DPD, but behaviors must be consistent and dominant across settings to qualify for the DPD diagnosis.

ASSESSMENT

There are several measures that specifically examine DPD as conceptualized by the DSM-IV-TR criteria (APA, 2000) including the Rorschach Oral Dependency scale (ROD; Masling, Rabie, & Blondheim, 1967), the Structured Clinical Interview for DSM Personality Disorders (SCID-II; Spitzer, Williams, Gibbons, & First, 1990), the Structured Interview for DSM Personality-Revised (SIDP-R; Pfohl, Blum, Zimmerman, & Stangl, 1989), and the Interpersonal Dependency Inventory (IDI; Hirschfeld et al., 1977). Each of these measures has been used reliably to determine DPD symptoms and diagnosis. A review of psychometric properties of diagnostic interviews and construct validity of self-report measures has been conducted by Bornstein, (1999b, 2005b).

On the Millon Multiaxial Clinical Inventory, Third Edition (MCMI; Millon, Millon, & Davis, 1994), a DPD individual is likely to produce high scores on scale 3 and scale A, which is indicative of feelings of incapability and incompetence when functioning independently, inadequacy and insecurity, submissiveness in relationships (Choca & Van Denburg, 1997), tendency to minimize problems, and high anxiety (especially when distressed). On the Minnesota Multiphasic Personality Inventory, Second Edition (MMPI-2), the anticipated profile of an individual with DPD would be 2-7/7-2, which illustrates a passive, dependent, and docile tendency (Meyer & Deitsch, 1996).

CASE EXAMPLE – MALE

Marlon has been friends with Ray for the last five years. They go everywhere together and have worked at the Gas-N-Sip on the same shift since they both started working there. Ray typically makes all the decisions and Marlon is eager is oblige. The new manager is cutting down on the hours and employees and is changing the shift for both Marlon and Ray, one in the evening and one in afternoon. Marlon thinks this is really being done so the new manager can become better friends with Ray and pull him away and he will be left alone and will never have friends again. Marlon asks Ray several times each day what he wants to do, as the new shift begins in one week. Ray is not certain if he wants to quit or not and this uncertainty only causes Marlon to ask more frequently, which is starting to frustrate him. Ray has told Marlon what job to take, they dress alike (as Marlon has bought the same clothing style as Ray since they met), and they engage in the same activities that Ray has done for years, such as hunting and working out. As the new shift begins with Marlon in the evening, he is calling Ray asking him questions about basic work activities in the store that they have done for years, such as stocking the shelf, how many items to put on the shelf, and cleaning the store to make it neat and clean for Ray when he starts in the afternoon. After Marlon's shift, he waits around the store for Ray to spend time with him. He is sleeping very little to be with Ray, trying to make sure that Ray is comfortable at work, and to find time to hunt and work out with him. Ray is becoming more and more frustrated with Marlon as Marlon increases his need to be reassured and obtain a sense of importance from Ray since the shifts changed. In a huge argument, Ray tells Marlon to leave him alone and that he does not want to be friends with him any longer. Marlon begins to have panic attacks again, which he has not had in five years, and soon Marlon and the manager are starting up a new and close friendship and hanging out each morning after Marlon's shift to go to breakfast and jogging, as the manager is a marathon runner and has been for years; Marlon told him he has always wanted to take up running.

CASE EXAMPLE – FEMALE

Paula just began treatment with Sean, who started working at the community mental health clinic two weeks ago after earning his degree. He is eager and excited to get started. Paula's presenting problems are anxiety and attachment issues. She grew up in "a good home" with a lot of love and caring. She recently graduated from college and is having trouble finding a job in hotel management. She is always on time for her sessions with Sean, and calls in-between sessions to get Sean's advice about where to apply for a job or if she should go out with friends or not, as these issues cause her intense anxiety as she feels she is never sure what is right. Sean tells Paula that he will be away from the practice for a while as he is moving into a new apartment. After hearing this, Paula breaks down in session about how lonely she feels and how uncertain her life is, and that she feels desperate without any answers in her life. Sean attempts to comfort her and gives her his cell phone number in case of an emergency. Paula begins to call every day to get confirmation about how to properly follow through on Sean's advice. After a few weeks, Sean and Paula have one session in the office and another at a coffee shop two blocks from Sean's new apartment. The manager of the practice sees them at one of their "coffee-shop sessions" and confronts Sean, who is then placed on probation and Paula is removed from his caseload. When Paula is told about this, she breaks down in session, feels that her life is over, that no one loves, her, and that all people are "just meant to hurt you and leave." Following the practice manager's intervening and Paula leaving, she immediately goes to another therapist's office two floors down and begins treatment the next day.

TREATMENT

Borge and colleagues (2010) examined pre-treatment predictors and in-treatment components in 77 participants who were diagnosed with at least one personality disorder: 57% AVD, 11% paranoid personality disorder (PPD), 9% OCPD, 6% BPD, and 4% DPD. There were two treatment groups, one utilizing a cognitive therapy modality and the other an interpersonal treatment modality. Results showed that the proportion of personality disorder symptomatology was decreased at one-year follow-up, individuals diagnosed with AVD and DPD showed a decrease from pre-treatment levels at one-year follow-up, and dimensions of DPD showed a greater decrease among the residential cognitive therapy group.

In the psychodynamic approach to DPD, the goal of treatment is to contend with earlier relationships and bring them to a sufficient and beneficial resolution. The clinician should symbolize the object losses; therapy success is achieved when the clinician becomes a better object than the earlier objects in the DPD individual's childhood (Sperry, 2003). Simon (2009) examined the maintenance of treatment gains in 15 studies conducted between 1982 and 2006 in individuals diagnosed with a cluster C disorder and found that individuals with AVD, OCPD, and DPD make significant progress during therapy and post-treatment when therapy utilized a psychodynamic or cognitive-behavioral modality, with social skills training producing larger effect sizes during post-treatment follow-up. This illustrates the benefit the cluster C individual can derive from treatment.

Rathus and colleagues (1995) examined the efficacy of cognitive-behavioral treatment (CBT) on 18 patients with personality disorders who also met criteria for panic disorder with agoraphobia (in DSM-5, these conditions are separated into two distinct categories). They found a decrease in dependency scores on the MCMI-II when assessed at pre- and post-treatment after 12 weeks of treatment. Bartak and colleagues (2009) conducted a study that utilized 371 participants from six mental health centers in the Netherlands to examine the effect of six therapeutic modalities in terms of setting and duration. Interventions included short-term outpatient (up to 6 months), long-term outpatient (more than 6 months), short-term day hospital, long-term day hospital, short-term in-patient, and long-term in-patient. Results showed that "patients in all treatment groups had improved psychiatric symptoms, psychosocial functioning, and quality of life after 12 months. Most improvement was observed in the short-term in-patient group" (p. 27).

Beck and colleagues (2004) outline treatment for working with a DPD individual with the goal of achieving autonomy and helping him or her to become more separate from significant others, including the therapist, along with increased self-confidence and self-efficacy. The therapist is advised to allow a degree of dependence initially, and to recognize that the majority of the workload may be on the therapist, but this changes through the course of treatment as the workload shifts to the client as therapy proceeds. Guided discovery and Socratic questioning is recommended to force the client to come up with his or her own solutions to questions and to encourage decision-making. As treatment progresses, goal attainment can be utilized as an intensive tool to illustrate the DPD individual's autonomous functioning and ability to make decisions and lessen helplessness.

The therapist must be vigilant of the tendency to see the client as helpless and in need of rescue as this stance would only serve to strengthen the initial belief in his or her helplessness. Techniques, such as challenging and disputing automatic thoughts, using a dysfunctional thought record, and assertiveness training and behavioral experiments can be useful when working with individuals with intensive dependency issues. The therapist needs to be aware that the DPD individual is likely to develop romantic feelings for the therapist. It is recommended that these feelings be discussed in session and processed sensitively, focusing on pin pointing the root and purpose, to feel safe with an identified figure. As treatment moves towards its conclusion, the therapist and client must address this issue openly and challenge any catastrophic thinking regarding the loss of this important relationship. The processing of grief must be discussed and addressed, and the therapist should help the DPD individual to see that even though it is an end, he or she will survive and continue on. To lessen the angst associated with the end of treatment, therapy can be augmented to include group therapy. This can dilute the intensive one-on-one relationship, or booster sessions can be utilized if the client experiences difficulties in the future.

Benjamin (1996) outlines treatment with the DPD individual utilizing her categories of correct response. The first step is to facilitate collaboration with the client against "it,"—the old way of being. This is very challenging with the DPD client as he or she will tend to see that changing the treatment plan is not helpful, but has the emphasis on building psychological strength as opposed to neediness and that this will encourage growth. It should be expected that the DPD individual is going to be uninterested in this treatment plan. Facilitating pattern recognition is the next step and achieved by illustrating that separation can be a viable life option, as opposed to the typical response pattern of giving control to another through submission. Assertiveness training can be beneficial in teaching these patients how to avoid situations that they may misinterpret as necessitating the relinquishment of control. Change may be required in the client's family as well.

The next step entails blocking the maladaptive pattern of dependency in times of distress or perceived need, and instead providing support and encouragement when the DPD individual is doing well. The focus needs to be on the DPD client's intense wish to be submissive and, instead, building a greater sense of competence. That the DPD client recognizes his or her pattern of dependency and the cost and benefits of living in the adult world is central to this step. Alternatives to dependency must be discussed and considered while strengthening the desire to give up old maladaptive patterns. Lastly, the DPD client must be willing to learn new patterns of interaction once the previous steps have been successfully completed, and he or she is receptive to new patterns of identification and expression of affect and effective communication.

Psychopharmacology

There have been no controlled pharmacological trials for DPD (Koenigsberg et al., 2002). However, many individuals with DPD have anxiety and depressive disorders as well (Bornstein, 2007; Brennan et al., 1998; Millon, 2011; Ng & Bornstein, 2005). Kimmel and Roy-Byrne (2012) examined the efficacy of antidepressants as a treatment for anxiety disorders, and Kelsey and colleagues (2006) take a more global approach and examine when and why a medication is appropriate, when not to use medication, and potential side effects when used for a variety of disorders including personality disorders.

FILM AND POPULAR MEDIA EXAMPLES

Blue Velvet (1986) – Dorothy Vallens, played by Isabella Rossellini

Arrested Development (2003–2006) – Buster Bluth, played by Tony Hale

All in the Family (1968–1979) – Edith Bunker, played by Jean Stapleton

Checklist: Dependent Personality Disorder

Below is a complete list to best identify and Dependent Personality Disorder. DSM-5 (APA, 2013) criteria are first, followed by discernible components, and lastly, associated features.

- ❑ Has difficulty making everyday decisions without an excessive amount of advice and reassurance from others*

- ❑ Needs others to assume responsibility for most major areas of his or her life*

- ❑ Has difficulty expressing disagreement with others because of fear of loss of support or approval.*

- ❑ Has difficulty initiating projects or doing things on his or her own (because of a lack of self-confidence in judgment or abilities rather than a lack of motivation or energy)*

- ❑ Goes to excessive lengths to obtain nurturance and support from others, to the point of volunteering to do things that are unpleasant*

- ❑ Feels uncomfortable or helpless when alone because of exaggerated fears of being unable to care for himself or herself*

- ❑ Urgently seeks another relationship as a source of care and support when a close relationship ends*

- ❑ Is unrealistically preoccupied with fears of being left to take care of himself or herself*

- ❑ Tendency to be childlike and unsophisticated; inexperienced and gullible; incapable of assuming adult responsibilities

- ❑ Tendency to be unproductive, incompetent; seeks a quiet life; refuses to deal with difficulties; untroubled by inadequacies

- ❑ Willingly merges with another and willingly gives up his or her own identity

- ❑ Is restlessly anxious, feels dread and apprehension when alone, and is lonely unless near supportive figures

- ❑ Is compliant, obliging, and agreeable; tends to block disturbing emotions and adopts a submissive as well as inferior role

*distinguishing characteristics

THERAPIST CLIENT ACTIVITY

Use these probes to explore your DPD client's dependency, feelings of inadequacy, fear of loneliness, and submissive views and presentation that are central to the pathology and enhance the socioeconomic dysfunction.

> ➤ What is the first thing that comes to your mind when you think about being alone?
> ➤ Can you imagine ways to increase your autonomy?
> ➤ Have you ever tried to be more autonomous; if so, how?
> ➤ What is the best relationship you have ever had?
> ➤ What made your best relationship so good?
> ➤ What was your worst relationship?
> ➤ What made it the worst relationship?
> ➤ Can you tell me something you have done that you regretted but felt you could not tell your partner?
> ➤ When was the last time you were mad and did you express it?
> ➤ Do you think people can be mad at you and still love you?
> ➤ Whom do you identify most with in this world?
> ➤ What is your greatest fear?
> ➤ What would you do to keep someone close to you?
> ➤ How do you see therapy helping you?
> ➤ How will you know you are successful in therapy?
> ➤ What do you think you are good at, regardless of how minor?
> ➤ What do you think you will never be able to do?
> ➤ If you were a machine, what would you replace and why?

CLIENT QUESTIONNAIRE

The following questions are to be given to your client to help him or her identify past challenges and provide guidance for treatment.

What is your earliest recollection? Describe only as much as you feel comfortable with.

List three things that you get out of giving others control and responsibility?

Draw a picture of you with your family of origin:

Draw a picture of your most recent relationship; include yourself and significant other:

Draw how you anticipate you will look after therapy is successful:

Obsessive-Compulsive Personality Disorder

Obsessive-Compulsive personality disorder (OCPD) is characterized by a continuous pattern of rigidity, orderliness, structure, and intensive mental and interpersonal control. OCPD is one of the few personality disorders to have been included in each edition of the *Diagnostic and Statistical Manual of Mental Disorders* (DSM). Its early conceptualization dates back to Freud (1906–1908/1959) who described a character style that is "anal retentive" or the "anal character" due to retentive bowel habits and sublimation of anal erotic impulses. He identified the main character traits as a preoccupation with orderliness, frugality, and obstinacy. Freud further explained that orderliness is manifested in cleanliness and over-conscientiousness; frugality manifests in miserliness; and obstinacy manifests in a negativistic and obstinate manner.

Abraham (1923) expanded on Freud's anal retentive character analysis by identifying the intrinsic satisfaction that OCPD individuals derive from orderliness, symmetrical structure of their environment, and making lists of tasks that they typically fail to follow through on. Abraham further contended that perseverance is often offset by procrastination behaviors, and that owning items in itself provides a sense of fulfillment that is so intense it precludes their disposal. Today this is called hoarding and is classified as 'hoarding disorder' in the DSM-5 (APA, 2013). When interacting with others, these individuals are intractable, demanding to control interplay between themselves and others, and highly critical (Abraham, 1923). Reich (1949) expanded the psychoanalytic viewpoint and described these compulsive individuals as "living machines," and noted their drive for orderliness and their attention to structure and organization, indecision, skepticism, flat affective reactions, and disregard for others.

In the first edition of the DSM (DSM-I; APA, 1952), compulsive personality is described as follows:

> Such individuals are characterized by chronic, excessive, or obsessive, concern with adherence to standards of conscience or of conformity. They may be over-inhibited, over-conscientious, and may have an inordinate capacity for work. Typically they are rigid and lack a normal capacity for relaxation. While their chronic tension may lead to neurotic illness, this is not an invariable consequence. The reaction may appear as a persistence of an adolescent pattern of behavior, or as a regression from more mature functioning as a result of stress (p. 37).

As evidenced by the description, this definition is derived from the psychoanalytic viewpoint of the disorder, particularly Abraham's (1923). Shapiro (1965) conceptualized

OCPD from a cognitive standpoint and identified three areas of problematic functioning: (1) intellectual rigidity to the point of impaired attention due to intensive focus on details and constricted spontaneity; (2) inconsistent drive to produce that is thwarted by a lack of follow-through or conviction; it is the will alone that is satisfying, not the actual task; (3) impaired reality as these individuals oscillate between doubt and dogma. Dogma serves a practical purpose in these individuals, in that strict adherence to an idea or process makes up for and potentially surmounts doubt, which is strengthened by an intensive and provincial cognitive style permitting avoidance of new information while these individuals are easily contented by the resulting limited beliefs (Shapiro, 1965).

In the DSM-II (APA, 1968), obsessive compulsive personality (anankastic personality) emerges and is defined as follows:

> The behavior pattern is characterized by excessive concern with conformity and adherence to standards of conscience. Consequently, individuals in this group may be rigid, over-inhibited, over-conscientious, over-dutiful, and unable to relax easily. This disorder may lead to an *obsessive compulsive neurosis* (q.v.), from which it must be distinguished (p. 43).

The DSM-II definition adds many clinical components compared to the DSM-I, and addresses the condition, obsessive compulsive neurosis, now called obsessive-compulsive disorder (OCD). In the DSM-III (APA, 1980), the definition of compulsive personality disorder, as it was still called, was modified to include difficulty with emotional expressiveness to include warm and tender emotions and affective constriction. These cold and uncaring traits replaced over-inhibition and over-conscientiousness. Additional criteria were added to address perfectionism that interferes with task completion, demanding and controlling interpersonal style, poor insight into the impact the individual's behavior has upon others, being overly committed to occupational tasks to the point of excluding interpersonal relationships and pleasure, and fear of making a mistake that is so great that it impedes decision-making.

The term obsessive-compulsive personality disorder emerges in the DSM-III-R (APA, 1987) and "over-conscientiousness, scrupulousness, and inflexibility," "lack of generosity," and "inability to discard worn out, worthless objects" are included as criteria.

In reviewing criteria and research for the DSM-IV (APA, 1994), Pfohl and Blum (1991) identified the essential feature of OCPD to include "a preoccupation with perfectionism, mental and interpersonal control, and orderliness at the expense of flexibility, openness, and efficiency" (p.373). The three best criteria for predicting a diagnosis of OCPD were "preoccupied with details," "rigid and stubborn," and "reluctant to delegate," and the OCPD individual could best be described in terms of interpersonal and psychological behaviors (Grilo, 2004). Sanislow and colleagues (2002) explored the diagnostic construct of OCPD and other personality disorders within the DSM-IV. Results indicated that OCPD is independent of the other three clusters and the criteria "reluctant to delegate tasks" and "perfectionism" loaded most heavily within the factor analysis.

ETIOLOGY

The etiology of obsessive-compulsive personality disorder has been conceptualized in a variety of ways and from various theoretical perspectives. One of the key questions is whether or not OCPD has a biological component. Reichborn-Kjennerud and colleagues (2007) examined the genetic and environmental influence associated with Cluster C personality disorders, the cluster that contains OCPD as well as avoidant and dependent personality disorders, in a sample of 1,386 young adult twin pairs from the Norwegian Institute of Public Health Twin Panel (NIPHTP). Results showed that genetic influences were distinct for OCPD as compared to the other disorders in Cluster C, and correlated strongly with the personality construct of conscientiousness and negatively with the personality construct of neuroticism. Genetic and environmental factors accounted for only 11% of the variance for OCPD. In another study to determine genetic influence of OCPD, Lochner and colleagues (2011) utilized a sample of individuals diagnosed with obsessive-compulsive disorder (OCD), with and without OCPD, and found that those with OCPD do not have a unique genetic profile. Rather, OCPD is a marker of severity for OCD (OCD and OCPD will be discussed later in this chapter). Additionally, a study found that genetics accounted for 45% of the variance, whereas non-shared environment accounted for 55% of the variance (Taylor, Asmundson, & Jang, 2011). Noting the vast array of results, the question remains as as to what degree biological factors are at work in OCPD.

Pollak (1979) conducted a comprehensive review of the literature regarding obsessive-compulsive personality, now called OCPD, and found "meager support" (p. 227) for bowel training as a significant etiological factor, but identified a link between parental anal traits and children who go on to develop OCPD. Additionally, it has been postulated that OCPD is derived from modeling and learned behaviors related to parents and their rigid, controlling, and obsessional style of relating to their children (Carr, 1974).

Benjamin (1996) proposes a pathogenic hypothesis for the development of OCPD symptoms. The developmental pathway for the OCPD individual was filled with "relentless coercion to perform correctly and follow the rules, regardless of personal cost" (p. 243). Within the home environment there was little warmth, and intensive focus on perfection and orderliness. Toilet training can be a time when the OCPD individual learns strict control, and principles of performance are set throughout early developmental periods. As the child has both success and failure, and at times is defiant toward excessive rules and practices, he ultimately tries to please the parent and improve his performance. As he or she internalizes the ideals of the parent, the future OCPD individual projects these ideals onto others who are expected to function in the same manner. Rigid moral views and beliefs perpetuate complicity with cruel practices under the pretense of "proper training." Very little, if any, acknowledgment was provided for success, but imperfections or failure, no matter how slight, were met with harsh consequences and criticism. With the internalized view of perfection, the OCPD individual is consumed with indecision and becomes stagnated due to the perceived need to move forward without flaws. Affection was in limited supply as the household tended to lack physical contact and levity. Due to the variability and difficulty in gaining 100%

emotional control, the OCPD-to-be learned to minimize feelings which were not considered important or a source of concern.

PREVALENCE

The DSM-5 (APA, 2013) reports that OCPD "is one of the most prevalent personality disorders in the general population, with estimated prevalence ranging from 2.1% to 7.9%" (p. 681). Grant and colleagues (2008) reported a prevalence rate of 7.88% for OCPD in a nationally representative sample derived from the National Epidemiologic Survey on Alcohol and Related Conditions (NESARC). It was found to be the most prevalent personality disorder in the general population. The authors also found no gender, income, marital status, or socioeconomic differences for those with OCPD. The risk of developing OCPD was higher for those with some college, and higher still for those with a bachelor's degree, when compared to those with less than a high school education.

Prevalence rates have varied greatly for OCPD depending upon context and assessment instrument used. Lenzenweger and colleagues (2007) found a prevalence rate of 2.4% using the International Personality Disorder Examination (IPDE; Loranger et al., 1987) with a sample of 5,692 participants from the National Comorbidity Survey Replication (NCS-R). Using the Structured Clinical Interview for DSM-IV Axis II personality disorders (SCID-II), Crawford and colleagues (2005) found a prevalence rate of 4.7% for OCPD in 644 participants from a sample first assessed in 1975 and then subsequently spanning the next 25 years.

ATTACHMENT

Nordahl and Stiles (1997) examined the relationship between parental bonding and personality disorders and found that OCPD individuals experienced lower levels of care along with higher levels of overprotection from both parents when compared to individuals who did not meet criteria for a personality disorder. In addition, there was a paucity of paternal care and significantly higher levels of overprotection from both parents when compared to those with a history of outpatient psychiatric care. The relationship between maternal overprotection and OCPD was tempered when "comorbidity with a lifetime depressive disorder was accounted for" (p. 399). The authors link this latter result with psychoanalytic theories that state poor paternal parenting causes the individual to be at significant risk to develop OCPD (see Nordahl & Stiles, 1997).

Lyddon and Sherry (2001) propose that OCPD individuals will fall within the preoccupied attachment style due to their demand for perfection from self and others. Love from a caregiver was typically based upon level of performance (Ivey, 1991, as cited in Lyddon & Sherry, 2001). Interpersonally, they are domineering with subordinates, while being submissive to those of higher rank or status. The view of self becomes negative due to the idea of needing to be perfect and continually falling short of the expectations and standards of parental figures. While others may not live up to expectations, OCPD individuals find themselves at fault so the tendency is to see others in a positive light. Sperry (2003) further substantiates the contention that OCPD individuals possess a preoccupied attachment style.

DIAGNOSIS

The most commonly used criteria to diagnose OCPD are the seven listed below in Table 1 from the DSM-5 (APA, 2013):

TABLE 1: DSM-5 DIAGNOSTIC CRITERIA FOR OBSESSIVE-COMPULSIVE PERSONALITY DISORDER

A. A pervasive pattern of preoccupation with orderliness, perfectionism, and mental and interpersonal control, at the expense of flexibility, openness, and efficiency, beginning by early adulthood and present in a variety of contexts, as indicated by four (or more) of the following:

(1) Is occupied with details, rules, lists, order, organization, or agenda to the point that the key part of the activity is gone

(2) Shows perfectionism that interferes with task completion

(3) Is extremely dedicated to work and efficiency to the elimination of spare time activities

(4) Is meticulous, scrupulous, and rigid about etiquettes of morality, ethics, or values

(5) Is not capable of disposing worn out or insignificant things even when they have no sentimental meaning

(6) Is unwilling to pass on tasks or work with others except if they surrender to exactly their way of doing things

(7) Takes on a stingy spending style towards self and others

(8) Shows stiffness and stubbornness

Reprinted with permission from the *Diagnostic and Statistical Manual of Mental Disorders, Fifth Edition*, (Copyright ©2013). American Psychiatric Association. All Rights Reserved.

Consistent with all of the criteria listed in the DSM, these are not hard and fast rules of diagnosis, but rather guidelines and criteria to make diagnoses, as individual and cultural differences will impact the presentation and expression of the OCPD individual. The first criterion pertains to the intensive focus on structure and organization that is so severe that the individual loses sight of the task itself. The OCPD individual gets lost in the process, so much so that the task is never completed. "The devil is in the details" has new meaning for the OCPD individual, as the details are what will consume him or her to the point of losing jobs and having tasks withdrawn. Criterion two entails the mental idea of the task that is so specific and perfect that it cannot be achieved. Due to this, the OCPD individual is continually on phase one, as phase one of a several-step task will never be completed perfectly enough to permit moving on to the next phase. The third criterion relates to the OCPD individual's adherence to completing activities to such an extent that he or she loses sight of outside relationships and connections. Hobbies are out of the question, as these individuals ensconce themselves so thoroughly in tasks that anything external to these is not even considered. Work in this case consists not of employment activities, but tasks or jobs to be completed in an allotted time. A family trip is hampered by the need to get to the destination in the time frame allotted, rather than taking time to stop along the way, see sights, or even go to the restroom.

Criterion four addresses the strict cognitive beliefs about what is right and wrong. Rules are to be followed without question, and these rules can range from societal rules, such as do not steal, to rules of a game with others, such as who goes next and when someone gets a point or not. The OCPD individual will distance himself or herself from others who may interpret rules or laws more liberally or more realistically, and see such people as "a bad influence" or "corrupted." The fifth criterion entails the OCPD individual's tendency to hold onto items such as newspapers, old technology, papers, and paystubs, as they may someday be needed. This attempt at control hampers relationships as there is only so much space to store items, and significant others typically become frustrated as space becomes filled with hoarded objects.

Criterion six is related to the OCPD individual's inclination to take on all tasks and not work well with others without their strict adherence to his rules and methods of operation. This relates to work relationships as well as familial and social relationships. The details must be followed and completed precisely as outlined, and any deviation is not tolerated. The seventh criterion pertains to the view that money, like items in criterion five, must be saved and not parted with. These individuals are exceptionally stingy with spending on themselves and others. This is not due to having little money or means, but about collecting, stashing, and stockpiling it for the inescapable "rainy day." Criterion eight provides a global and defining nature of the OCPD individual: He or she is strict, inflexible, and unyielding in regard to every aspect of life. This includes family, friends, and co-workers. The OCPD individual is not able to "go with the flow" or adjust to unscheduled change or circumstances, and when such issues arise, depression, anxiety, or panic are likely to follow.

The DSM-5 (APA, 2013) lists several additional features associated with OCPD. The OCPD individual is likely to be fixated on rules and procedures when explicit guidelines or steps are not provided and may have considerable difficulty making a decision as to which step should go first, second, and so on. Anger and frustration are likely when the OCPD individual is not able to control the situation but it is typically not directly expressed and may manifest as self-righteousness and passive-aggressive attack. Affect is restricted, and the OCPD individual may become uncomfortable in the presence of those who are openly affectionate. Relationships possess a very serious tone and utilize cognitive processes to understand emotions. These individuals are likely to hold back until a point is reached where she can say exactly what she wants to say. Within an occupational environment, the OCPD individual may experience problems when new situations that require flexibility and compromise arise.

It is Millon's (2004) view that there are few pure personality prototypes and that, instead, there are mixed variants of one major type with one or more secondary or subsidiary subtypes.

Millon and colleagues (2004) have identified five subtypes of OCPD, which they refer to as compulsive personality, shown below.

Conscientious

(dependent features)

Rule and duty bound; painstakingly meticulous; considerable and generalized self-doubt; hates errors and mistakes

Bureaucratic

(narcissistic features)

Feels a sense of power in formal organizations; group rules provide identity and security; unimaginative, nosy, and intrusive; closed-minded

Puritanical

(paranoid features)

Self-righteous, bigoted, zealous; grim and prudish morality; intensive need for control and to oppose own abhorrent impulses and fantasies

Parsimonious

(schizoid features)

Tight-fisted, miserly, hoarding; protects against self-loss; fears intrusion into empty inner world; afraid of exposure of personal improprieties and contrary impulses

Bedeviled

(negativistic features)

Unresolved ambivalence; feels tormented and confused; plagued with intrapsychic conflicts, confusions, and frustrations; contradictory emotions are controlled by condensed obsessions and compulsions

Millon's Five Subtypes of OCPD

Benjamin (1996) proposes a link between the OCPD individual's interpersonal history and the manifestation of the DSM criteria. She identifies the "total OCD" (she uses the abbreviation OCD to identify OCPD) as meeting all criteria listed in the DSM. During development, the future OCPD individual experienced intense pressure to be perfect without considering the consequences to self, which causes preoccupation with details and rules (criterion 1), task interference derived from perfectionism (criterion 2), and disproportionate devotion to work to the point of exclusion of leisure interests (criterion 3). Perfection is a strong foundational component of the OCPD individual's tendency to be judgmental, over-conscientious, and fixated on scrupulousness (criterion 4). In an effort for complete control over his or her life, the OCPD individual hoards items, regardless of worth, in case he or she needs them in the future (criterion 5). In an additional attempt at complete control, he or she will insist on doing things himself or herself. The OCPD individual may work with others but complete submission to his or her way of task completion must be achieved (criterion 6). Dedication to control, lack of warmth, and the condoning of self-restraint in the parental home is associated with miserliness (criterion 7), rigidity, and stubbornness (criterion 8). Benjamin (1996) states: "The DSM-IV discarded the DSM-III-R item 5, *restricted expression of affection*, an attribute that does belong in this group. It is a consequence of lack of warmth and a high value on self-control" (p. 247). When working with OCPD individuals, this item is an ever-present core issue.

Skodol and colleagues (2011) identified several personality traits and domains for inclusion in the upcoming DSM-5 proposed types and traits. Though they were not utilized in the manual, they do provide insight into the disorder. They found the following 11 traits within four domains shown below:

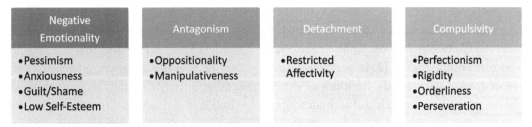

Negative Emotionality	Antagonism	Detachment	Compulsivity
•Pessimism •Anxiousness •Guilt/Shame •Low Self-Esteem	•Oppositionality •Manipulativeness	•Restricted Affectivity	•Perfectionism •Rigidity •Orderliness •Perseveration

OCPD Domains and Traits

This figure provides a visual format in which to conceptualize the areas within OCPD and those traits that drive the behaviors often seen in individuals diagnosed with this personality disorder.

Obsessive-Compulsive Spectrum

It has been postulated that there is an obsessive-compulsive spectrum of disorders (Hollander, 1993) that includes obsessive-compulsive disorder (OCD), body dysmorphic disorder (BDD), Tourette's disorder, trichotillomania, hypochondriasis (HYS), certain eating disorders, and autism spectrum disorders (Allen, King, & Hollander, 2003; Phillips et al., 2010; Stein, 2000; Sulkowski, Mariaskin, & Storch, 2011). The notion of a spectrum of disorders is related to each of the aforementioned disorders having varying degrees of obsessive and compulsive features. Sulkowski and colleagues (2011) explored the occurrence of obsessive-compulsive spectrum disorders (OCSDs) in a sample of 358 college students and found strong associations between OCD and BDD, OCD and health-anxiety symptoms (used to assess the degree of hypochondriasis), BDD and skin-picking symptoms, and health-anxiety and pathological skin-picking symptoms. Weak associations were found between OCD and trichotillomania, OCD and pathological skin-picking symptoms, and health anxiety and trichotillomania symptoms. The authors discuss the adaptive nature of the behaviors and other components that make up the disorders studied, but also functional impairment when severe. OCPD and OCD share many overlapping features such as age of onset, course, heritability; executive neurocognitive impairment; cognitive rigidity; and clinical response to medication, specifically SSRIs. Evidence continues to build for OCPD being a component of the obsessive-compulsive spectrum (Fineberg, Sharma, Sivakumaran, Sahakian, & Chamberlain, 2007).

Lochner and colleagues (2011) examined the association of OCD and OCPD using a sample of 403 individuals in which 66% met criteria for OCD without OCPD and 34% met criteria for OCD and criteria for OCPD. They found that those with OCD were not distinguished from OCPD by gender and age of onset, but those individuals with OCD and OCPD were at an increased likelihood to meet criterion 5 (is unable to discard worn-out or worthless objects when they have no sentimental value; hoarding) had significantly greater OCD symptomatology, comorbidity, functional impairment, and poorer insight. These authors concluded that OCPD is marker of OCD severity. In line with this finding is that individuals who meet criteria for both OCD and OCPD tend to show greater frequency of obsessions and compulsions including symmetry, ordering, repeating, cleaning, and hoarding, and a greater degree of functional impairment (Coles, Pinto, Mancebo, Rasmussen, & Eisen, 2008). These two studies did not agree on the age of onset, as Coles and colleagues (2008) found that those with OCD and OCPD had an earlier age of onset of initial obsession and compulsions.

Eisen and colleagues (2006) explored OCD and OCPD in a sample of 629 participants from the Collaborative Longitudinal Personality Disorders Study and found that individuals who met criteria for OCD showed significantly greater rates of hoarding, perfectionism, and preoccupation with details. Results also showed that other anxiety disorders including, social phobia, panic disorder with and without agoraphobia (in DSM-5 these conditions are separated into two distinct categories), and major depression were not indicative of developing OCPD. The authors found that individuals who met criteria for generalized anxiety disorder (GAD) were at an increased risk to be preoccupied with details and reluctant to delegate tasks, and this finding was attributed to the overlap in operationally defining both constructs.

In the DSM-5 (APA, 2013), the associated features attempted to clarify the relationship between anxiety disorders (particularly obsessive-compulsive disorder; OCD) and OCPD.

> Individuals with anxiety disorders, including generalized anxiety disorder, social anxiety disorder (social phobia), and specific phobias, and obsessive-compulsive disorder (OCD) have an increased likelihood of having a personality disturbance that meets criteria for obsessive-compulsive personality disorder. Even so, it appears that the majority of individuals with OCD do not have a pattern of behavior that meets criteria for this personality disorder (p. 680–681).

No changes were made to the criteria for OCPD in the DSM-5 (APA, 2013).

Differential Diagnosis

According to the DSM-5 (APA, 2013), OCPD individuals are at an increased risk to develop GAD, OCD, social anxiety disorder (social phobia), and specific phobias. Grant and colleagues (2012) utilized a sample of 43,093 participants from the National Epidemiologic Survey on Alcohol and Related Conditions (NESARC) and found that 57.78% of the sample that met criteria for OCPD also had a substance use disorder, and 30.63% of individuals with OCPD were found to have a mood disorder (in the DSM-5 broken into two categories – bipolar disorders and depressive disorders). Specifically, 46.05% met criteria for major depressive disorder, 15.54% met criteria for dysthymic disorder, 16.18% met criteria for bipolar I disorder, and 6.48% met criteria for bipolar II disorder. In examining OCPD and other anxiety disorders, overall rates of comorbidity were found to be 36.98%. Specific anxiety disorders and OCPD co-morbidity rates are as follows: 11.39% for OCPD and panic disorder with agoraphobia, 5.37% for OCPD and panic disorder without agoraphobia, 20.92% for OCPD and social phobia, 25.14% for OCPD and specific phobia, and 16.42% for OCPD and GAD.

Individuals with OCPD are typically confused or comorbid with several other personality disorders (APA, 2000), and the clinician is required to assess and distinguish each disorder for accurate diagnoses. If an individual meets criteria for more than one personality disorder, it should be diagnosed along with OCPD. Narcissistic personality disorder (NPD) and OCPD tend to share a drive for perfectionism and a belief that others cannot complete tasks to their level of satisfaction, but the NPD individual is likely to feel that he or she has achieved that level of perfection, whereas the OCPD individual does not. Both the NPD and the antisocial personality disorder (ASPD) individual lack generosity, similar to the OCPD individual, but the NPD and ASPD individual will treat himself or herself to extravagant gifts, which is contrary to the OCPD individual who is "tight" with money and spending. The schizoid personality disorder (SPD) and the OCPD individual share the tendency to be formal and socially detached, but in the SPD individual this tendency is based upon a basic lack of interest in others, whereas the OCPD individual is uncomfortable with emotional content.

The DSM-5 (APA, 2013) lists hoarding disorder as a differential diagnosis when the hoarding behaviors are severe, such as their home is filled with old newspapers and worthless objects. In instances where criteria for both OCPD and hoarding disorder are met, both diagnoses should be made.

ASSESSMENT

There are several methods to assess OCPD, the most common being the unstructured clinical interview, followed by the structured clinical interview such as the Structured Clinical Interview for DSM-IV personality disorders (SCID-II) (First et al., 1997) and the Structured Interview for DSM-IV Personality (SIDP-IV) (Pfohl et al., 1997). Screening and self-report instruments available to the qualified clinician are very useful in providing accurate diagnosis of OCPD. These instruments include the Personality Diagnostic Questionnaire-IV (PDQ-IV) (Hyler, 1994), Wisconsin Personality Inventory (WISPI) (Klein et al., 1993; Smith et al., 2003), Personality Assessment Inventory (PAI) (Morey, 1991), and Schedule for Normal and Abnormal Personality (SNAP) (Clark, 1993a). The Minnesota Multiphasic Personality Inventory, Second Edition (MMPI-2) and the Millon Multiaxial Clinical Inventory, Third Edition (MCMI) (Millon et al., 1997) have been used most widely in research and clinical settings. When the MMPI-2 is given to an individual with OCPD, a 2-7/7-2 code type is likely. Individuals with this code type are likely to be anxious and tense, worry excessively, and be vulnerable to real or imagined threat. He or she is likely to interpret problems before they occur and react in a stressed manner. Obsessive thoughts are common and behaviors to manage such thoughts frequently ensue. Clinical depressive symptoms are likely, as well as a pessimistic view of the world along with a strong need for achievement and recognition of accomplishments.

Results on the MCMI when given to an individual with OCPD are likely to show elevations on scale 7 (compulsive). Results indicate an individual who possesses conformity, discipline, and self-restraint, while adhering to social norms in a strict manner. In addition, he or she is conscientious, meticulous, and self-righteous, fears social disapproval, and approaches problems with maturity and competence. These individuals are likely to express their anxiety through somatic complaints, which can produce elevations on scale H (somatoform).

On the Rorschach, individuals with OCPD are likely to show an emphasis on Dd (unusual detail) and D (common detail), high F+% (form plus), and few W (whole) responses and color responses. Above average attention to detail and criticisms of the inkblots should be expected with these individuals as well (Meyer & Deitsch, 1996). The Thematic Apperception Test (TAT), when given to the OCPD individual, is likely to show results that are highly detailed and have various themes. Due to so much information, the details of the story can become lost (Bellak & Abrams, 1997).

CASE STUDY – MALE

Marvin just started working at a new software company after being let go by his previous employer of six years for failing to complete a project as well as continual issues with his co-workers. Marvin spent four hours completing paperwork related to his taxes, retirement, and other benefit forms due to his scrupulous attention to every detail. The human resources manager checked on him several times out of concern as it typically requires 30 to 60 minutes to complete the forms. Once he was shown his desk, Marvin cleaned it very well and then took two hours to set up his note pads and position his computer monitor and computer, as well as organizing his pens "just right based upon frequency of use." On Marvin's second day, he was introduced to his project manager and the work team as they were assigned the task of devising a new user-friendly interface for a professional architecture program. During the meeting, Marvin would continually ask questions about the basic design of the software, as opposed to addressing the usability of the software. The project manager told Marvin, "We are not here for that, but to address other aspects of the software." "Without a good foundation, how can other aspects of the software work well?" Marvin retorted. Typically, these meetings last 1 to 1 ½ hours, but "the new guy kept us there for 3 ½ hours talking about the little stuff and minute details," the project manager complained to the department head. When Marvin was informed that a particular aspect of the software design was going to be left out, because they were running behind schedule, Marvin became upset and openly questioned the department head's and the company's ethics: "people pay for the whole program, not part of it. This is not right!" Marvin was typically the last to leave the office as he would stay and work on the basic aspects of the design program to get it running "smooth, just right, and without bugs," though this was not his job. After six months, Marvin was sent to the employee assistance program (EAP) for help in working with others, but after three sessions, he refused to return which resulted in his termination.

CASE STUDY – FEMALE

Joan was recently put in charge of the 8-year-old girls' dance troupe schedule and production for the season. All the other parents were taken aback when they found this out. Typically people are chosen at random, and it was Joan's turn. Joan was known as a "taskmaster," "impatient busybody," and "the queen bee of perfection." She started sending out e-mails regarding times of each practice, appropriate dress for each practice, appropriate times to arrive at each practice, and explicit details regarding refreshments, decorations, and the flyer design for the end-of-the-year show. With each e-mail came a verification button to show that each parent had read it. Many parents did not click, which prompted Joan to send continual e-mails until all the parents did respond. This occurred for each e-mail, for each practice. When they showed up at practice, Joan would mark off each parent and child on an attendance form she had created to "keep accountability." During practice, Joan was known to critique her daughter Janet loudly from the waiting area. These critiques typically entailed "perfect form, show us perfect form" or noted a "sloppy, sloppy, sloppy" performance. Joan demands that Janet practice 2 hours before and after each practice and 4 hours before any show. One day, another parent noticed that Joan's trunk was filled with all of the past dance flyers and old newspapers. Joan saw her look of surprise and said, "You never know when you'll need to refer back something," without a hint of embarrassment or concern. When the season finale arrived, no other parents were given tasks as Joan took them all upon herself to execute "perfectly." However, no refreshments were prepared, no decorations were put up, and only the draft flyers were available in time for the show due to Joan working tirelessly on making a "perfect flyer for all to see."

TREATMENT

It is important for the clinician to be aware that most individuals with OCPD who seek treatment do so due to mental health conditions such as anxiety attacks, sexual dysfunction, fatigue, immobilization, or at the forceful request of spouses or family members (Millon, 1996). Dimaggio and colleagues (2011) conducted a qualitative analysis of a session transcript to determine the efficacy of metacognitive interpersonal therapy (MIT) as a treatment modality for OCPD. Treatment lasted for more than one year utilizing MIT. The authors reported a positive outcome and reduction in symptoms when the therapist was cognizant of the client's metacognitive dysfunctions, promoted emotional awareness if emotional language was restricted, and enhanced shared understanding of emotional triggers and outcomes. Barber and colleagues (1997) utilized a supportive-expressive dynamic psychotherapy approach with 24 individuals diagnosed with avoidant personality disorder (AVD) and 14 individuals diagnosed with OCPD. Treatment lasted for 52 sessions, and results indicated that 84.6% of OCPD individuals no longer qualified for the OCPD diagnosis at termination whereas 61.5% of AVD individuals no longer met criteria for the AVD diagnosis. OCPD participants were found to remain in treatment longer and improve, while those with AVD were more likely to drop out earlier due to avoidance tendencies.

Beck and colleagues (2004) discuss a cognitive-behavioral therapy (CBT) approach to treatment with individuals with OCPD. They recommend teaching the client about emotions and their importance at the very early stages of treatment. Goals should be listed in a specific and clear manner then rank-ordered by importance and ease of solvability. The OCPD individual should be exposed to the concept that emotions and behaviors are founded upon perceptions, thoughts, and interpretation of life events. A dysfunctional thought record can be helpful to list situations, feelings, and thoughts when issues occur. As with any treatment modality, collaboration and the therapeutic alliance are key. This is no different when working with OCPD individuals although it is typically more complex due to their perfectionism, reluctance to ask for help, and tendency to accept only the surface nature of somatic complaints, such as headaches, sexual dysfunction, etc. being addressed as opposed to being explored in depth as in more psychodynamically oriented approaches.

Beck and colleagues (2004) report several techniques that are beneficial when working with the OCPD individual, such as defining session structure via setting an agenda, problem prioritization, and problem solving. These techniques allow the OCPD individual to identify and work on specific issues until he or she improves and recognizes change. Once the OCPD individual recognizes and accepts that his or her chronic pattern of worry, structure, and perfectionism is dysfunctional, thought-stopping and refocusing techniques to redirect their cognitive process can be put into place. Once OCPD individuals have significantly reduced their dysfunctional thoughts and ensuing behaviors, a maintenance schedule with "booster sessions" can be put into place to prevent relapse.

Benjamin (1996) identifies treatment strategies when working with OCPD individuals using her five correct responses. She notes that, "the effect of interventions is assessed in terms of the actual impact on the patient, not in terms of the therapist's intention" (p. 156). When the OCPD individual responds with righteous indignation or abject submission, the therapist should be alert that an error has occurred. Facilitating collaboration is the foundational step when working with the OCPD individual, but also one of the most challenging as the control of therapy is likely to shift between client and therapist due to the OCPD client's control tendencies. A clear and rational explanation regarding his or her desire for control, submission, and self-control can be very valuable as well as identifying how these patterns developed. This is a concept he or she can understand quickly and that friendly differentiation, as opposed to hostile control, can serve as a more adaptive and beneficial collaborative relationship within treatment. Assisting with pattern recognition and emphasizing the benefit of developing compassion and empathy toward himself or herself can assist in finding connections to earlier life experiences that are rooted in current functioning.

Benjamin (1996) uses the example of couples' therapy as a stage for learning and modifying maladaptive patterns and utilizing a collaborative strategy as opposed to one of domination. In some cases, the therapist may "order" the OCPD client to work with the partner to develop "rules" to address contentious marital problems. Blocking maladaptive patterns entails disrupting power struggles, especially when present in sexual relationships, and this can entail the therapist telling "who will do what to whom and when" (Benjamin, 1996, p. 258). Sexual exercises can assist in modeling and encouraging more balanced interactive patterns, but the OCPD individual needs to learn to stop blocking feelings and integrate warmth. The therapist should be aware of "generic" affective expression and address it accordingly. Benjamin goes on to explain that anxiety is derived from fear of certain failure in his or her attempt to achieve perfection. The underlying issues of control and perfectionism should remain as therapeutic targets: "If one does not need to be perfect to survive, then one doesn't have to be frightened about not being perfect" (p. 259). In working with the OCPD client to give up maladaptive patterns in excchn, empathy for him or her as a child and gaining understanding of the parents and their past behaviors, but not doing this as a means to "point fingers" or demand retribution, assist the client in relinquishing old patterns in exchange for more adaptive new ones. After this work is completed, other therapeutic techniques, such as CBT, can be employed as the OCPD client is open and receptive to learning new strategies and moving forward in a less perfectionistic, structured, and anxious manner.

Psychopharmacology

There are no research studies that examine the impact of specific medications on OCPD (Bartz, Kaplan, & Hollander, 2007; Simeon & Hollander, 2006; Sperry, 2003). Sperry (2003) outlines a medication protocol for treating individuals with OCPD and recommends addressing anxiety symptoms first using a selective serotonin reuptake inhibitor (SSRI). If the individual does not respond to a particular SSRI, attempt another, but following an additional failure to reduce symptoms, a long-acting benzodiazepine or clonazepam can be added or used in lieu of the SSRI (Reich, 2002, as cited in Sperry, 2003). Sadock and Sadock (2007) also mention using clonazepam to reduce severe obsessive-compulsive disorder, but are uncertain as to its efficacy in OCPD. They recommend using clomipramine (Anafranil) and other serotonergic medications such as fluoxetine (Prozac) at a dosage of 60 mg to 80 mg to reduce obsessive-compulsive signs and symptoms. Lastly, they mention that nafazodone (Serzone) may be beneficial.

FILM AND POPULAR MEDIA EXAMPLES

Matchstick Men (2003) – Roy Waller, played by Nicholas Cage

The Big Bang Theory (2007 – Present) – Sheldon Cooper, played by Jim Parsons

Friends (1994–2004) – Monica Geller, played by Courtney Cox

Monk (2002–2009) – Adrian Monk, played by Tony Shalhoub

CHECKLIST: OBSESSIVE-COMPULSIVE PERSONALITY DISORDER

Below is a complete list to best identify and diagnose Obsessive-Compulsive Personality Disorder. DSM-5 (APA, 2013) criteria are first, followed by discernible components, and lastly, associated features.

- ❏ A pervasive pattern of preoccupation with orderliness, perfectionism, and mental and interpersonal control at the expense of flexibility, openness, and efficiency, beginning by early adulthood and present in a variety of contexts*
- ❏ Is occupied with details, rules, lists, order, organization, or agenda to the point that the key part of the activity is gone*
- ❏ Demonstrates perfectionism that hampers the completion of tasks*
- ❏ Is extremely dedicated to work and efficiency to the elimination of spare-time activities*
- ❏ Is meticulous, scrupulous, and rigid about etiquettes of morality, ethics, or values*
- ❏ Is not capable of disposing of worn-out or insignificant things even when they have no sentimental meaning*
- ❏ Is unwilling to pass on tasks or work with others unless others surrender to exactly their way of doing things*
- ❏ Takes on a stingy spending style toward self and others*
- ❏ Shows stiffness and stubbornness*
- ❏ Possesses intense feelings of excessive doubt and caution
- ❏ Difficulty determining task priority
- ❏ Tends to become agitated in situations where he or she lacks the ability to maintain control of the physical and interpersonal environment
- ❏ Acutely aware of his or her dominance or submission status within relationships
- ❏ Excessive deference to authority he or she respects
- ❏ Excessive resistance to authority he or she does not respect

*distinguishing characteristics

THERAPIST CLIENT ACTIVITY

Use these probes to explore your OCPD client's need for perfection, structure, and self-reliance that are central to the pathology and enhance the socioeconomic dysfunction.

> ➢ What do you see happening if things are not the way you envision them?
>
> ➢ What would it feel like to relax?
>
> ➢ Can you describe how you feel when you start and finish task?
>
> ➢ How do you think therapy would be best structured for you?
>
> ➢ How much time do you spend making lists and schedules?
>
> ➢ Have you ever lost a job or not completed a task "well enough" due to getting lost in the details? Can you describe how this felt for you?
>
> ➢ Can you walk me through how you prioritize tasks?
>
> ➢ When you think of the word perfect, what comes to mind and how do you define it?
>
> ➢ How much work is too much?
>
> ➢ Do you think you have ever lost an opportunity due to being too work oriented? Can you describe what happened and how it felt?
>
> ➢ When was the last time you were able to relax?
>
> ➢ Do you have a clear idea of what is right and what is wrong? Can you give me an example that applies to you and your life?
>
> ➢ What is it like for you when you know something is unjust or immoral?
>
> ➢ Do you believe you can ever be too strict or too structured?
>
> ➢ Do you tend to save things? What type of things and how come?
>
> ➢ What is it like for you to work with a team of others to complete a task?
>
> ➢ What is it like for you to delegate tasks to others and what are your expectations?
>
> ➢ What does money mean to you? If you were to buy anything frivolous, what would it be?
>
> ➢ Do you think other people see you as stubborn?
>
> ➢ How would you know therapy is or was helpful?
>
> ➢ Do you want to do things differently?

CLIENT QUESTIONNAIRE

The following questions are to be given to your client to help him or her identify past challenges and provide guidance for treatment.

What is your earliest recollection? Describe only as much as your feel comfortable with.

List three things that have helped you in the past to achieve your goals:

Can you list three people who you trust most and why?

Can you list the most important people in your life and why?

If you were your therapist, what are three things you would make sure to cover during the course of treatment?

References

Abraham, K. (1923). Contributions to the theory of the anal character. *The International Journal of Psychoanalysis*, *4*, 400–418.

Abraham, Karl, Bryan, D., & Strachey, A. (1991). The influence of oral erotism on character-formation. In M. F. R. Kets de Vries & S. M. Perzow (Eds.), *Handbook of character studies: Psychoanalytic explorations.* (pp. 55–67). Madison, CT: International Universities Press, Inc. Retrieved from http://ezproxy.shsu.edu/login?url=http://search. ebscohost.com/login.aspx?direct=true&db=psyh&AN=1991-98935-004&site=ehost-live&scope=site

Adams, H. E., Bernat, J. A., & Luscher, K. A. (2001). Borderline personality disorder: An overview. In P. B. Sutker & H. E. Adams (Eds.), *Comprehensive handbook of psychopathology (3rd ed.).* (pp. 491–507). New York: Kluwer Academic/Plenum Publishers. Retrieved from http://ezproxy.shsu.edu/login?url=http://search.ebscohost. com/login.aspx?direct=true&db=psyh&AN=2001-01406-017&site=ehost-live&scope=site

Adler, G. (1981). The borderline-narcissistic personality disorder continuum. *The American Journal of Psychiatry*, *138*(1), 46–50.

Afifi, T. O., Mather, A., Boman, J., Fleisher, W., Enns, M. W., MacMillan, H., & et al. (2011). Childhood adversity and personality disorders: Results from a nationally representative population-based study. *Journal of Psychiatric Research*, *45*(6), 814–822.

Agrawal, H. R., Gunderson, J., Holmes, B. M., & Lyons-Ruth, K. (2004). Attachment studies with borderline patients: A review. *Harvard Review of Psychiatry*, *12*(2), 94–104.

Ainsworth, M. D. S., Blehar, M. C., Waters, E., & Wall, S. (1978). *Patterns of attachment: A psychological study of the strange situation.* Oxford, England: Lawrence Erlbaum.

Ainsworth, M. S., & Bowlby, J. (1991). An ethological approach to personality development. *American Psychologist*, *46*(4), 333–341.

Akhtar, S. (1987). Schizoid personality disorder: A synthesis of developmental, dynamic, and descriptive features. *American Journal of Psychotherapy*, *41*(4), 499–518.

Akhtar, S. (1995). *Quest for answers: A primer of understanding and treating severe personality disorders.* Lanham, MD: Jason Aronson. Retrieved from http://ezproxy.shsu.edu/login?url=http://search.ebscohost.com/login. aspx?direct=true&db=psyh&AN=1995-98155-000&site=ehost-live&scope=site

Akhtar, S. (1990). Paranoid personality disorder: A synthesis of developmental, dynamic and descriptive features. American Journal Of Psychotherapy, 44(1), 5–25.

Alarcón, R. D., Foulks, E. F., & Vakkur, M. (1998). *Personality Disorders and Culture: Clinical and Conceptual Interactions* (1st ed.). New York: John Wiley & Sons.

Alden, L. (1989). Short-term structured treatment for avoidant personality disorder. *Journal of Consulting and Clinical Psychology*, *57*(6), 756–764.

Alden, L. E., Laposa, J. M., Taylor, C. T., & Ryder, A. G. (2002). Avoidant personality disorder: Current status and future directions. *Journal of Personality Disorders*, *16*(1), 1–29.

Alexander, P. C. (2009). Childhood trauma, attachment, and abuse by multiple partners. *Psychological Trauma: Theory, Research, Practice, and Policy*, *1*(1), 78–88.

Allen, A., King, A., & Hollander, E. (2003). Obsessive-compulsive spectrum disorders. *Dialogues In Clinical Neuroscience, 5*(3), 259–271.

Allnutt, S., & Links, P. S. (1996). Diagnosing specific personality disorders and the optimal criteria. *Clinical assessment and management of severe personality disorders*, Clinical practice, No. 35. (pp. 21–47). Washington, DC: American Psychiatric Association.

Alperin, R. M. (2001). Barriers to intimacy: An object relations perspective. *Psychoanalytic Psychology, 18*(1), 137–156. doi:10.1037/0736-9735.18.1.137

Anderson, C. L., & Alexander, P. C. (1996). The relationship between attachment and dissociation in adult survivors of incest. *Psychiatry: Interpersonal and Biological Processes, 59*(3), 240–254.

Anderson, C. M. (1983). A psychoeducational program for families of patients with schizophrenia. *Family Therapy in Schizophrenia*. New York: Guilford Press.

Anglin, D. M., Cohen, P. R., & Chen, H. (2008). Duration of early maternal separation and prediction of schizotypal symptoms from early adolescence to midlife. *Schizophrenia Research, 103*(1–3), 143–150. doi:10.1016/j.schres.2008.02.016

American Psychiatric Association. (1952). *DSM I: Diagnostic and Statistical Manual Mental Disorders* (Limited.). American Psychiatric Association.

American Psychiatric Association. (1968). *DSM-II Diagnostic and Statistical Manual of Mental Disorders* (2nd ed.).

American Psychiatric Association. (1980). *DSM-III. Diagnostic and Statistical Manual of Mental Disorders (Third Edition)*. American Psychiatric Association.

American Psychiatric Association. (1987). *Diagnostic and Statistical Manual of Mental Disorders: DSM-III-R*. American Psychiatric In.

American Psychiatric Association. (1994). *Diagnostic and Statistical Manual of Mental Disorders DSM-IV* (4th ed.). American Psychiatric Association.

American Psychiatric Association. (2000). *Diagnostic and Statistical Manual of Mental Disorders DSM-IV-TR Fourth Edition* (4th ed.). Amer Psychiatric Pub.

American Psychiatric Association. (2013). *Diagnostic and Statistical Manual of Mental Disorders DSM-5 Fifth Edition* (5th ed.). Amer Psychiatric Pub.

Appel, G. (1974). An approach to the treatment of schizoid phenomena. *Psychoanalytic Review, 61*(1), 99–113.

Attwood, T. (2007). Asperger's disorder: Exploring the schizoid spectrum. *Personality disorders in childhood and adolescence* (pp. 299–340). Hoboken, NJ: New York: John Wiley & Sons & Sons Inc.

Auther, A. M. (2003). *Social anhedonia and schizophrenia-spectrum personality traits in genetic high-risk adolescents and young adults*. ProQuest Information & Learning.

Bachrach, N., Croon, M. A., & Bekker, M. H. J. (2012). Factor structure of self-reported clinical disorders and personality disorders: A review of the existing literature and a factor analytical study. *Journal of Clinical Psychology, 68*(6), 645–660.

Baity, M. R., Blais, M. A., Hilsenroth, M. J., Fowler, J. C., & Padawer, J. R. (2009). Self-mutilation, severity of borderline psychopathology, and the Rorschach. *Bulletin of the Menninger Clinic, 73*(3), 203–225.

Baker, J. D., Capron, E. W., & Azorlosa, J. (1996). Family environment characteristics of persons with histrionic and dependent personality disorders. *Journal of Personality Disorders, 10*(1), 82–87.

Bakkevig, J. F., & Karterud, S. (2010). Is the Diagnostic and Statistical Manual of Mental Disorders, Fourth Edition, histrionic personality disorder category a valid construct? *Comprehensive Psychiatry, 51*(5), 462–470.

Bandelow, B., Krause, J., Wedekind, D., Broocks, A., Hajak, G., & Rüther, E. (2005). Early traumatic life events, parental attitudes, family history, and birth risk factors in patients with borderline personality disorder and healthy controls. *Psychiatry Research, 134*(2), 169–179.

Barber, J. P., Morse, J. Q., Krakauer, I. D., Chittams, J., & Crits-Christoph, K. (1997). Change in obsessive-compulsive and avoidant personality disorders following time-limited supportive-expressive therapy. *Psychotherapy: Theory, Research, Practice, Training, 34*(2), 133–143.

Barratt, E. S., Stanford, M. S., Felthous, A. R., & Kent, T. A. (1997). The effects of phenytoin on impulsive and premeditated aggression: A controlled study. *Journal of Clinical Psychopharmacology, 17*(5), 341–349.

Bartak, A., Spreeuwenberg, M. D., Andrea, H., Holleman, L., Rijnierse, P., Rossum, B. V., Hamers, E. F. M., et al. (2009). Effectiveness of different modalities of psychotherapeutic treatment for patients with cluster C personality disorders: Results of a large prospective multicentre study. *Psychotherapy and Psychosomatics, 79*(1), 20–30.

Bartholomew, K. (1990). Avoidance of intimacy: An attachment perspective. *Journal of Social and Personal Relationships, 7*(2), 147–178. doi:10.1177/0265407590072001

Bartholomew, K., & Horowitz, L. M. (1991). Attachment styles among young adults: A test of a four-category model. *Journal of Personality and Social Psychology, 61*(2), 226–244. doi:10.1037/0022-3514.61.2.226

Bartholomew, K., Kwong, M. J., & Hart, S. D. (2001). Attachment. *Handbook of Personality Disorders: Theory, research, and treatment* (pp. 196–230). New York, NY: Guilford Press.

Bartz, J., Kaplan, A., & Hollander, E. (2007). Obsessive-compulsive personality disorder. In W. O'Donohue, K. A. Fowler, & S. O. Lilienfeld (Eds.), *Personality disorders: Toward the DSM-V.* (pp. 325–351). Thousand Oaks, CA: Sage Publications, Inc. Retrieved from http://ezproxy.shsu.edu/login?url=http://search.ebscohost.com/login.aspx?direct=true&db=psyh&AN=2007-00410-013&site=ehost-live&scope=site

Battaglia, M., Gasperini, M., Sciuto, G., Scherillo, P., Diaferia, G., & Bellodi, L. (1991). Psychiatric Disorders in the Families of Schizotypal Subjects. *Schizophrenia Bulletin, 17*(4), 659–668.

Beck, A. T., Freeman, A., & Davis, D. D. (2004). *Cognitive therapy of personality disorders (2nd ed.).* New York: Guilford Press. Retrieved from http://ezproxy.shsu.edu/login?url=http://search.ebscohost.com/login.aspx?direct=true&db=psyh&AN=2004-00033-000&site=ehost-live&scope=site

Becker, D. F., Grilo, C. M., Edell, W. S., & McGlashan, T. H. (2000). Comorbidity of borderline personality disorder with other personality disorders in hospitalized adolescents and adults. *The American Journal of Psychiatry, 157*(12), 2011–2016.

Becker, D. F., Masheb, R. M., White, M. A., & Grilo, C. M. (2010). Psychiatric, behavioral, and attitudinal correlates of avoidant and obsessive-compulsive personality pathology in patients with binge-eating disorder. *Comprehensive Psychiatry, 51*(5), 531–537.

Becker, D., & Lamb, S. (1994). Sex bias in the diagnosis of borderline personality disorder and posttraumatic stress disorder. *Professional Psychology: Research and Practice, 25*(1), 55–61.

Behrens, K. Y. (2004). A Multifaceted View of the Concept of Amae: Reconsidering the Indigenous Japanese Concept of Relatedness. *Human Development, 47*(1), 1–27.

Bekker, M. H. J. B. (2007). The relationships of antisocial behavior with attachment styles, autonomy-connectedness, and alexithymia. *Journal of Clinical Psychology, 63*(6), 507–527. doi:Article

Bellak, L., & Abrams, D. M. (1997). *The Thematic Apperception Test, the Children's Apperception Test, and the Senior Apperception Technique in clinical use (6th ed.).* Needham Heights, MA: Allyn & Bacon.

Belsky, D. W., Caspi, A., Arseneault, L., Bleidorn, W., Fonagy, P., Goodman, M., Houts, R., et al. (2012). Etiological features of borderline personality related characteristics in a birth cohort of 12-year-old children. *Development and Psychopathology*, A Developmental Psychopathology Perspective on Emotional Availability Research, *24*(1), 251–265.

Benjamin, L. S. (1996). *Interpersonal Diagnosis and Treatment of personality disorders: Second Edition.* The Guilford Press.

Benjamin, L. S., & Wonderlich, S. A. (1994). Social perceptions and borderline personality disorder: The relation to mood disorders. *Journal of Abnormal Psychology, 103*(4), 610–624.

Berenbaum, H., Valera, E. M., & Kerns, J. G. (2003). Psychological Trauma and Schizotypal Symptoms. *Schizophrenia Bulletin, 29*(1), 143–152.

Bernstein, D. P., & Useda, J. (2007). Paranoid personality disorder. In W. O'Donohue, K. A. Fowler, S. O. Lilienfeld (Eds.), *Personality disorders: Toward the DSM-V* (pp. 41–62). Thousand Oaks, CA: Sage Publications, Inc.

Berry, K., Barrowclough, C., & Wearden, A. (2008). Attachment theory: A framework for understanding symptoms and interpersonal relationships in psychosis. *Behaviour Research and Therapy, 46*(12), 1275–1282. doi:10.1016/j.brat.2008.08.009

Binzer, M., & Eisemann, M. (1998). Childhood experiences and personality traits in patients with motor conversion symptoms. *Acta Psychiatrica Scandinavica, 98*(4), 288–295.

Birtchnell, J. (1988). Defining dependence. *British Journal of Medical Psychology, 61*(2), 111–123.

Blagov, P. S., Fowler, K. A., & Lilienfeld, S. O. (2007). Histrionic personality disorder. In W. O'Donohue, K. A. Fowler, & S. O. Lilienfeld (Eds.), *Personality disorders: Toward the DSM-V.* (pp. 203–232). Thousand Oaks, CA: Sage Publications, Inc. Retrieved from http://ezproxy.shsu.edu/login?url=http://search.ebscohost.com/login.aspx?direct=true&db=psyh&AN=2007-00410-008&site=ehost-live&scope=site

Blais, M. A., & Baity, M. R. (2006). Rorschach Assessment of Histrionic personality disorder. In Steven K. Huprich (Ed.), *Rorschach assessment to the personality disorders.*, The LEA series in personality and clinical psychology (pp. 205–221). Mahwah, NJ: Lawrence Erlbaum Associates Publishers. Retrieved from http://ezproxy.shsu.edu/login?url=http://search.ebscohost.com/login.aspx?direct=true&db=psyh&AN=2005-14852-008&site=ehost-live&scope=site

Blashfield, R., Blum, N., & Pfohl, B. (1992). The effects of changing Axis II diagnostic criteria. *Comprehensive Psychiatry, 33*(4), 245–252.

Blashfield, R. K., & Breen, M. J. (1989). Face validity of the DSM-III—R personality disorders. *The American Journal of Psychiatry, 146*(12), 1575–1579.

Blashfield, R. K., & Davis, R. T. (1993). Dependent and histrionic personality disorders. In P. B. Sutker & H. E. Adams (Eds.), *Comprehensive handbook of psychopathology (2nd ed.).* (pp. 395–409). New York: Plenum Press. Retrieved from http://ezproxy.shsu.edu/login?url=http://search.ebscohost.com/login.aspx?direct=true&db=psyh&AN=1993-97447-016&site=ehost-live&scope=site

Blashfield, R. K., & Flanagan, E. H. (1998). A prototypic nonprototype of a personality disorder. *Journal of Nervous and Mental Disease, 186*(4), 244–246.

Blashfield, R. K., Sprock, J., & Fuller, A. K. (1990). Suggested guidelines for including or excluding categories in the DSM-IV. *Comprehensive Psychiatry, 31*(1), 15–19.

Blatt, S. J., & Levy, K. N. (2003). Attachment theory, psychoanalysis, personality development, and psychopathology. *Psychoanalytic Inquiry*, Attachment research and psychoanalysis III: Further reflections on theory and clinical experience, *23*(1), 102–150.

Bleuler, E. (1924). *Textbook of Psychiatry.* New York: Macmillan.

Bleuler, E. (1987). The prognosis of dementia praecox: The group of schizophrenias. In J. Cutting & M. Shepherd (Eds.), *The clinical roots of the schizophrenia concept: Translations of seminal European contributions on schizophrenia.* (pp. 59–74). New York: Cambridge University Press. Retrieved from http://ezproxy.shsu.edu/login?url=http://search.ebscohost.com/login.aspx?direct=true&db=psyh&AN=1987-97125-007&site=ehost-live&scope=site

Bogdanoff, M., & Elbaum, P. L. (1978). Role lock: Dealing with monopolizers, mistrusters, isolates, "helpful Hannahs," and other assorted characters in group psychotherapy. *International Journal of Group Psychotherapy, 28*(2), 247–262.

Bögels, S. M., Alden, L., Beidel, D. C., Clark, L. A., Pine, D. S., Stein, M. B., & Voncken, M. (2010). Social anxiety disorder: Questions and answers for the DSM-5. *Depression and Anxiety, 27*(2), 168–189.

Bogenschutz, M. P., & Nurnberg, H. G. (2004). Olanzapine Versus Placebo in the Treatment of Borderline personality disorder. *Journal of Clinical Psychiatry*, *65*(1), 104–109.

Bollini, A. M., & Walker, E. F. (2007). Schizotypal personality disorder. *Personality disorders: Toward the DSM-V* (pp. 81–108). Thousand Oaks, CA: Sage Publications, Inc.

Bond, M., & Perry, J. (2004). Long-term changes in defense styles with psychodynamic psychotherapy for depressive, anxiety, and personality disorders. *The American Journal Of Psychiatry*, *161*(9), 1665–1671. doi:10.1176/appi.ajp.161.9.1665

Booth, T. (1986). Institutional regimes and induced dependency in homes for the aged. *The Gerontologist*, *26*(4), 418–423.

Borge, F.-M., Hoffart, A., Sexton, H., Martinsen, E., Gude, T., Hedley, L. M., & Abrahamsen, G. (2010). Pre-treatment predictors and in-treatment factors associated with change in avoidant and dependent personality disorder traits among patients with social phobia. *Clinical Psychology & Psychotherapy*, *17*(2), 87–99.

Bornovalova, M. A., Hicks, B. M., Iacono, W. G., & McGue, M. (2009). Stability, change, and heritability of borderline personality disorder traits from adolescence to adulthood: A longitudinal twin study. *Development and Psychopathology*, Precursors and diverse pathways to personality disorder in children and adolescents: Part 2, *21*(4), 1335–1353.

Bornstein, R. F. (2005a). The dependent patient: Assessment and treatment. *Professional Psychology: Research and Practice*, *36*(1), 82–89.

Bornstein, R. F. (2005b). *The dependent patient: A practitioner's guide.* The dependent patient: A practitioner's guide. Washington, DC: American Psychological Association. Retrieved from http://ezproxy.shsu.edu/login?url=http://search.ebscohost.com/login.aspx?direct=true&db=psyh&AN=2005-01370-000&site=ehost-live&scope=site

Bornstein, R. F. (1993). *The dependent personality.* New York: Guilford Press. Retrieved from http://ezproxy.shsu.edu/login?url=http://search.ebscohost.com/login.aspx?direct=true&db=psyh&AN=1993-97914-000&site=ehost-live&scope=site

Bornstein, R. F. (1995). Sex differences in objective and projective dependency tests: A meta-analytic review. *Assessment*, *2*(4), 319–331.

Bornstein, R. F. (1997). Dependent personality disorder in the DSM-IV and beyond. *Clinical Psychology: Science and Practice*, *4*(2), 175–187.

Bornstein, R. F. (1999a). Dependent and histrionic personality disorders. In T. Millon, P. H. Blaney, & R. D. Davis (Eds.), *Oxford textbook of psychopathology.*, Oxford textbooks in clinical psychology, Vol. 4 (pp. 535–554). New York: Oxford University Press. Retrieved from http://ezproxy.shsu.edu/login?url=http://search.ebscohost.com/login.aspx?direct=true&db=psyh&AN=1999-04377-021&site=ehost-live&scope=site

Bornstein, R. F. (1999b). Criterion validity of objective and projective dependency tests: A meta-analytic assessment of behavioral prediction. *Psychological Assessment*, *11*(1), 48–57.

Bornstein, R. F. (2007). Dependent personality disorder. In W. O'Donohue, K. A. Fowler, & S. O. Lilienfeld (Eds.), *Personality disorders: Toward the DSM-V.* (pp. 307–324). Thousand Oaks, CA: Sage Publications, Inc. Retrieved from http://ezproxy.shsu.edu/login?url=http://search.ebscohost.com/login.aspx?direct=true&db=psyh&AN=2007-00410-012&site=ehost-live&scope=site

Bornstein, R. F. (2011). Reconceptualizing personality pathology in DSM-5: Limitations in evidence for eliminating dependent personality disorder and other DSM-IV syndromes. *Journal of Personality Disorders*, Proposals for DSM-5, *25*(2), 235–247.

Bornstein, R. F., & Gold, S. H. (2008). Comorbidity of personality disorders and somatization disorder: A meta-analytic review. *Journal of Psychopathology and Behavioral Assessment*, *30*(2), 154–161.

Bornstein, R. F., & Malka, I. L. (2009). Dependent and histrionic personality disorders. In P. H. Blaney & T. Millon (Eds.), *Oxford textbook of psychopathology (2nd ed.).* (pp. 602–621). New York: Oxford

University Press. Retrieved from http://ezproxy.shsu.edu/login?url=http://search.ebscohost.com/login. aspx?direct=true&db=psyh&AN=2008-17157-023&site=ehost-live&scope=site

Bornstein, R. F., Rossner, S., Hill, E. L., & Stepanian, M. (1994). Face Validity and Fakability of Objective and Projective Measures of Dependency. *Journal of Personality Assessment, 63*(2), 363.

Bowlby, J. (1944). Forty-four juvenile thieves: their characters and home-life. *The International Journal of Psychoanalysis, 25,* 19–53.

Bowlby, John. (1958). The nature of the child's tie to his mother. *The International Journal of Psychoanalysis, 39,* 350–373.

Bowlby, John. (1977). The making and breaking of affectional bonds: I. Aetiology and psychopathology in the light of attachment theory. *The British Journal of Psychiatry, 130,* 201–210.

Bowlby, John. (1980). *Attachment and loss.* New York, NY: Basic Books.

Bowlby, John. (1988). *A Secure Base: Parent-Child Attachment and Healthy Human Development.* Basic Books.

Bowlby, John. (1989). The role of attachment in personality development and psychopathology. In S. I. Greenspan & G. H. Pollock (Eds.), *The Course of life, Vol. 1: Infancy.* (pp. 229–270). Madison, CT: International Universities Press, Inc. Retrieved from http://ezproxy.shsu.edu/login?url=http://search.ebscohost.com/login. aspx?direct=true&db=psyh&AN=1989-98540-006&site=ehost-live&scope=site

Bradley, R., Conklin, C. Z., & Westen, D. (2007). Borderline personality disorder. In W. O'Donohue, K. A. Fowler, & S. O. Lilienfeld (Eds.), *Personality disorders: Toward the DSM-V.* (pp. 167–201). Thousand Oaks, CA: Sage Publications, Inc. Retrieved from http://ezproxy.shsu.edu/login?url=http://search.ebscohost.com/login.aspx? direct=true&db=psyh&AN=2007-00410-007&site=ehost-live&scope=site

Bradley, R., Jenei, J., & Westen, D. (2005). Etiology of Borderline personality disorder: Disentangling the Contributions of Intercorrelated Antecedents. *Journal of Nervous and Mental Disease, 193*(1), 24–31.

Bradley, R., & Westen, D. (2005). The psychodynamics of borderline personality disorder: A view from developmental psychopathology. *Development and Psychopathology, 17*(4), 927–957.

Bradley, S. J. (1979). The relationship of early maternal separation to borderline personality in children and adolescents: A pilot study. *The American Journal of Psychiatry, 136*(4-A), 424–426.

Brand, B. L., Armstrong, J. G., Loewenstein, R. J., & McNary, S. W. (2009). Personality differences on the Rorschach of dissociative identity disorder, borderline personality disorder, and psychotic inpatients. *Psychological Trauma: Theory, Research, Practice, and Policy, 1*(3), 188–205.

Brennan, K. A., Clark, C. L., & Shaver, P. R. (1998). Self-report measurement of adult attachment: An integrative overview. In J. A. Simpson & W. S. Rholes (Eds.), *Attachment theory and close relationships.* (pp. 46–76). New York: Guilford Press. Retrieved from http://ezproxy.shsu.edu/login?url=http://search.ebscohost.com/login. aspx?direct=true&db=psyh&AN=1997-36873-002&site=ehost-live&scope=site

Brennan, K. A., & Shaver, P. R. (1998). Attachment styles and personality disorders: Their connections to each other and to parental divorce, parental death, and perceptions of parental caregiving. *Journal of Personality, 66*(5), 835–878.

Brown, G. K., Newman, C. F., Charlesworth, S. E., Crits-Christoph, P., & Beck, A. T. (2004). An Open Clinical Trial of Cognitive Therapy for Borderline personality disorder. *Journal of Personality Disorders, 18*(3), 257–271.

Buss, D. M. (2005). *The murderer next door: Why the mind is designed to kill.* New York: Penguin Press.

Butler, T., Schofield, P. W., Greenberg, D., Allnutt, S. H., Indig, D., Carr, V., D'Este, C., et al. (2010). Reducing impulsivity in repeat violent offenders: An open label trial of a selective serotonin reuptake inhibitor. *Australian and New Zealand Journal of Psychiatry, 44*(12), 1137–1143.

Cadoret, R. J., Cain, C. A., & Crowe, R. R. (1983). Evidence for gene–environment interaction in the development of adolescent antisocial behavior. *Behavior Genetics, 13*(3), 301–310.

Callaghan, G. M., Summers, C. J., & Weidman, M. (2003). The Treatment of Histrionic and Narcissistic personality disorder Behaviors: A Single-Subject Demonstration of Clinical Improvement Using Functional Analytic Psychotherapy. *Journal of Contemporary Psychotherapy, 33*(4), 321–339.

Cameron, N. (1963). *Personality development and psychopathology: A dynamic approach.* Boston: Houghton, Mifflin Co.

Campbell, R. J. (1989). *Psychiatric dictionary.* Oxford University Press.

Capron, E. W. (2004). Types of pampering and the narcissistic personality trait. *Journal of Individual Psychology, 60*(1), 76–93. doi:Article

Carey, G., & Goldman, D. (1997). The genetics of antisocial behavior. In D. M. Stoff, J. Breiling, & J. D. Maser (Eds.), *Handbook of antisocial behavior.* (pp. 243–254). Hoboken, NJ: John New York: John Wiley & Sons & Sons Inc. Retrieved from http://ezproxy.shsu.edu/login?url=http://search.ebscohost.com/login.aspx?direct=true&db=psyh&AN=1997-36421-023&site=ehost-live&scope=site

Carnelley, K. B., Pietromonaco, P. R., & Jaffe, K. (1994). Depression, working models of others, and relationship functioning. *Journal of Personality and Social Psychology, 66*(1), 127–140. doi:10.1037/0022-3514.66.1.127

Carr, A. T. (1974). Compulsive neurosis: A review of the literature. *Psychological Bulletin, 81*(5), 311–318.

Carr, S., & Francis, A. (2010). Do early maladaptive schemas mediate the relationship between childhood experiences and avoidant personality disorder features? A preliminary investigation in a non-clinical sample. *Cognitive Therapy & Research, 34*(4), 343–358.

Coccaro, E. F., & Kavoussi, R. J. (1997). Fluoxetine and impulsive aggressive behavior in personality-disordered subjects. *Archives Of General Psychiatry, 54*(12), 1081–1088. doi:10.1001/archpsyc.1997.01830240035005

Carrillo, M., Ricci, L. A., Coppersmith, G. A., & Melloni, R. H. J. (2009). The effect of increased serotonergic neurotransmission on aggression: A critical meta-analytical review of preclinical studies. *Psychopharmacology, 205*(3), 349–368.

Chen, Y., Nettles, M. E., & Chen, S.-W. (2009). Rethinking dependent personality disorder: comparing different human relatedness in cultural contexts. *The Journal Of Nervous And Mental Disease, 197*(11), 793–800.

Choca, J. P., & Van Denburg, E. J. (1997). *Interpretive guide to the Millon Clinical Multiaxial Inventory (2nd ed.).* Washington, DC: American Psychological Association.

Clark, L. A. (1993a). *Manual for the schedule for nonadaptive and adaptive personality.* Minneapolis, MN: University of Minnesota.

Clark, L. A. (1993b). *Manual for the schedule for nonadaptive and adaptive personality (SNAP).* Minneapolis, MN: University of Minnesota Press.

Cleckley, H. (1941). *The mask of sanity; an attempt to reinterpret the so-called psychopathic personality.* Oxford England: Mosby. Retrieved from http://ezproxy.shsu.edu/login?url=http://search.ebscohost.com/login.aspx?direct=true&db=psyh&AN=1941-02603-000&site=ehost-live&scope=site

Cloninger, C. (1987). A systematic method for clinical description and classification of personality variants: A proposal. *Archives Of General Psychiatry, 44*(6), 573–588. doi:10.1001/archpsyc.1987.01800180093014

Cloninger, C. R., Reich, T., & Guze, S. B. (1978). Genetic-environmental interactions ad antisocial behaviour. *Psychopathic behaviour: Approaches to research* (pp. 225–237). New York, NY: John Wiley & Sons.

Cohen, P., & Cohen, J. (1995). *Life Values and Adolescent Mental Health.* Psychology Press.

Cohen, P., Crawford, T. N., Johnson, J. G., & Kasen, S. (2005). The Children in the Community Study of developmental course of personality disorder. *Journal of Personality Disorders, 19*(5), 466–486. doi:10.1521/pedi.2005.19.5.466

Coie, J. D., & Dodge, K. A. (1998). Aggression and antisocial behavior. In N. Eisenberg (Ed.), *Handbook of child psychology, 5th ed.: Vol 3. Social, emotional, and personality development* (pp. 779–862). Hoboken, NJ: John New York: John Wiley & Sons & Sons Inc.

Coles, M. E., Pinto, A., Mancebo, M. C., Rasmussen, S. A., & Eisen, J. L. (2008). OCD with comorbid OCPD: A subtype of OCD? *Journal of Psychiatric Research, 42*(4), 289–296.

Comtois, K. A., Koons, C. R., Kim, S. A., Manning, S. Y., Bellows, E., & Dimeff, L. A. (2007). Implementing standard dialectical behavior therapy in an outpatient setting. In L. A. Dimeff & K. Koerner (Eds.), *Dialectical behavior therapy in clinical practice: Applications across disorders and settings.* (pp. 37–68). New York: Guilford Press. Retrieved from http://ezproxy.shsu.edu/login?url=http://search.ebscohost.com/login.aspx?direct=true&db=psyh&AN=2007-14074-003&site=ehost-live&scope=site

Condray, R., & Steinhauer, S. R. (1992). Schizotypal personality disorder in individuals with and without schizophrenic relatives: Similarities and contrasts in neurocognitive and clinical functioning. *Schizophrenia Research, 7*(1), 33–41. doi:10.1016/0920-9964(92)90071-C

Cowdry, R. W., & Gardner, D. L. (1988). Pharmacotherapy of borderline personality disorder: Alprazolam, carbamazepine, trifluoperazine, and tranylcypromine. *Archives of General Psychiatry, 45*(2), 111–119.

Cox, B. J. P. (2009). The relationship between generalized social phobia and avoidant personality disorder in a national mental health survey. *Depression & Anxiety (1091–4269), 26*(4), 354–362. Cox, B. J., Turnbull, D. L., Robinson, J. A., Grant, B. F., & Stein, M. B. (2011). The effect of avoidant personality disorder on the persistence of generalized social anxiety disorder in the general population: Results from a longitudinal, nationally representative mental health survey. *Depression and Anxiety, 28*(3), 250–255.

Crawford, T. N., Cohen, P., & Brook, J. S. (2001). Dramatic-erratic personality disorder symptoms: II. Developmental pathways from early adolescence to adulthood. *Journal of Personality Disorders, 15*(4), 336–350.

Crawford, T. N., Cohen, P., Johnson, J. G., Kasen, S., First, M. B., Gordon, K., & Brook, J. S. (2005). Self-reported personality disorder in the children in the community sample: convergent and prospective validity in late adolescence and adulthood. *Journal of Personality Disorders, 19*(1), 30–52. doi:10.1521/pedi.19.1.30.62179

Crawford, T., Shaver, P., Cohen, P., Pilkonis, P., Gillath, O., & Kasen, S. (2006). Self-reported attachment, interpersonal aggression, and personality disorder in a prospective community sample of adolescents and adults. *Journal Of Personality Disorders, 20*(4), 331–351.

Crits-Christoph, P., & Barber, J. P. (2002). Psychological treatments for personality disorders. *A guide to treatments that work (2nd ed.)* (pp. 611–623). New York, NY: Oxford University Press.

Cummings, J. A., Hayes, A. M., Newman, C. F., & Beck, A. T. (2011). Navigating therapeutic alliance ruptures in cognitive therapy for avoidant and obsessive-compulsive personality disorders and comorbid Axis I disorders. *International Journal of Cognitive Therapy, 4*(4), 397–414.

Cunningham, M. D. R. (1998). Antisocial personality disorder and psychopathy: diagnostic dilemmas in classifying patterns of antisocial behavior in sentencing evaluations. *Behavioral Sciences & the Law, 16*(3), 333–351. doi:Article

Curtis, J. M., & Cowell, D. R. (1993). Relation of birth order and scores on measures of pathological narcissism. *Psychological Reports, 72*(1), 311–315.

Dahl, A. A. (1985). Borderline disorders—the validity of the diagnostic concept. *Psychiatric Developments, 3*(2), 109–152.

Deltito, J., Martin, L., Riefkohl, J., Austria, B., Kissilenko, A., & Morse, P. C. C. (2001). Do patients with borderline personality disorder belong to the bipolar spectrum? *Journal of Affective Disorders*, Millenial issue: The new bipolar era, *67*(1–3), 221–228.

Dickinson, K. A., & Pincus, A. L. (2003). Interpersonal analysis of grandiose and vulnerable narcissism. *Journal of Personality Disorders, 17*(3), 188–207.

Diehl, M., Elnick, A. B., Bourbeau, L. S., & Labouvie-Vief, G. (1998). Adult attachment styles: Their relations to family context and personality. *Journal of Personality and Social Psychology, 74*(6), 1656–1669. doi:10.1037/0022-3514.74.6.1656

Digre, E. I., Reece, J., Johnson, A. L., & Thomas, R. A. (2009). Treatment response in subtypes of borderline personality disorder. *Personality and Mental Health, 3*(1), 56–67.

Dimaggio, G., Carcione, A., Salvatore, G., Nicolò, G., Sisto, A., & Semerari, A. (2011). Progressively promoting metacognition in a case of obsessive-compulsive personality disorder treated with metacognitive interpersonal therapy. *Psychology and Psychotherapy: Theory, Research and Practice, 84*(1), 70–83.

Dishion, T. J., McCord, J., & Poulin, F. (1999). When interventions harm: Peer groups and problem behavior. *American Psychologist, 54*(9), 755–764.

Distel, M. A., Trull, T. J., Derom, C. A., Thiery, E. W., Grimmer, M. A., Martin, N. G., Willemsen, G., et al. (2008). Heritability of borderline personality disorder features is similar across three countries. *Psychological Medicine, 38*(9), 1219–1229.

Done, D. J., Crow, T. J., Johnstone, E. C., & Sacker, A. (1994). Childhood antecedents of schizophrenia and affective illness: social adjustment at ages 7 and 11. *British Medical Journal, 309*(6956), 699–703.

Donegan, N. H., Sanislow, C. A., Blumberg, H. P., Fulbright, R. K., Lacadie, C., Skudlarski, P., Gore, J. C., et al. (2003). Amygdala Hyperreactivity in Borderline personality disorder: Implications for Emotional Dysregulation. *Biological Psychiatry, 54*(11), 1284–1293.

Drake, R. E., & Vaillant, G. E. (1985). A validity study of axis II of DSM-III. *The American Journal of Psychiatry, 142*(5), 553–558.

Eaton, N. R., Keyes, K. M., Krueger, R. F., Balsis, S., Skodol, A. E., Markon, K. E., Grant, B. F., et al. (2012). An invariant dimensional liability model of gender differences in mental disorder prevalence: Evidence from a national sample. *Journal of Abnormal Psychology, 121*(1), 282–288.

Edell, W. S. (1987). Relationship of borderline syndrome disorders to early schizophrenia on the MMPI. *Journal of Clinical Psychology, 43*(2), 163–176. doi:10.1002/1097-4679(198703)43:2<163::AID-JCLP2270430202>3.0.CO;2-S

Edens, J. F., Poythress, N. G., & Watkins, M. M. (2001). Further validation of the Psychopathic Personality Inventory among offenders: Personality and behavioral correlates. *Journal of Personality Disorders, 15*(5), 403–415.

Eichelman, B. (1988). Toward a rational pharmacotherapy for aggressive and violent behavior. *Hospital & Community Psychiatry, 39*(1), 31–39.

Eisen, J. L., Coles, M. E., Shea, M. T., Pagano, M. E., Stout, R. L., Yen, S., Grilo, C. M., et al. (2006). Clarifying the convergence between obsessive compulsive personality disorder criteria and obsessive compulsive disorder. *Journal of Personality Disorders, 20*(3), 294–305.

Elzy, M. B. (2011). Examining the relationship between childhood sexual abuse and borderline personality disorder: Does social support matter? *Journal of Child Sexual Abuse: Research, Treatment, & Program Innovations for Victims, Survivors, & Offenders, 20*(3), 284–304.

Ericson, M., Tuvblad, C., Raine, A., Young-Wolff, K., & Baker, L. A. (2011). Heritability and longitudinal stability of schizotypal traits during adolescence. *Behavior Genetics, 41*(4), 499–511. doi:10.1007/s10519-010-9401-x

Exner, J E. (1986). Some Rorschach data comparing schizophrenics with borderline and schizotypal personality disorders. *Journal of Personality Assessment, 50*(3), 455–471. doi:10.1207/s15327752jpa5003_14

Exner, John E. (1986). *The Rorschach: a comprehensive system.* New York: John Wiley & Sons.

Eyring, W. E., & Sobelman, S. (1996). Narcissism and birth order. *Psychological Reports, 78*(2), 403–406.

Eysenck, H. J., & Eysenck, S. B. G. (1978). *Psychopathy, personality, and genetics.* New York, NY: John Wiley & Sons.

Fairbairn, W. R. D. (1952). *Psychoanalytic studies of the personality.* Oxford, England: Routledge & Kegan Paul.

Fairbairn, W. R. D. (2002). *Psychoanalytic Studies of the Personality* (1st ed.). Taylor & Francis.

Feighner, J. P., Robins, E., Guze, S. B., Woodruff, R. A., Jr, Winokur, G., & Munoz, R. (1972). Diagnostic criteria for use in psychiatric research. *Archives of General Psychiatry, 26*(1), 57–63.

Fieve, R. (1994). *Prozac: Questions and answers for patients, family and physicians.* New York: Avon Books.

Fineberg, N. A., Sharma, P., Sivakumaran, T., Sahakian, B., & Chamberlain, S. R. (2007). Does obsessive-compulsive personality disorder belong within the obsessive-compulsive spectrum? *CNS Spectrums, 12*(6), 467–482.

First, M. B., France, A., & Pincus, H. A. (2004). *DSM-IV-TR guidebook.* Arlington, VA: American Psychiatric Publishing, Inc. Retrieved from http://ezproxy.shsu.edu/login?url=http://search.ebscohost.com/login.aspx?direct=true&db=psyh&AN=2004-13884-000&site=ehost-live&scope=site

First, M. B., Gibbon, M., Spitzer, R. L., Benjamin, L. S., & Williams, J. B. W. (1997). *Structured Clinical Interview for DSM-IV Axis II personality disorders: SCID-II.* American Psychiatric Pub.

Fonagy, P., Target, M., Steele, M., Steele, H., Leigh, T., Levinson, A., & Kennedy, R. (1997). Morality, disruptive behavior, borderline personality disorder, crime and their relationship to security of attachment. In L. Atkinson & K. J. Zucker (Eds.), *Attachment and psychopathology.* (pp. 223–274). New York: Guilford Press. Retrieved from http://ezproxy.shsu.edu/login?url=http://search.ebscohost.com/login.aspx?direct=true&db=psyh&AN=1997-08324-007&site=ehost-live&scope=site

Forsman, M., Lichtenstein, P., Andershed, H., & Larsson, H. (2010). A longitudinal twin study of the direction of effects between psychopathic personality and antisocial behaviour. *Journal of Child Psychology & Psychiatry, 51*(1), 39–47.

Fossati, A., Beauchaine, T. P., Grazioli, F., Borroni, S., Carretta, I., De Vecchi, C., Cortinovis, F., et al. (2006). Confirmatory factor analyses of DSM-IV cluster C personality disorder criteria. *Journal Of Personality Disorders, 20*(2), 186–203.

Fraley, R. C., Waller, N. G., & Brennan, K. A. (2000). An item response theory analysis of self-report measures of adult attachment. *Journal of Personality and Social Psychology, 78*(2), 350–365.

Frank, H., & Paris, J. (1981). Recollections of family experience in borderline patients. *Archives Of General Psychiatry, 38*(9), 1031–1034.

Freedman, B., & Chapman, L. J. (1973). Early subjective experiences in schizophrenic episodes. *Journal of Abnormal Psychology, 82*(1), 46–54. doi:10.1037/h0034952

Freud, S. (1906). Character and anal eroticism. In J. Strachey (Ed.), *The standard editon of the complete psychological works of Sigmund Freud* (Vol. 9, pp. 169–175). London, U.K.: Hogarth Press.

Freud, S. (1914). On narcissism: An introduction. In J. Strachey (Ed.), *The standard edition of the complete psychological works of Sigmund Freud* (Vol. 14, pp. 73–102). London, U.K.: Hogarth Press.

Freud, S. (1963). *Three case histories.* New York: Collier Books/Macmillan Publishing Co.

Freud, S. (1984). The defence neuro-psychoses: An endeavor to provide a psychological theory of acquired hysteria, many phobias and obsessions, and certain hallucinatory psychoses. In Dan J. Stein & M. H. Stone (Eds.), *Essential papers on obsessive-compulsive disorder.*, Essential papers in psychoanalysis (pp. 33–44). New York: New York University Press. Retrieved from http://ezproxy.shsu.edu/login?url=http://search.ebscohost.com/login.aspx?direct=true&db=psyh&AN=1997-08667-001&site=ehost-live&scope=site

Freud, S., Breuer, J., & Luckhurst, N. (2004). *Studies in hysteria.* New York: Penguin Press. Retrieved from http://ezproxy.shsu.edu/login?url=http://search.ebscohost.com/login.aspx?direct=true&db=psyh&AN=2004-15778-000&site=ehost-live&scope=site

Friedel, R. O. (2004). *Borderline personality disorder demystified: An essential guide for understanding and living with BPD.* New York: Marlowe & Company. Retrieved from http://ezproxy.shsu.edu/login?url=http://search.ebscohost.com/login.aspx?direct=true&db=psyh&AN=2004-21808-000&site=ehost-live

Frodi, A., Dernevik, M., Sepa, A., Philipson, J., & Bragesjö, M. (2001). Current attachment representations of incarcerated offenders varying in degree of psychopathy. *Attachment & Human Development,* Attachment in mental health institutions, *3*(3), 269–283.

Gabbard, G. O. (1989). Two subtypes of narcissistic personality disorder. *Bulletin of the Menninger Clinic, 53*(6), 527–532.

Gabbard, G. O. (1990). *Psychodynamic psychiatry in clinical practice.* Washington, DC: American Psychiatric Association. Retrieved from http://ezproxy.shsu.edu/login?url=http://search.ebscohost.com/login.aspx?direct=true&db=psyh&AN=1990-98189-000&site=ehost-live&scope=site

Gabbard, G. O. (1994a). *Psychodynamic psychiatry in clinical practice: The DSM-IV edition.* Washington, DC: American Psychiatric Association.

Gabbard, G. O. (1994b). *Psychodynamic psychiatry in clinical practice: The DSM-IV edition.* Washington, DC: American Psychiatric Association. Retrieved from http://ezproxy.shsu.edu/login?url=http://search.ebscohost. com/login.aspx?direct=true&db=psyh&AN=1994-97173-000&site=ehost-live&scope=site

Gabbard, G. O. (1998). Transference and countertransference in the treatment of narcissistic patients. In E. F. Ronningstam (Ed.), *Disorders of narcissism: Diagnostic, clinical, and empirical implications.* (pp. 125–145). Washington, DC: American Psychiatric Association. Retrieved from http://ezproxy.shsu.edu/login?url=http:// search.ebscohost.com/login.aspx?direct=true&db=psyh&AN=1997-36386-006&site=ehost-live&scope=site

Gabbard, G. O. (2005). *Psychodynamic psychiatry in clinical practice (4th ed.).* Arlington, VA: American Psychiatric Publishing, Inc. Retrieved from http://ezproxy.shsu.edu/login?url=http://search.ebscohost.com/login. aspx?direct=true&db=psyh&AN=2005-02871-000&site=ehost-live&scope=site

Gabbard, G. O. (2010). The therapeutic action in psychoanalytic psychotherapy of borderline personality disorder. In P. Williams (Ed.), *The psychoanalytic therapy of severe disturbance.*, Psychoanalytic ideas (pp. 1–19). London, U.K.: Karnac Books. Retrieved from http://ezproxy.shsu.edu/login?url=http://search.ebscohost.com/login. aspx?direct=true&db=psyh&AN=2010-13836-001&site=ehost-live&scope=site

Gacono, C. B., & Meloy, J. R. (1991). A Rorschach investigation of attachment and anxiety in antisocial personality disorder. *Journal of Nervous and Mental Disease, 179*(9), 546–552.

Gacono, C. B., & Meloy, J. R. (1997). Rorschach research and the psychodiagnosis of antisocial and psychopathic personalities. *Rorschachiana, 22*(1), 130–148.

Gardner, K., & Qualter, P. (2009). Emotional intelligence and borderline personality disorder. *Personality and Individual Differences, 47*(2), 94–98.

Giffin, J. (2008). Family Experience of Borderline personality disorder. *Australian & New Zealand Journal of Family Therapy, 29*(3), 133–138.

Glickauf-Hughes, C., & Wells, M. (1997). *Object relations psychotherapy: An individualized and interactive approach to diagnosis and treatment.* Lanham, MD: Jason Aronson. Retrieved from http://ezproxy. shsu.edu/login?url=http://search.ebscohost.com/login.aspx?direct=true&db=psyh&AN=2007-01875-000&site=ehost-live&scope=site

Glueck, S., & Glueck, E. (1950). *Unraveling Juvenile delinquency.* Oxford, U.K.: Commonwealth Fund. Retrieved from http://ezproxy.shsu.edu/login?url=http://search.ebscohost.com/login.aspx?direct=true&db= psyh&AN=1951-02578-000&site=ehost-live&scope=site

Goldberg, J. F., & Garno, J. L. (2009). Age at onset of bipolar disorder and risk for comorbid borderline personality disorder. *Bipolar Disorders, 11*(2), 205–208.

Goldberg, S. C., & et al. (1986). Borderline and schizotypal personality disorders treated with low-dose thiothixene vs placebo. *Archives of General Psychiatry, 43*(7), 680–686. doi:10.1001/archpsyc.1986.01800070070009

Golomb, A., Ludolph, P., Westen, D., Block, M. J., Maurer, P., & Wiss, F. C. (1994). Maternal empathy, family chaos, and the etiology of borderline personality disorder. *Journal Of The American Psychoanalytic Association, 42*(2), 525–548.

Graham, J. R. (2011). *MMPI-2: Assessing Personality and Psychopathology* (Fifth ed.). New York: Oxford University Press.

Grant, B. F., Chou, S. P., Goldstein, R. B., Huang, B., Stinson, F. S., Saha, T. D., Smith, S. M., et al. (2008). Prevalence, correlates, disability, and comorbidity of DSM-IV borderline personality disorder: Results from the Wave 2 National Epidemiologic Survey on Alcohol and Related Conditions. *Journal of Clinical Psychiatry, 69*(4), 533–545.

Grant, B. F., Harford, T. C., Dawson, D. D., & Chou, P. S. (1995). The Alcohol Use Disorder and Associated Disabilities Interview Schedule (AUDADIS): Reliability of alcohol and drug modules in a general population sample. *Drug and Alcohol Dependence, 39*(1), 37–44.

Grant, J. E., Mooney, M. E., & Kushner, M. G. (2012). Prevalence, correlates, and comorbidity of DSM-IV obsessive-compulsive personality disorder: Results from the National Epidemiologic Survey on Alcohol and Related Conditions. *Journal of Psychiatric Research*, *46*(4), 469–475.

Graves, R. (1993). *The Greek Myths: Complete Edition* (Cmb Rep.). Penguin Books.

Greenberg, R. P., & Bornstein, R. F. (1989). Length of psychiatric hospitalization and oral dependency. *Journal of Personality Disorders*, *3*(3), 199–204.

Grilo, C. M. S. (2004). Longitudinal diagnostic efficiency of DSM-IV criteria for obsessive–compulsive personality disorder: a 2-year prospective study. *Acta Psychiatrica Scandinavica*, *110*(1), 64–68.

Grinker, R. R., Werble, B., & Drye, R. C. (1968). *The borderline syndrome: a behavioral study of ego functions*. Basic Books.

Gross, R., Olfson, M., Gameroff, M., Shea, S., Feder, A., Fuentes, M., Lantigua, R., et al. (2002). Borderline personality disorder in primary care. *Archives Of Internal Medicine*, *162*(1), 53–60.

Gruzelier, J., & Raine, A. (1994). Bilateral electrodermal activity and cerebral mechanisms in syndromes of schizophrenia and the schizotypal personality. *International Journal of Psychophysiology*, *16*(1), 1–16. doi:10.1016/0167-8760(94)90037-X

Gude, T., Karterud, S., Pedersen, G., & Falkum, E. (2006). The quality of the Diagnostic and Statistical Manual of Mental Disorders, Fourth Edition dependent personality disorder prototype. *Comprehensive Psychiatry*, *47*(6), 456–462.

Guitart-Masip, M., Pascual, J. C., Carmona, S., Hoekzema, E., Bergé, D., Pérez, V., Soler, J., et al. (2009). Neural correlates of impaired emotional discrimination in borderline personality disorder: An fMRI study. *Progress in Neuro-Psychopharmacology & Biological Psychiatry*, *33*(8), 1537–1545.

Gunderson, J G, & Phillips, K. A. (1991). A current view of the interface between borderline personality disorder and depression. *The American Journal Of Psychiatry*, *148*(8), 967–975.

Gunderson, John G. (1994). Building structure for the borderline construct. *Acta Psychiatrica Scandinavica*, *89*(379, Suppl), 12–18.

Gunderson, John G. (1996). Borderline patient's intolerance of aloneness: Insecure attachments and therapist availability. *The American Journal of Psychiatry*, *153*(6), 752–758.

Gunderson, John G., Ronningstam, E., & Smith, L. E. (1991). Narcissistic personality disorder: A review of data on DSM-III—R descriptions. *Journal of Personality Disorders*, Special Series: DSM-IV and personality disorders, *5*(2), 167–177.

Gunderson, John G., & Singer, M. T. (1975). Defining borderline patients: An overview. *The American Journal of Psychiatry*, *132*(1), 1–10.

Gutmann, P. (2006). [Julius Ludwig August Koch (1841–1908). Psychiatrist, philosopher, and Christian]. *Würzburger Medizinhistorische Mitteilungen/Im Auftrage Der Würzburger Medizinhistorischen Gesellschaft Und in Verbindung Mit Dem Institut Für Geschichte Der Medizin Der Universität Würzburg*, *25*, 215–230.

Hall, J., Olabi, B., Lawrie, S. M., & McIntosh, A. M. (2010). Hippocampal and amygdala volumes in borderline personality disorder: A meta-analysis of magnetic resonance imaging studies. *Personality and Mental Health*, *4*(3), 172–179.

Hallquist, M. N., & Pilkonis, P. A. (2012). Refining the phenotype of borderline personality disorder: Diagnostic criteria and beyond. *Personality Disorders: Theory, Research, and Treatment*, *3*(3), 228–246.

Hare, R. D. (1996). Psychopathy: A clinical construct whose time has come. *Criminal Justice and Behavior*, *23*(1), 25–54.

Hare, R. D. (1999). *Without Conscience: The Disturbing World of the Psychopaths Among Us* (1st ed.). The Guilford Press.

Hare, R. D. (2003). *Manual for the hare psychopathy checklist* (2nd ed.). Toronto, ON: Multi-Health Systems.

Hare, R. D., Hart, S. D., & Harpur, T. J. (1991). Psychopathy and the DSM-IV criteria for antisocial personality disorder. *Journal of Abnormal Psychology*, Diagnoses, Dimensions, and DSM-IV: The Science of Classification, *100*(3), 391–398.

Hare, R. D., & Neumann, C. S. (2006). The PCL-R Assessment of Psychopathy: Development, Structural Properties, and New Directions. In C. J. Patrick (Ed.), *Handbook of psychopathy.* (pp. 58–88). New York: Guilford Press. Retrieved from http://ezproxy.shsu.edu/login?url=http://search.ebscohost.com/login.aspx?direct=true&db=psyh&AN=2006-01001-004&site=ehost-live&scope=site

Harlow, H. F., & Harlow, M. K. (1962). The effect of rearing conditions on behavior. *Bulletin of the Menninger Clinic, 26*(5), 213–224.

Harris, G. T., Rice, M. E., & Quinsey, V. L. (1994). Psychopathy as a taxon: Evidence that psychopaths are a discrete class. *Journal of Consulting and Clinical Psychology, 62*(2), 387–397.

Hart, S. D., & Hare, R. D. (1989). Discriminant validity of the Psychopathy Checklist in a forensic psychiatric population. *Psychological Assessment: A Journal of Consulting and Clinical Psychology, 1*(3), 211–218.

Head, S. B., Baker, J. D., & Williamson, D. A. (1991). Family environment characteristics and dependent personality disorder. *Journal of Personality Disorders, 5*(3), 256–263.

Hendin, H. M., & Cheek, J. M. (1997). Assessing hypersensitive narcissism: A reexamination of Murray's Narcism Scale. *Journal of Research in Personality, 31*(4), 588–599.

Henry Maudsley. (1874). *Responsibility in Mental Disease.* King. Retrieved from http://archive.org/details/responsibilityi04maudgoog

Herbert, J. D. (2007). Avoidant personality disorder. In W. O'Donohue, K. A. Fowler, & S. O. Lilienfeld (Eds.), *Personality disorders: Toward the DSM-V.* (pp. 279–305). Thousand Oaks, CA: Sage Publications, Inc. Retrieved from http://ezproxy.shsu.edu/login?url=http://search.ebscohost.com/login.aspx?direct=true&db=psyh&AN=2007-00410-010&site=ehost-live&scope=site

Herman, J. L., Perry, J. C., & Van der Kolk, B. A. (1989). Childhood trauma in borderline personality disorder. *The American Journal of Psychiatry, 146*(4), 490–495.

Hill, E. L., Gold, S. N., & Bornstein, R. F. (2000). Interpersonal dependency among adult survivors of childhood sexual abuse in therapy. *Journal of Child Sexual Abuse: Research, Treatment, & Program Innovations for Victims, Survivors, & Offenders, 9*(2), 71–86.

Hill, J., Pilkonis, P., Morse, J., Feske, U., Reynolds, S., Hope, H., Charest, C., et al. (2008). Social domain dysfunction and disorganization in borderline personality disorder. *Psychological Medicine, 38*(1), 135–146.

Hill, Jonathan, Stepp, S. D., Wan, M. W., Hope, H., Morse, J. Q., Steele, M., Steele, H., et al. (2011). Attachment, borderline personality, and romantic relationship dysfunction. *Journal of Personality Disorders, 25*(6), 789–805.

Hines, D. J., & Saudino, K. J. (2008). Personality and intimate partner aggression in dating relationships: the role of the "Big Five". *Aggressive Behavior, 34*(6), 593–604.

Hirschfeld, R. M., Klerman, G., Gouch, H., Barrett, J., Korchin, S., & Chodoff, P. (1977). A measure of interpersonal dependency. *Journal of Personality Assessment, 41*(6), 610.

Hirschfeld, R. M., Shea, M. T., & Weise, R. E. (1991). Dependent personality disorder: Perspectives for DSM-IV. *Journal of Personality Disorders, 5*(2), 135–149.

Hoare, P. (1984). Does illness foster dependency? A study of epileptic and diabetic children. *Developmental Medicine And Child Neurology, 26*(1), 20–24.

Hobson, R. P., Patrick, M. P. H., Hobson, J. A., Crandell, L., Bronfman, E., & Lyons-Ruth, K. (2009). How mothers with borderline personality disorder relate to their year-old infants. *The British Journal of Psychiatry, 195*(4), 325–330.

Hodgins, S., De Brito, S. A., Chhabra, P., & Côté, G. (2010). Anxiety disorders among offenders with antisocial personality disorders: A distinct subtype? *The Canadian Journal of Psychiatry/La Revue Canadienne de Psychiatrie, 55*(12), 784–791.

Hollander. (1993). *Obsessive-compulsive related disorders*. Washington, D.C: American Psychiatric Press.

Hollander, E., Swann, A. C., Coccaro, E. F., Jiang, P., & Smith, T. B. (2005). Impact of trait impulsivity and state aggression on divalproex versus placebo response in borderline personality disorder. *The American Journal of Psychiatry*, *162*(3), 621–624.

Hollander, E., Tracy, K. A., Swann, A. C., Coccaro, E. F., McElroy, S. L., Wozniak, P., Sommerville, K. W., et al. (2003). Divalproex in the treatment of impulsive aggression: Efficacy in cluster B personality disorders. *Neuropsychopharmacology*, *28*(6), 1186–1197.

Hooley, J. M., & Wilson-Murphy, M. (2012). Adult attachment to transitional objects and borderline personality. *Journal of Personality Disorders*, *26*(2), 179–191.

Huang, J., Yang, Y., Wu, J., Napolitano, L. A., Xi, Y., & Cui, Y. (2012). Childhood abuse Chinese patients with borderline personality disorder. *Journal of Personality Disorders*, *26*(2), 238–254.

Huprich, Steven Ken. (2006). *Rorschach Assessment Of The personality disorders*. Psychology Press.

Hyler, S. E. (1994). *Personality Diagnostic Questionnaire-4*. New York: New York State Psychiatric Institute.

Ingoldsby, E. M. S. (2002). Neighborhood Contextual Factors and Early-Starting Antisocial Pathways. *Clinical Child & Family Psychology Review*, *5*(1), 21–55.

Ivey, A. E. (1991). *Developmental strategies for helpers: Individual, family, and network interventions*. Developmental strategies for helpers: Individual, family, and network interventions. Belmont, CA: Thomson Brooks/Cole Publishing Co. Retrieved from http://ezproxy.shsu.edu/login?url=http://search.ebscohost.com/login.aspx?direct=true&db=psyh&AN=1990-98843-000&site=ehost-live&scope=site

Johnson, B. A., Brent, D. A., Connolly, J., & Bridge, J. (1995). Familial aggregation of adolescent personality disorders. *Journal of the American Academy of Child & Adolescent Psychiatry*, *34*(6), 798–804.

Johnson, D. M., Shea, M. T., Yen, S., Battle, C. L., Zlotnick, C., Sanislow, C. A., Grilo, C. M., et al. (2003). Gender differences in borderline personality disorder: Findings from the Collaborative Longitudinal personality disorders Study. *Comprehensive Psychiatry*, *44*(4), 284–292.

Johnson, F. A. (1993). *Dependency and Japanese socialization: Psychoanalytic and anthropological investigations into amae*. Dependency and Japanese socialization: Psychoanalytic and anthropological investigations into amae. New York: New York University Press. Retrieved from http://ezproxy.shsu.edu/login?url=http://search.ebscohost.com/login.aspx?direct=true&db=psyh&AN=1993-97319-000&site=ehost-live&scope=site

Johnson, J. G., Cohen, P., Brown, J., Smailes, E., & Bernstein, D. P. (1999). Childhood maltreatment increases risk for personality disorders during early adulthood. *Archives of General Psychiatry*, *56*(7), 600–606.

Kagan, J. (1989). Temperamental contributions to social behavior. *American Psychologist*, *44*(4), 668–674.

Karpman, Benjamin. (1955). Criminal psychodynamics: a platform. *Archives of Criminal Psychodynamics*, *1*, 3–100.

Karpman, Benjamin. (1948). Conscience in the psychopath: another version. *American Journal of Orthopsychiatry*, *18*, 455–491.

Kelsey, J. E., Newport, D. J., & Nemeroff, C. B. (2006). *Principles of psychopharmacology for mental health professionals*. Hoboken, NJ: John New York: John Wiley & Sons & Sons Inc. Retrieved from http://ezproxy.shsu.edu/login?url=http://search.ebscohost.com/login.aspx?direct=true&db=psyh&AN=2006-08160-000&site=ehost-live&scope=site

Kernberg, O. (1967). Borderline Personality Organization. *Journal of the American Psychoanalytic Association.*, *15*, 641–685.

Kernberg, O. F. (1970). Factors in the psychoanalytic treatment of narcissistic personalities. *Journal of the American Psychoanalytic Association*, *18*(1), 51–85.

Kernberg, O. F. (1975). *Borderline conditions and pathological narcissism*. J. Aronson.

Kernberg, O. F. (1984). *Severe personality disorders: Psychotherapeutic Strategies*. Yale University Press.

Kernberg, O. F. (1992). *Aggression in personality disorders and perversions*. New Haven, CT: Yale University Press. Retrieved from http://ezproxy.shsu.edu/login?url=http://search.ebscohost.com/login.aspx?direct=true& db=psyh&AN=1992-98914-000&site=ehost-live&scope=site

Kernberg, O. F. (2009). Narcissistic personality disorders: Part 1. *Psychiatric Annals, 39*(3), 105–107, 110, 164–166.

Kernberg, Otto. (1968). The treatment of patients with borderline personality organization. *The International Journal of Psychoanalysis, 49*(4), 600–619.

Kety, S. S., Wender, P. H., Jacobsen, B., Ingraham, L. J., & et al. (1994). Mental illness in the biological and adoptive relatives of schizophrenic adoptees: Replication of the Copenhagen study in the rest of Denmark. *Archives of General Psychiatry, 51*(6), 442–455. doi:10.1001/archpsyc.1994.03950060006001

Kim-Cohen, J., Caspi, A., Moffitt, T. E., Harrington, H., Milne, B. J., & Poulton, R. (2003). Prior juvenile diagnoses in adults with mental disorder: Developmental follow-back of a prospective-longitudinal cohort. *Archives of General Psychiatry, 60*(7), 709–717.

Kimmel, R. J., & Roy-Byrne, P. P. (2012). Anxiety disorders. In A. J. Rothschild (Ed.), *The evidence-based guide to antidepressant medications.* (pp. 57–88). Arlington, VA: American Psychiatric Publishing, Inc. Retrieved from http://ezproxy.shsu.edu/login?url=http://search.ebscohost.com/login.aspx?direct=true& db=psyh&AN=2012-00703-003&site=ehost-live&scope=site

Kirk, S. A., & Kutchins, H. (1994). The myth of the reliability of DSM. *Journal of Mind and Behavior, 15*(1–2), 71–86.

Klein, M. H., Benjamin, L. S., Rosenfeld, R., & Treece, C. (1993). The Wisconsin personality disorders Inventory: Development, reliability, and validity. *Journal of Personality Disorders, 7*(4), 285–303.

Koenigsberg, H. W., Harvey, P. D., Mitropoulou, V., New, A. S., Goodman, M., Silverman, J., & ... Siever, L. J. (2001). Are the interpersonal and identity disturbances in the borderline personality disorder criteria linked to the traits of affective instability and impulsivity?. *Journal Of personality disorders, 15*(4), 358–370. doi:10.1521/pedi.15.4.358.19181

Koenigsberg, H. W., Reynolds, D., Goodman, M., New, A. S., Mitropoulou, V., Trestman, R. L., Silverman, J., et al. (2003). Risperidone in the treatment of schizotypal personality disorder. *Journal of Clinical Psychiatry, 64*(6), 628–634. doi:10.4088/JCP.v64n0602

Koenigsberg, H. W., Woo-Ming, A. M., & Siever, L. J. (2002). Pharmacological treatments for personality disorders. In P. E. Nathan J. M. Gorman (Ed.), *A guide to treatments that work (2nd ed.)* (pp. 625–641). New York, NY: Oxford University Press.

Koenigsberg, H. W., Woo-Ming, A. M., & Siever, L. J. (2007). Psychopharmacological treatment of personality disorders. *A guide to treatments that work (3rd ed.)* (pp. 659–680). New York, N.Y: Oxford University Press.

Kohut, H. (1979). The two analyses of Mr. Z. *The International Journal Of Psycho-Analysis, 60*(1), 3–27.

Kohut, H. (1966). Forms and transformations of narcissism. *Journal of the American Psychoanalytic Association, 14*(2), 243–272.

Kohut, Heinz. (1971). *The analysis of the self: A systematic approach to the psychoanalytic treatment of narcissistic personality disorders.* Chicago: University of Chicago Press. Retrieved from http://ezproxy.shsu.edu/login?url=http://search.ebscohost.com/login.aspx?direct=true&db=psyh&AN=2009-16139-000&site=ehost-live&scope=site

Kohut, Heinz. (1972). Thoughts on narcissism and narcissistic rage. *The Psychoanalytic Study of the Child, 27*, 360–400.

Kohut, Heinz. (1977). *The restoration of the self.* Chicago: University of Chicago Press. Retrieved from http://ezproxy.shsu.edu/login?url=http://search.ebscohost.com/login.aspx?direct=true&db=psyh&AN=2009-16135-000&site=ehost-live&scope=site

Kohut, Heinz. (1984). Introspection, empathy, and semicircle of mental health. *Emotions & Behavior Monographs, MO 3*, 347–375.

Kohut, Heinz, & Ornstein, P. H. (2011). *The search for the self: Selected writings of Heinz Kohut: 1950–1978, Vol 2.* (P. H. Ornstein, Ed.). London, U.K.: Karnac Books. Retrieved from http://ezproxy.shsu.edu/login?url=http://search. ebscohost.com/login.aspx?direct=true&db=psyh&AN=2011-14153-000&site=ehost-live&scope=site

Kohut, Hienz. (1968). The psychoanalytic treatment of narcissistic personality disorders: Outline of a systematic approach. *The Psychoanalytic Study of the Child, 23,* 86–113.

Kraepelin, E. (1904). *Psychiatrie: Ein Lehrbuch [Psychiatry: A textbook]* (7th ed.). Leipzig, Germany: Barth.

Kraepelin, E. (1915). *Psychiatrie: Ein Lehrbuch [Psychiatry: A textbook]* (8th ed., Vol. 4). Leipzig, Germany: Barth.

Kraepelin, E. (1921). *Physique and character.* London, U.K.: Kegan Paul.

Kraus, G., & Reynolds, D. J. (2001). The "A-B-C"s' of the cluster B's: Identifying, understanding, and treating cluster B personality disorders. *Clinical Psychology Review, 21*(3), 345–373.

Kretschmer, E. (1925). *Physique and character. (2nd ed. rev.).* Oxford, U.K.: Harcourt, Brace.

Krueger, R. F., Hicks, B. M., Patrick, C. J., Carlson, S. R., Iacono, W. G., & McGue, M. (2002). Etiologic connections among substance dependence, antisocial behavior and personality: Modeling the externalizing spectrum. *Journal of Abnormal Psychology, 111*(3), 411–424.

Krueger, R. F. M. (1998). Assortative Mating for Antisocial Behavior: Developmental and Methodological Implications. *Behavior Genetics, 28*(3), 173.

Lafreniere, P. (2009). A functionalist perspective on social anxiety and avoidant personality disorder. *Development And Psychopathology, 21*(4), 1065–1082.

Lazare, A. (1971). The hysterical character in psychoanalytic theory. Evolution and confusion. *Archives Of General Psychiatry, 25*(2), 131–137.

Leible, T. L., & Snell, W. E. J. (2004). Borderline personality disorder and multiple aspects of emotional intelligence. *Personality and Individual Differences, 37*(2), 393–404.

Lempert, T., Dieterich, M., Huppert, D., & Brandt, T. (1990). Psychogenic disorders in neurology: Frequency and clinical spectrum. *Acta Neurologica Scandinavica, 82*(5), 335–340.

Lenzenweger, M F, Loranger, A. W., Korfine, L., & Neff, C. (1997). Detecting personality disorders in a nonclinical population. Application of a 2-stage procedure for case identification. *Archives Of General Psychiatry, 54*(4), 345–351.

Lenzenweger, Mark F., Lane, M. C., Loranger, A. W., & Kessler, R. C. (2007). DSM-IV personality disorders in the National Comorbidity Survey Replication. *Biological psychiatry, 62*(6), 553–564. doi:10.1016/j. biopsych.2006.09.019

Leszcz, M. (1989). Group psychotherapy of the characterologically difficult patient. *International Journal of Group Psychotherapy, 39*(3, Spec Issue), 311–335.

Levels of Personality Functioning | APA DSM-5. (n.d.). Retrieved October 1, 2012, from http://www.dsm5.org/ ProposedRevisions/pages/proposedrevision.aspx?rid=468

Levenson, M. R., Kiehl, K. A., & Fitzpatrick, C. M. (1995). Assessing psychopathic attributes in a noninstitutionalized population. *Journal of Personality and Social Psychology, 68*(1), 151–158.

Levy, K. N., Meehan, K. B., Kelly, K. M., Reynoso, J. S., Weber, M., Clarkin, J. F., & Kernberg, O. F. (2006). Change in attachment patterns and reflective function in a randomized control trial of transference-focused psychotherapy for borderline personality disorder. *Journal of Consulting and Clinical Psychology,* Special Section: Attachment Theory and Psychotherapy, 74(6), 1027–1040.

Levy, K. N., Meehan, K. B., Weber, M., Reynoso, J., & Clarkin, J. F. (2005). Attachment and Borderline personality disorder: Implications for Psychotherapy. *Psychopathology, 38*(2), 64–74.

Levy, K. N., Reynoso, J. S., Wasserman, R. H., & Clarkin, J. F. (2007). Narcissistic personality disorder. In W. O'Donohue, K. A. Fowler, & S. O. Lilienfeld (Eds.), *Personality disorders: Toward the DSM-V.* (pp. 233–277).

Thousand Oaks, CA: Sage Publications, Inc. Retrieved from http://ezproxy.shsu.edu/login?url=http://search. ebscohost.com/login.aspx?direct=true&db=psyh&AN=2007-00410-009&site=ehost-live&scope=site

Levy, K. N., Wasserman, R. H., Scott, L. N., & Yeomans, F. E. (2009). Empirical evidence for transference-focused psychotherapy and other psychodynamic psychotherapy for borderline personality disorder. In R. A. Levy & J. S. Ablon (Eds.), *Handbook of evidence-based psychodynamic psychotherapy: Bridging the gap between science and practice.* (pp. 93–119). Totowa, NJ: Humana Press. Retrieved from http://ezproxy. shsu.edu/login?url=http://search.ebscohost.com/login.aspx?direct=true&db=psyh&AN=2008-14828-005&site=ehost-live&scope=site

Lewis, C. E. (1991). Neurochemical mechanisms of chronic antisocial behavior (psychopathy): A literature review. *Journal of Nervous and Mental Disease, 179*(12), 720–727.

Lilienfeld, S O, & Penna, S. (2001). Anxiety sensitivity: relations to psychopathy, DSM-IV personality disorder features, and personality traits. *Journal Of Anxiety Disorders, 15*(5), 367–393.

Lilienfeld, Scott O. (1994). Conceptual problems in the assessment of psychopathy. *Clinical Psychology Review, 14*(1), 17–38.

Lilienfeld, Scott O., & Fowler, K. A. (2006). The Self-Report Assessment of Psychopathy: Problems, Pitfalls, and Promises. In C. J. Patrick (Ed.), *Handbook of psychopathy.* (pp. 107–132). New York: Guilford Press. Retrieved from http://ezproxy.shsu.edu/login?url=http://search.ebscohost.com/login. aspx?direct=true&db=psyh&AN=2006-01001-006&site=ehost-live&scope=site

Linde, J. A., & Clark, L. A. (1998). Diagnostic assignment of criteria: Clinicians and DSM-IV. *Journal of Personality Disorders, 12*(2), 126–137.

Linehan, M. M. (1993). *Cognitive-behavioral treatment of borderline personality disorder.* Diagnosis and treatment of mental disorders. New York: Guilford Press. Retrieved from http://ezproxy.shsu.edu/login?url=http://search. ebscohost.com/login.aspx?direct=true&db=psyh&AN=1993-97864-000&site=ehost-live&scope=site

Linehan, M. M., Armstrong, H. E., Suarez, A., & Allmon, D. (1991). Cognitive-behavioral treatment of chronically parasuicidal borderline patients. *Archives of General Psychiatry, 48*(12), 1060–1064.

Lingiardi, V., Lonati, C., Delucchi, F., Fossati, A., Vanzulli, L., & Maffei, C. (1999). Defense mechanisms and personality disorders. *The Journal Of Nervous And Mental Disease, 187*(4), 224–228.

Links, P. S. (1990). *Family environment and borderline personality disorder.* (P. S. Links, Ed.)Progress in psychiatry series. Washington, DC: American Psychiatric Association. Retrieved from http://ezproxy. shsu.edu/login?url=http://search.ebscohost.com/login.aspx?direct=true&db=psyh&AN=1990-98652-000&site=ehost-live&scope=site

Links, P. S., Steiner, M., & Huxley, G. (1988). The occurrence of borderline personality disorder in the families of borderline patients. *Journal of Personality Disorders, 2*(1), 14–20.

Lochner, C., Serebro, P., van der Merwe, L., Hemmings, S., Kinnear, C., Seedat, S., & Stein, D. J. (2011). Comorbid obsessive–compulsive personality disorder in obsessive–compulsive disorder (OCD): A marker of severity. *Progress in Neuro-Psychopharmacology & Biological Psychiatry, 35*(4), 1087–1092.

Loeber, R., DeLamatre, M. S., Keenan, K., & Zhang, Q. (1998). A prospective replication of developmental pathways in disruptive and delinquent behavior. In R. B. Cairns, L. R. Bergman, & J. Kagan (Eds.), *Methods and models for studying the individual.* (pp. 185–218). Thousand Oaks, CA: Sage Publications, Inc. Retrieved from http:// ezproxy.shsu.edu/login?url=http://search.ebscohost.com/login.aspx?direct=true&db=psyh&AN=1998-06623-008&site=ehost-live&scope=site

Loeber, R., Green, S. M., Keenan, K., & Lahey, B. B. (1995). Which boys will fare worse? Early predictors of the onset of conduct disorder in a six-year longitudinal study. *Journal of the American Academy of Child & Adolescent Psychiatry, 34*(4), 499–509.

Loeber, R., & Hay, D. (1997). Key issues in the development of aggression and violence from childhood to early adulthood. *Annual Review of Psychology, 48*, 371–410.

Lombroso, C. (1911). *Crime, Its Causes and Remedies*. Little, Brown.

Loranger, A. W., Susman, V. L., Oldham, J. M., & Russakoff, L. M. (1987). The personality disorder Examination: A preliminary report. *Journal of Personality Disorders, 1*(1), 1–13.

Ludolph, P. S., Westen, D., Misle, B., Jackson, A., Wixom, J., & Wiss, F. C. (1990). The borderline diagnosis in adolescents: symptoms and developmental history. *The American Journal Of Psychiatry, 147*(4), 470–476.

Lyddon, W. J., & Sherry, A. (2001). Developmental personality styles: An attachment theory conceptualization of personality disorders. *Journal of Counseling & Development, 79*(4), 405–414. doi:10.1002/j.1556-6676.2001.tb01987.x

Lykken, D. T. (1995). Antisocial Personalities. Retrieved from http://ezproxy.shsu.edu/login?url=http://search.ebscohost.com/login.aspx?direct=true&db=sih&AN=SM155470&site=ehost-live&scope=site

Lynam, D. R. (1998). Early identification of the fledgling psychopath: Locating the psychopathic child in the current nomenclature. *Journal of Abnormal Psychology, 107*(4), 566–575.

Lyons-Ruth, K., & Jacobvitz, D. (1999). Attachment disorganization: Unresolved loss, relational violence, and lapses in behavioral and attentional strategies. In J. Cassidy & P. R. Shaver (Eds.), *Handbook of attachment: Theory, research, and clinical applications.* (pp. 520–554). New York: Guilford Press. Retrieved from http://ezproxy.shsu.edu/login?url=http://search.ebscohost.com/login.aspx?direct=true&db=psyh&AN=1999-02469-023&site=ehost-live&scope=site

Mack, T. D., Hackney, A. A., & Pyle, M. (2011). The relationship between psychopathic traits and attachment behavior in a non-clinical population. *Personality and Individual Differences, 51*(5), 584–588.

MacKinnon, D. F., & Pies, R. (2006). Affective instability as rapid cycling: Theoretical and clinical implications for borderline personality and bipolar spectrum disorders. *Bipolar Disorders, 8*(1), 1–14.

Maffei, C., Fossati, A., Agostoni, I., Barraco, A., Bagnato, M., Deborah, D., Namia, C., et al. (1997). Interrater reliability and internal consistency of the Structured Clinical Interview for DSM-IV Axis II personality disorders (SCID-II), version 2.0. *Journal of Personality Disorders, 11*(3), 279–284. doi:10.1521/pedi.1997.11.3.279

Magnavita, J. J., Levy, K. N., Critchfield, K. L., & Lebow, J. L. (2010). Ethical considerations in treatment of personality dysfunction: Using evidence, principles, and clinical judgment. *Professional Psychology: Research and Practice, 41*(1), 64–74.

Mahler, M. S., Pine, F., & Bergman, A. (1975). *The Psychological Birth of the Human Infant: Symbiosis and Individuation* (1st ed.). Basic Books.

Maier, W., Lichtermann, D., Klingler, T., & Heun, R. (1992). Prevalences of personality disorders (DSM-III—R) in the community. *Journal of Personality Disorders, 6*(3), 187–196.

Main, M., Kaplan, N., & Cassidy, J. (1985). Security in infancy, childhood, and adulthood: A move to the level of representation. *Monographs of the Society for Research in Child Development, 50*(1–2), 66–104.

Markovitz, P. J., Calabrese, J. R., Schulz, S. C., & Meltzer, H. Y. (1991). Fluoxetine in the treatment of borderline and schizotypal personality disorders. *The American Journal of Psychiatry, 148*(8), 1064–1067.

Markovitz, P. J., & Wagner, S. C. (1995). Venlafaxine in the treatment of borderline personality disorder. *Psychopharmacology Bulletin, 31*(4), 773–777.

Martens, W. H. J. (2010). Schizoid personality disorder linked to unbearable and inescapable loneliness. *The European Journal of Psychiatry, 24*(1), 38–45.

Masling, J., Rabie, L., & Blondheim, S. H. (1967). Obesity, level of aspiration, and Rorschach and TAT measures of oral dependence. *Journal of Consulting Psychology, 31*(3), 233–239.

Mayes, R., & Horwitz, A. V. (2005). DSM-III and the revolution in the classification of mental illness. *Journal Of The History Of The Behavioral Sciences, 41*(3), 249–267.

McCormack, C. C. (1989). The borderline/schizoid marriage: The holding environment as an essential treatment construct. *Journal of Marital and Family Therapy, 15*(3), 299–309. doi:10.1111/j.1752-0606.1989.tb00811.x

McCrae, R. R. (1994). A reformulation of Axis II: Personality and personality-related problems. In P. T. Costa & T. A. Widiger (Eds.), *Personality disorders and the five-factor model of personality.* (pp. 303–309). Washington, DC: American Psychological Association. Retrieved from http://ezproxy.shsu.edu/login?url=http://search. ebscohost.com/login.aspx?direct=true&db=psyh&AN=1993-99107-020&site=ehost-live&scope=site

McGlashan, T. H. (2005). Two-Year Prevalence and Stability of Individual DSM-IV Criteria for Schizotypal, Borderline, Avoidant, and Obsessive-Compulsive personality disorders: Toward a Hybrid Model of Axis II Disorders. *American Journal of Psychiatry, 162*(5), 883–889. doi:10.1176/appi.ajp.162.5.883

McGlashan, Thomas H. (1987). Testing DSM-III symptoms criteria for schizotypal and borderline personality disorders. *Archives of General Psychiatry, 44*(2), 143–148. doi:10.1001/archpsyc.1987.01800140045007

McGowan, A., King, H., Frankenburg, F. R., Fitzmaurice, G., & Zanarini, M. C. (2012). The course of adult experiences of abuse in patients with borderline personality disorder and axis II comparison subjects: A 10-year follow up study. *Journal of Personality Disorders, 26*(2), 192–202.

McGuffin, P., & Thapar, A. (1992). The genetics of personality disorder. *The British Journal Of Psychiatry: The Journal Of Mental Science, 160,* 12–23.

Mednick, S. A., Parnas, J., & Schulsinger, F. (1987). The Copenhagen High-Risk Project, 1962-86. *Schizophrenia Bulletin, 13*(3), 485–495.

Meehl, P. E. (1962). Schizotaxia, schizotypy, schizophrenia. *American Psychologist, 17*(12), 827–838. doi:10.1037/ h0041029

Meehl, P. E. (1990). Toward an integrated theory of schizotaxia, schizotypy, and schizophrenia. *Journal of Personality Disorders, 4*(1), 1–99. doi:10.1521/pedi.1990.4.1.1

Meins, E., Jones, S. R., Fernyhough, C., Hurndall, S., & Koronis, P. (2008). Attachment dimensions and schizotypy in a non-clinical sample. *Personality and Individual Differences, 44*(4), 1000–1011. doi:10.1016/j. paid.2007.10.026

Meissner, W. W. (1986). The Oedipus complex and the paranoid process. *The Annual Of Psychoanalysis, 14,* 221–243.

Meissner, W. W. (1988). *Treatment of patients in the borderline spectrum.* Lanham, MD: Jason Aronson. Retrieved from http://ezproxy.shsu.edu/login?url=http://search.ebscohost.com/login.aspx?direct=true&db=psyh&AN= 1989-97140-000&site=ehost-live&scope=site

Meissner, W. W. (1989). Theoretical perspectives. In R. Fine (Ed.), *Current and historical perspectives on the borderline patient* (pp. 161-197). Philadelphia, PA: Brunner/Mazel.

Mellsop, G., Varghese, F., Joshua, S., & Hicks, A. (1982). The reliability of axis II of DSM-III. *The American Journal Of Psychiatry, 139*(10), 1360–1361.

Meloy, J. R. (1988). *The psychopathic mind: Origins, dynamics, and treatment.* Lanham, MD: Jason Aronson. Retrieved from http://ezproxy.shsu.edu/login?url=http://search.ebscohost.com/login.aspx?direct=true&db= psyh&AN=1988-98198-000&site=ehost-live&scope=site

Meloy, J. R. (1992). *Violent attachments.* Lanham, MD: Jason Aronson. Retrieved from http://ezproxy.shsu. edu/login?url=http://search.ebscohost.com/login.aspx?direct=true&db=psyh&AN=1992-98924-000&site=ehost-live&scope=site

Meyer, A. (1904). A review of recent problems. *Nervous and mental diseases* (4th ed.). Baltimore, MD: Williams & Wilkins Co.

Meyer, Bjorn, & Carver, C. S. (2000). Negative childhood accounts, sensitivity and pessimism: A study of avoidant personality disorder features in college students. *Journal of Personality Disorders, 14*(3), 233–248.

Meyer, Björn, Pilkonis, P. A., & Beevers, C. G. (2004). What's in a (neutral) face? Personality disorders, attachment styles, and the appraisal of ambiguous social cues. *Journal Of Personality Disorders, 18*(4), 320–336.

Meyer, R. G., & Deitsch, S. E. (1996). *The clinician's handbook: Integrated diagnostics, assessment, and intervention in adult and adolescent psychopathology (4th ed.).* Needham Heights, MA: Allyn & Bacon. Retrieved from http://

ezproxy.shsu.edu/login?url=http://search.ebscohost.com/login.aspx?direct=true&db=psyh&AN=1996-97385-000&site=ehost-live&scope=site

Mikulincer, M., & Shaver, P. R. (2007). *Attachment in Adulthood: Structure, Dynamics, and Change* (1st ed.). The Guilford Press.

Miller, J. D., Campbell, W. K., & Pilkonis, P. (2007).Narcissistic personality disorder: Relations with distress and functional impairment. *Comprehensive Psychiatry, 48*, 170–177.

Miller, J. D., & Lynam, D. R. (2008). Dependent personality disorder: Comparing an expert generated and empirically derived five-factor model personality disorder count. *Assessment, 15*(1), 4–15.

Miller, J. D., Morse, J. Q., Nolf, K., Stepp, S. D., & Pilkonis, P. A. (2012). Can DSM–IV Borderline personality disorder Be Diagnosed via Dimensional Personality Traits? Implications for the DSM-5 personality disorder Proposal. *Journal of Abnormal Psychology.* Retrieved from http://ezproxy.shsu.edu/login?url=http://search.ebscohost.com/login.aspx?direct=true&db=psyh&AN=2012-06738-001&site=ehost-live&scope=site

Miller, M. B., Useda, D. J., Trull, T. J., Burr, R. M., & Minks-Brown, C. (2004). Paranoid, Schizoid, and Schizotypal personality disorders. *Comprehensive Handbook of Psychopathology* (Third ed., pp. 535–557). Boston: Kluwer Academic Publishers. Retrieved from http://www.springerlink.com/content/plqk1r22x5q54017/

Miller, P., Byrne, M., Hodges, A., Lawrie, S. M., Owens, D. G. C., & Johnstone, E. C. (2002). Schizotypal components in people at high risk of developing schizophrenia: Early findings from the Edinburgh high-risk study. *The British Journal of Psychiatry, 180*(2), 179–184. doi:10.1192/bjp.180.2.179

Millon, T. (1969). *Modern psychopathology: a biosocial approach to maladaptive learning and functioning.* Saunders.

Millon, T. (1981). *Disorders of Personality: DSM-III: Axis II* (1st ed.). New York: John Wiley & Sons.

Millon, T. (1996). Compulsive personality disorders: The conforming pattern. In T. Millon & R. D. Davis (Eds.), *Disorders of personality: DSM-IV and beyond* (pp. 505–539). New York: John Wiley & Sons.

Millon, T. (2011). *Disorders of personality: Introducing a DSM/ICD spectrum from normal to abnormal (3rd ed.).* Hoboken, NJ: New York: John Wiley & Sons. Retrieved from http://ezproxy.shsu.edu/login?url=http://search.ebscohost.com/login.aspx?direct=true&db=psyh&AN=2011-02661-000&site=ehost-live&scope=site

Millon, T., Davis, R., & Millon, C. (1997). *Millon clinical multiaxial inventory-III manual.* Minneapolis, MN: National Computer Systems.

Millon, T., Davis, R., Millon, C., Escovar, L., & Meagher, S. (2000). *Personality disorders in modern life.* Hoboken, NJ: New York: John Wiley & Sons.

Millon, T., Grossman, S., Millon, C., Meagher, S., & Ramnath, R. (2004). *Personality disorders in modern life (2nd ed.).* New York: John Wiley & Sons. Retrieved from http://ezproxy.shsu.edu/login?url=http://search.ebscohost.com/login.aspx?direct=true&db=psyh&AN=2004-18756-000&site=ehost-live&scope=site

Millon, T., Grossman, S., & Tringone, R. (2010). The Millon Personality Spectrometer: A tool for personality spectrum analyses, diagnoses, and treatments. In T. Millon, R. F. Krueger, & E. Simonsen (Eds.), *Contemporary directions in psychopathology: Scientific foundations of the DSM-V and ICD-11.* (pp. 391–416). New York: Guilford Press. Retrieved from http://ezproxy.shsu.edu/login?url=http://search.ebscohost.com/login.aspx?direct=true&db=psyh&AN=2010-13146-021&site=ehost-live&scope=site

Millon, T., Millon, C., & Davis, R. (1994). *Millon clinical multiaxial inventory-III.* Minneapolis, MN: National Computer Systems.

Millon, T., Simonsen, E., & Birket-Smith, M. (1998). Historical conceptions of psychopathy in the United States and Europe. In T. Millon, E. Simonsen, M. Birket-Smith, & R. D. Davis (Eds.), *Psychopathy: Antisocial, criminal, and violent behavior.* (pp. 3–31). New York: Guilford Press. Retrieved from http://ezproxy.shsu.edu/login?url=http://search.ebscohost.com/login.aspx?direct=true&db=psyh&AN=1998-08069-001&site=ehost-live&scope=site

Mittal, V. A., Kalus, O., Bernstein, D. P., & Siever, L. J. (2007). Schizoid personality disorder. *Personality disorders: Toward the DSM-V* (pp. 63–79). Thousand Oaks, CA: Sage Publications, Inc.

Mongrain, M. (1993). Dependency and Self-Criticism located within the five-factor model of personality. *Personality and Individual Differences, 15*(4), 455–462.

Morey, L. C. (1988). Personality disorders in DSM-III and DSM-III-R: Convergence, coverage, and internal consistency. *The American Journal of Psychiatry, 145*(5), 573–577.

Morey, L. C. (1991). *Personality Assessment Inventory: Professional Manual.* Odessa, FL: Psychological Assessment Resources.

Morey, L. C. (2007). *The personality assessment inventory professional manual.* Lutz, FL: Psychological Assessment Resources.

Moss, H. B., Yao, J. K., & Panzak, G. L. (1990). Serotonergic responsivity and behavioral dimensions in antisocial personality disorder with substance abuse. *Biological Psychiatry, 28*(4), 325–338.

Mueser, K. T., Gottlieb, J. D., Cather, C., Glynn, S. M., Zarate, R., Smith, M. F., Clark, R. E., et al. (2012). Antisocial personality disorder in people with co-occurring severe mental illness and substance use disorders: Clinical, functional, and family relationship correlates. *Psychosis: Psychological, Social and Integrative Approaches,* Psychosis and personality disorder, *4*(1), 52–62.

Nannarello, J. J. (1953). Schizoid. *Journal of Nervous and Mental Disease, 118,* 237–249. doi:10.1097/00005053-195309000-00004

Narrow, W. E., Rae, D. S., Robins, L. N., & Regier, D. A. (2002). Revised prevalence based estimates of mental disorders in the United States: using a clinical signficance criterion to reconcile 2 surveys' estimates. *Archives of General Psychiatry, 59*(2), 115–123.

Nathan, P. E. (1998). The DSM-IV and its antecedents: Enhancing syndromal diagnosis. In J. W. Barron (Ed.), *Making diagnosis meaningful: Enhancing evaluation and treatment of psychological disorders.* (pp. 3–27). Washington, DC: American Psychological Association. Retrieved from http://ezproxy.shsu.edu/login?url=http://search.ebscohost.com/login.aspx?direct=true&db=psyh&AN=1998-07858-001&site=ehost-live&scope=site

Nathanson, B. J., & Jamison, S. C. (2011). Psychotherapeutic and pharmacologic treatment of schizotypal personality disorder: The heuristic utility of stressing function over form. *Clinical Case Studies, 10*(5), 395–407. doi:10.1177/1534650111427076

Nestadt, G., Romanoski, A. J., Chahal, R., Merchant, A., Folstein, M. F., Gruenberg, E. M., & McHugh, P. R. (1990). An epidemiological study of histrionic personality disorder. *Psychological Medicine, 20*(2), 413–422.

Nestor, P. G. (2002). Mental disorder and violence: Personality dimensions and clinical features. *The American Journal Of Psychiatry, 159*(12), 1973–1978. doi:10.1176/appi.ajp.159.12.1973

Neumann, C. S., & Walker, E. F. (2003). Neuromotor functioning in adolescents with schizotypal personality disorder: Associations with symptoms and neurocognition. *Schizophrenia Bulletin, 29*(2), 285–298.

Newman, J. P., & Brinkley, C. A. (1998). Psychopathy: Rediscovering Cleckley's Construct. *Psychopathy Research: The Newsletter of the Society for Research in Psychopathology, 9*(1), 1–5, 7–8.

Ng, H. M., & Bornstein, R. F. (2005). Comorbidity of dependent personality disorder and anxiety disorders: A meta-analytic review. *Clinical Psychology: Science and Practice, 12*(4), 395–406.

Nordahl, H. M., & Stiles, T. C. (1997). Perceptions of parental bonding in patients with various personality disorders, lifetime depressive disorders, and healthy controls. *Journal Of personality disorders, 11*(4), 391–402.

O'Neill, F. A., & Kendler, K. S. (1998). Longitudinal study of interpersonal dependency in female twins. *The British Journal Of Psychiatry: The Journal Of Mental Science, 172,* 154–158.

Ogata, S. N., Silk, K. R., Goodrich, S., & Lohr, N. E. (1990). Childhood sexual and physical abuse in adult patients with borderline personality disorder. *The American Journal of Psychiatry, 147*(8), 1008–1013.

Oldham, J M, Skodol, A. E., Kellman, H. D., Hyler, S. E., Doidge, N., Rosnick, L., & Gallaher, P. E. (1995). Comorbidity of axis I and axis II disorders. *The American Journal Of Psychiatry, 152*(4), 571–578.

Oldham, John M., Gabbard, G. O., Goin, M. K., Gunderson, J., Soloff, P., Spiegel, D., Stone, M., et al. (2002). Practice guideline for the treatment of patients with borderlne personality disorder. In N. C. Numerous Contributors

(Ed.), *American Psychiatric Association practice guidelines for the treatment of psychiatric disorders: Compendium 2002.* (pp. 767–855). Washington, DC: American Psychiatric Association. Retrieved from http://ezproxy.shsu.edu/login?url=http://search.ebscohost.com/login.aspx?direct=true&db=psyh&AN=2002-17057-011&site=ehost-live&scope=site

Olin, S. S., Raine, A., Cannon, T. D., Parnas, J., & et al. (1997). Childhood behavior precursors of schizotypal personality disorder. *Schizophrenia Bulletin, 23*(1), 93–103.

Onishi, M., Gjerde, P. F., & Block, J. (2001). Personality implications of romantic attachment patterns in young adults: A multi-method, multi-informant study. *Personality and Social Psychology Bulletin, 27*(9), 1097–1110. doi:10.1177/0146167201279003

Otway, L. J., & Vignoles, V. L. (2006). Narcissism and Childhood Recollections: A Quantitative Test of Psychoanalytic Predictions. *Personality and Social Psychology Bulletin, 32*(1), 104–116.

Padilla, A. M. (1995). *Hispanic psychology: Critical issues in theory and research.* (A. M. Padilla, Ed.). Thousand Oaks, CA: Sage Publications, Inc. Retrieved from http://ezproxy.shsu.edu/login?url=http://search.ebscohost.com/login.aspx?direct=true&db=psyh&AN=1996-97115-000&site=ehost-live&scope=site

Paris, J. (1994). The etiology of borderline personality disorder: A biopsychosocial approach. *Psychiatry: Interpersonal and Biological Processes, 57*(4), 316–325.

Paris, J. (1997). Childhood trauma as an etiological factor in the personality disorders. *Journal of Personality Disorders, 11*(1), 34–49.

Paris, J. (1999). Borderline personality disorder. In T. Millon, P. H. Blaney, & R. D. Davis (Eds.), *Oxford textbook of psychopathology.*, Vol. 4 (pp. 628–652). New York: Oxford University Press. Retrieved from http://ezproxy.shsu.edu/login?url=http://search.ebscohost.com/login.aspx?direct=true&db=psyh&AN=1999-04377-025&site=ehost-live&scope=site

Paris, J. (2003). *Personality disorders over time: Precursors, course, and outcome.* Arlington, VA: American Psychiatric Publishing, Inc. Retrieved from http://ezproxy.shsu.edu/login?url=http://search.ebscohost.com/login.aspx?direct=true&db=psyh&AN=2003-00332-000&site=ehost-live

Parker, G., & Lipscombe, P. (1980). The relevance of early parental experiences to adult dependency, hypochondriasis and utilization of primary physicians. *The British Journal Of Medical Psychology, 53*(4), 355–363.

Patrick, C. J. (2007). Antisocial personality disorder and psychopathy. In W. O'Donohue, K. A. Fowler, & S. O. Lilienfeld (Eds.), *Personality disorders: Toward the DSM-V.* (pp. 109–166). Thousand Oaks, CA: Sage Publications, Inc. Retrieved from http://ezproxy.shsu.edu/login?url=http://search.ebscohost.com/login.aspx?direct=true&db=psyh&AN=2007-00410-006&site=ehost-live&scope=site

Perry, J. Christopher, & Klerman, G. L. (1978). The borderline patient: A comparative analysis of four sets of diagnostic criteria. *Archives of General Psychiatry, 35*(2), 141–150.

Perry, J. Christopher, & Klerman, G. L. (1980). Clinical features of the borderline personality disorder. *The American Journal of Psychiatry, 137*(2), 165–173.

Petrides, K. V., Pérez-González, J. C., & Furnham, A. (2007). On the criterion and incremental validity of trait emotional intelligence. *Cognition and Emotion, 21*(1), 26–55.

Pfohl, B. (1991). Histrionic personality disorder: A review of available data and recommendations for DSM-IV. *Journal of Personality Disorders,* Special Series: DSM-IV and personality disorders, *5*(2), 150–166.

Pfohl, B., & Blum, N. S. (1991). Obsessive-compulsive personality disorder: A review of available data and recommendations for DSM-IV. *Journal of Personality Disorders, 5*(4), 363–375.

Pfohl, B., Blum, N., & Zimmerman, M. (1997). *Structured Interview for DSM-IV Personality: SIDP-IV.* American Psychiatric Pub.

Pfohl, B., Blum, N., Zimmerman, M., & Stangl, D. (1989). *Structured interview for DSM-III-R Personality SIDP-R.* Department of Psychiatry: University of Iowa.

Phillips, K. A., Stein, D. J., Rauch, S. L., Hollander, E., Fallon, B. A., Barsky, A., Fineberg, N., et al. (2010). Should an obsessive-compulsive spectrum grouping of disorders be included in DSM-V? *Depression and Anxiety, 27*(6), 528–555.

Pincus, A. L., & Gurtman, M. B. (1995). The three faces of interpersonal dependency: Structural analyses of self-report dependency measures. *Journal of Personality and Social Psychology, 69*(4), 744–758.

Pinel, P. (1806). *A treatise on insanity.* London, U.K.: Messers Cadell & Davies, Strand. Retrieved from http://ezproxy.shsu.edu/login?url=http://search.ebscohost.com/login.aspx?direct=true&db=psyh&AN=2004-16221-000&site=ehost-live&scope=site

Polatin, P. (1975). Paranoid States. *Comprehensive Textbook of Psychiatry-II* (Vols. 1-2, Vol. 1, pp. 992–1002). Baltimore, MD: Williams and Wilkins.

Poldrugo, F., & Forti, B. (1988). Personality disorders and alcoholism treatment outcome. *Drug And Alcohol Dependence, 21*(3), 171–176.

Pollak, J. M. (1979). Obsessive-compulsive personality: A review. *Psychological Bulletin, 86*(2), 225–241.

Pollock, V. E., Briere, J., Schneider, L., & Knop, J. (1990). Childhood antecedents of antisocial behavior: Parental alcoholism and physical abusiveness. *The American Journal of Psychiatry, 147*(10), 1290–1293.

Pretzer, J. L. (1990). Borderline personality disorder. In A. T. Beck & A. Freeman (Eds.), *Cognitive therapy of personality disorders* (pp. 176–207). New York: Guilford Press.

Pretzer, James L., & Beck, A. T. (2005). A cognitive theory of personality disorders. In Mark F. Lenzenweger & J. F. Clarkin (Eds.), *Major theories of personality disorder (2nd ed).* (pp. 43–113). New York: Guilford Press. Retrieved from http://ezproxy.shsu.edu/login?url=http://search.ebscohost.com/login.aspx?direct=true&db=psyh&AN=2005-02797-002&site=ehost-live&scope=site

Pulay, A. J., Stinson, F. S., Dawson, D. A., Goldstein, R. B., Chou, S. P., Huang, B., Saha, T. D., et al. (2009). Prevalence, correlates, disability, and comorbidity of DSM-IV schizotypal personality disorder: results from the wave 2 national epidemiologic survey on alcohol and related conditions. *Primary Care Companion to the Journal of Clinical Psychiatry, 11*(2), 53–67.

Quality Assurance Project. (1991). Treatment outlines for borderline, narcissistic and histrionic personality disorders. *Australian and New Zealand Journal of Psychiatry, 25*(3), 392–403.

Rado, S. (1953). Dynamics and classification of disordered behavior. *The American Journal of Psychiatry, 110,* 406–426.

Raine, A. (1991). The SPQ: A Scale for the Assessment of Schizotypal Personality Based on DSM-III-R Criteria. *Schizophrenia Bulletin, 17*(4), 555–564. doi:10.1093/schbul/17.4.555

Raine, A., & Benishay, D. (1995). The SPQ-B: A brief screening instrument for schizotypal personality disorder. *Journal of Personality Disorders, 9*(4), 346–355. doi:10.1521/pedi.1995.9.4.346

Raine, A., Lee, L., Yang, Y., & Colletti, P. (2010). Neurodevelopmental marker for limbic maldevelopment in antisocial personality disorder and psychopathy. *The British Journal of Psychiatry, 197*(3), 186–192.

Raskin, R. N., & Hall, C. S. (1979). A narcissistic personality inventory. *Psychological Reports, 45*(2). Retrieved from http://ezproxy.shsu.edu/login?url=http://search.ebscohost.com/login.aspx?direct=true&db=psyh&AN=1981-08131-001&site=ehost-live&scope=site

Rathus, J. H., Sanderson, W. C., Miller, A. L., & Wetzler, S. (1995). Impact of personality functioning on cognitive behavioral treatment of panic disorder: A preliminary report. *Journal of Personality Disorders, 9*(2), 160–168.

Reich, D. B., & Zanarini, M. C. (2001). Developmental aspects of borderline personality disorder. *Harvard Review of Psychiatry, 9*(6), 294–301.

Reich, J. (2002). Drug treatment of personality disorder traits. *Psychiatric Annals, 32*(10), 590–596.

Reich, W. (1949). *Character-analysis (3rd ed.).* Character-analysis (3rd ed.). Oxford, U.K.: Orgone Institute Press. Retrieved from http://ezproxy.shsu.edu/login?url=http://search.ebscohost.com/login.aspx?direct=true&db=psyh&AN=1949-06242-000&site=ehost-live&scope=site

Reichborn-Kjennerud, T., Czajkowski, N., Neale, M. C., Ørstavik, R. E., Torgersen, S., Tambs, K., Røysamb, E., et al. (2007). Genetic and environmental influences on dimensional representations of DSM-IV cluster C personality disorders: A population-based multivariate twin study. *Psychological Medicine, 37*(5), 645–653.

Reid, W. H., Balis, G. U., Wicoff, J. S., & Tomasovic, J. J. (1989). *The treatment of psychiatric disorders: Revised for the DSM-III-R.* Philadelphia, PA: Brunner/Mazel. Retrieved from http://ezproxy.shsu.edu/login?url=http://search. ebscohost.com/login.aspx?direct=true&db=psyh&AN=1989-97069-000&site=ehost-live&scope=site

Rhee, S. H., & Waldman, I. D. (2002). Genetic and environmental influences on antisocial behavior: A meta-analysis of twin and adoption studies. *Psychological Bulletin, 128*(3), 490–529.

Riggs, S. A., Paulson, A., Tunnell, E., Sahl, G., Atkison, H., & Ross, C. A. (2007). Attachment, personality, and psychopathology among adult inpatients: Self-reported romantic attachment style versus adult attachment interview states of mind. *Development and Psychopathology, 19*(01), 263–291. doi:10.1017/ S0954579407070149

Rinne, T., van den Brink, W., Wouters, L., & van Dyck, R. (2002). SSRI treatment of borderline personality disorder: A randomized, placebo-controlled clinical trial for female patients with borderline personality disorder. *The American Journal of Psychiatry, 159*(12), 2048–2054.

Robins, L. N. (1966). *Deviant children grown up: A sociological and psychiatric study of sociopathic personality.* Oxford, U.: Williams & Wilkins. Retrieved from http://ezproxy.shsu.edu/login?url=http://search.ebscohost.com/ login.aspx?direct=true&db=psyh&AN=1966-13320-000&site=ehost-live&scope=site

Robins, L. N., Tipp, J., & Przybeck, T. (1991). Antisocial personality. *Psychiatric disorders in America* (pp. 258–290). New York: Free Press.

Rocca, P., Marchiaro, L., Cocuzza, E., & Bogetto, F. (2002). Treatment of borderline personality disorder with risperidone. *Journal of Clinical Psychiatry, 63*(3), 241–244.

Rogers, R., Salekin, R. T., Sewell, K. W., & Cruise, K. R. (2000). Protoypical analysis of antisocial personality disorder: A study of inmate samples. *Criminal Justice and Behavior, 27*(2), 234–255.

Ronningstam, E. (2011). Narcissistic personality disorder: A clinical perspective. *Journal of Psychiatric Practice, 17,* 89 –99. doi:10.1097/01.pra.0000396060.67150.40

Ronningstam, E., & Gunderson, J. G. (1990). Identifying criteria for narcissistic personality disorder. *The American Journal of Psychiatry, 147*(7), 918–922.

Rosenstein, D. S., & Horowitz, H. A. (1996). Adolescent attachment and psychopathology. *Journal of Consulting and Clinical Psychology,* Special Section: Attachment and Psychopathology, Part 2., *64*(2), 244–253.

Rothbart, M. K., & Ahadi, S. A. (1994). Temperament and the development of personality. *Journal of Abnormal Psychology, 103*(1), 55–66.

Rush, B. (1835). *Medical Inquiries and Observations Upon the Diseases of the Mind.* Grigg and Elliot.

Russ, E., Shedler, J., Bradley, R., & Westen, D. (2008). Refining the construct of narcissistic personality disorder: Diagnostic criteria and subtypes. *The American Journal of Psychiatry, 165*(11), 1473–1481.

Sadock, B. J., & Sadock, V. A. (2007). *Kaplan & Sadock's synopsis of psychiatry: Behavioral sciences/clinical psychiatry (10th ed.).* Philadelphia: Lippincott Williams & Wilkins Publishers.

Samuels, J., Eaton, W. W., Bienvenu, O. J., 3rd, Brown, C. H., Costa, P. T., Jr, & Nestadt, G. (2002). Prevalence and correlates of personality disorders in a community sample. *The British Journal of Psychiatry: The Journal of Mental Science, 180,* 536–542.

Sanislow, C., Morey, L. C., Grilo, C. M., Gunderson, J. G., Shea, M. T., Skodol, A. E., Stout, R. L., et al. (2002). Confirmatory factor analysis of DSM-IV borderline, schizotypal, avoidant and obsessive-compulsive personality disorders: findings from the Collaborative Longitudinal Personality Disorders Study. *Acta Psychiatrica Scandinavica, 105*(1), 28–36.

Sansone, R. A., & Sansone, L. A. (2009). The families of borderline patients: The psychological environment revisited. *Psychiatry, 6*(2), 19–24.

Sargent, C. (2003). Gender, body, meaning: Anthropological perspectives on self-Injury and borderline personality disorder. *Philosophy, Psychiatry, & Psychology, 10*(1), 25–27.

Saxe, G. N., Van der Kolk, B. A., Berkowitz, R., & Chinman, G. (1993). Dissociative disorders in psychiatric inpatients. *The American Journal of Psychiatry, 150*(7), 1037–1042.

Schulz, S. C., Camlin, K. L., Berry, S. A., & Jesberger, J. A. (1999). Olanzapine safety and efficacy in patients with borderline personality disorder and comorbid dysthymia. *Biological Psychiatry, 46*(10), 1429–1435. doi:10.1016/S0006-3223(99)00128-6

Sellbom, M., Ben-Porath, Y. S., Lilienfeld, S. O., Patrick, C. J., & Graham, J. R. (2005). Assessing psychopathic personality traits with the MMPI-2. *Journal of Personality Assessment, 85*(3), 334–343.

Shapiro, D. (1965). *Neurotic styles.* Neurotic styles. Oxford, UK: Basic Books. Retrieved from http://ezproxy. shsu.edu/login?url=http://search.ebscohost.com/login.aspx?direct=true&db=psyh&AN=1965-35023-000&site=ehost-live&scope=site

Shearer, S. L. (1994). Dissociative phenomena in women with borderline personality disorder. *The American Journal Of Psychiatry, 151*(9), 1324–1328.

Sheldon, W. H., & Stevens, S. S. (1942). *The varieties of temperament; a psychology of constitutional differences.* Oxford England: Harper.

Sheldon, A. E., & West, M. (1990). Attachment pathology and low social skills in avoidant personality disorder: An exploratory study. *The Canadian Journal of Psychiatry/La Revue canadienne de psychiatrie, 35*(7), 596–599.

Siever, L. J., Bernstein, D. P., & Silverman, J. M. (1991). Schizotypal personality disorder: A review of its current status. *Journal of Personality Disorders, 5*(2), 178–193. doi:10.1521/pedi.1991.5.2.178

Siever, L. J., & Davis, K. L. (1991). A psychobiological perspective on the personality disorders. *The American Journal of Psychiatry, 148*(12), 1647–1658.

Silk, K. R., Lee, S., Hill, E. M., & Lohr, N. E. (1995). Borderline personality disorder symptoms and severity of sexual abuse. *The American Journal Of Psychiatry, 152*(7), 1059–1064.

Simeon, S., & Hollander, E. (2006). Treatment of personality disorders. *Essential of Clinical Psychopharmacology* (Second., pp. 689–705). Washington, DC: American Psychiatric Association.

Simon, W. (2009). Follow-up psychotherapy outcome of patients with dependent, avoidant and obsessive-compulsive personality disorders: A meta-analytic review. *International Journal of Psychiatry in Clinical Practice, 13*(2), 153–165.

Simons, C. P., Wichers, M. M., Derom, C. C., Thiery, E. E., Myin-Germeys, I. I., Krabbendam, L. L., & van Os, J. J. (2009). Subtle gene-environment interactions driving paranoia in daily life. *Genes, Brain & Behavior, 8*(1), 5–12. doi:10.1111/j.1601-183X.2008.00434.x

Sinclair, H., & Feigenbaum, J. (2012). Trait emotional intelligence and borderline personality disorder. *Personality and Individual Differences, 52*(6), 674–679.

Skodol, A. E., Clark, L. A., Bender, D. S., Krueger, R. F., Morey, L. C., Verheul, R., Alarcon, R. D., et al. (2011). Proposed changes in personality and personality disorder assessment and diagnosis for DSM-5 Part I: Description and rationale. *personality disorders: Theory, Research, and Treatment,* Personality and personality disorders in the DSM-5, *2*(1), 4–22.

Skodol, A. E., Gunderson, J. G., McGlashan, T. H., Dyck, I. R., Stout, R. L., Bender, D. S., Grilo, C. M., et al. (2002). Functional impairment in patients with schizotypal, borderline, avoidant, or obsessive-compulsive personality disorder. *The American Journal of Psychiatry, 159*(2), 276–283.

Skodol, A. E., Gunderson, J. G., Pfohl, B., Widiger, T. A., Livesley, W. J., & Siever, L. J. (2002). The borderline diagnosis I: Psychopathology, comorbidity, and personality structure. *Biological Psychiatry, 51*(12), 936–950.

Skodol, A. E., Siever, L. J., Livesley, W. J., Gunderson, J. G., Pfohl, B., & Widiger, T. A. (2002). The borderline diagnosis II: Biology, genetics, and clinical course. *Biological Psychiatry, 51*(12), 951–963.

Smith, A. M., Gacono, C. B., & Kaufman, L. (1997). A Rorschach comparison of psychopathic and nonpsychopathic conduct disordered adolescents. *Journal of Clinical Psychology, 53*(4), 289–300.

Smith, T. L., Klein, M. H., & Benjamin, L. S. (2003). Validation of the Wisconsin Personality Disorders Inventory-IV with the SCID-II. *Journal of Personality Disorders, 17*(3), 173–187.

Smolewska, K., & Dion,, K. (2005). Narcissism and adult attachment: A multivariate approach. *Self & Identity, 4*(1), 59–68. doi:Article

Solano, J. J. R., & De Chávez, M. G. (2000). Premorbid personality disorders in schizophrenia. *Schizophrenia Research, 44*(2), 137–144. doi:10.1016/S0920-9964(99)00203-0

Soloff, P. H. (1998). Algorithms for pharmacological treatment of personality dimensions: Symptom-specific treatments for cognitive-perceptual, affective, and impulsive-behavioral dysregulation. *Bulletin of the Menninger Clinic, 62*(2), 195–214.

Soloff, P. H., George, A., Nathan, R. S., Schulz, P. M., & et al. (1989). Amitriptyline versus haloperidol in borderlines: Final outcomes and predictors of response. *Journal of Clinical Psychopharmacology, 9*(4), 238–246. doi:10.1097/00004714-198908000-00002

Soloff, P. H., & Millward, J. W. (1983). Developmental histories of borderline patients. *Comprehensive Psychiatry, 24*(6), 574–588.

Sperry, L. (2003). *Handbook of Diagnosis and Treatment of DSM-IV-TR personality disorders* (2nd ed.). Routledge.

Sperry, L. (2006). *Cognitive behavior therapy of DSM-IV-TR personality disorders: Highly effective interventions for the most common personality disorders (2nd ed.)*. New York: Routledge/Taylor & Francis Group.

Spitzer, R. L., Endicott, J., & Gibbon, M. (1979). Crossing the border into borderline personality and borderline schizophrenia: The development of criteria. *Archives of General Psychiatry, 36*(1), 17–24. doi:10.1001/archpsyc.1979.01780010023001

Spitzer, R. L., Endicott, J., & Robins, E. (1975). Clinical criteria for psychiatric diagnosis and DSM-III. *The American Journal of Psychiatry, 132*(11), 1187–1192.

Spitzer, R. L., Endicott, J., & Robins, E. (1978). Research diagnostic criteria: Rationale and reliability. *Archives of General Psychiatry, 35*(6), 773–782.

Spitzer, R. L., Williams, J. B., & Skodol, A. E. (1980). DSM-III: The major achievements and an overview. *The American Journal of Psychiatry, 137*(2), 151–164.

Sprague, J., Javdani, S., Sadeh, N., Newman, J. P., & Verona, E. (2012). Borderline personality disorder as a female phenotypic expression of psychopathy? *personality disorders: Theory, Research, and Treatment, 3*(2), 127–139.

Sprock, J., Blashfield, R. K., & Smith, B. (1990). Gender weighting of DSM-III—R personality disorder criteria. *The American Journal of Psychiatry, 147*(5), 586–590.

Sroufe, L., Fox, N. E., & Pancake, V. R. (1983). Attachment and dependency in developmental perspective. *Child Development, 54*(6), 1615–1627.

Stein, D. J. (2000). Neurobiology of the obsessive-compulsive spectrum disorders. *Biological Psychiatry, 47*, 296–304.

Stern, A. (1938). Borderline group of neuroses. *The Psychoanalytic Quarterly, 7*, 467–489.

Stern, J., Murphy, M., & Bass, C. (1993). Personality disorders in patients with somatisation disorder: A controlled study. *The British Journal of Psychiatry, 163*, 785–789.

Stone, M. (1985). Schizotypal Personality: Psychotherapeutic Aspects. *Schizophrenia Bulletin, 11*(4), 576–589.

Stone, M. H. (1983). Psychotherapy with schizotypal borderline patients. *Journal of the American Academy of Psychoanalysis, 11*(1), 87–111.

Stout, M. (2005). *The Sociopath Next Door* (1st ed.). Broadway Books.

Stravynski, A., Elie, R., & Franche, R.-L. (1989). Perception of early parenting by patients diagnosed avoidant personality disorder: A test of the overprotection hypothesis. *Acta Psychiatrica Scandinavica, 80*(5), 415–420.

Stinson, F.S., Dawson, D.A., Goldstein, R.B., Chou, S.P., Huang, B., Smith, S.M., Ruan, W.J., Pulay, A.J., Saha, T.D., Pickering, R.P., & Grant, B.F. (2008). Prevalence, correlates, disability, and comorbidity of DSM-IV narcissistic personality disorder: results from the wave 2 national epidemiologic survey on alcohol and related conditions. *The Journal of Clinical Psychology*, 69 (7), 1033–1045.

Stuart, S., Pfohl, B., Battaglia, M., Bellodi, L., Grove, W., & Cadoret, R. (1998). The cooccurrence of DSM-III-R personality disorders. *Journal of Personality Disorders*, *12*(4), 302–315.

Sulkowski, M. L., Mariaskin, A., & Storch, E. (2011). Obsessive-Compulsive Spectrum Disorder Symptoms in College Students. *Journal of American College Health*, *59*(5), 342–348.

Sutker, P. B., & Allain, A. N. J. (2001). Antisocial personality disorder. In P. B. Sutker & H. E. Adams (Eds.), *Comprehensive handbook of psychopathology (3rd ed.)*. (pp. 445–490). New York: Kluwer Academic/ Plenum Publishers. Retrieved from http://ezproxy.shsu.edu/login?url=http://search.ebscohost.com/login. aspx?direct=true&db=psyh&AN=2001-01406-016&site=ehost-live&scope=site

Svartberg, M., Stiles, T. C., & Seltzer, M. H. (2004). Randomized, Controlled Trial of the Effectiveness of Short-Term Dynamic Psychotherapy and Cognitive Therapy for cluster C personality disorders. *The American Journal of Psychiatry*, *161*(5), 810–817.

Symington, N. (1980). The response aroused by the psychopath. *The International Journal of Psychoanalysis*, *7*(3), 291–298.

Tadić, A., Wagner, S., Hoch, J., Başkaya, Ö., von Cube, R., Skaletz, C., Lieb, K., et al. (2009). Gender differences in axis I and axis II comorbidity in patients with borderline personality disorder. *Psychopathology*, *42*(4), 257–263.

Taylor, J., Loney, B. R., Bobadillo, L., Iacono, W. G., & McGue, M. (2003). Genetic and environmental influence on psychopathy trait dimensions in a community sample of male twins. *Journal of Abnormal Child Psychology*, *31*, 633–645.

Taylor, S., Asmundson, G. J. G., & Jang, K. L. (2011). Etiology of obsessive–compulsive symptoms and obsessive–compulsive personality traits: Common genes, mostly different environments. *Depression and Anxiety*, *28*(10), 863–869.

Thomas, A., & Chess, S. (1977). *Temperament and development*. Oxford England: Brunner/Mazel. Retrieved from http:// ezproxy.shsu.edu/login?url=http://search.ebscohost.com/login.aspx?direct=true&db=psyh&AN=1978-03178-000&site=ehost-live&scope=site

Tiliopoulos, N., & Goodall, K. (2009). The neglected link between adult attachment and schizotypal personality traits. *Personality and Individual Differences*, *47*(4), 299–304. doi:10.1016/j.paid.2009.03.017

Tillfors, M., Furmark, T., Ekselius, L., & Fredrikson, M. (2001). Social phobia and avoidant personality disorder as related to parental history of social anxiety: A general population study. *Behaviour Research and Therapy*, *39*(3), 289–298.

Torgersen, S, Kringlen, E., & Cramer, V. (2001). The prevalence of personality disorders in a community sample. *Archives Of General Psychiatry*, *58*(6), 590–596.

Torgersen, S, Lygren, S., Oien, P. A., Skre, I., Onstad, S., Edvardsen, J., Tambs, K., et al. (2000). A twin study of personality disorders. *Comprehensive Psychiatry*, *41*(6), 416–425.

Torgersen, S., Czajkowski, N., Jacobson, K., Reichborn-Kjennerud, T., Røysamb, E., Neale, M. C., & Kendler, K. S. (2008). Dimensional representations of DSM-IV cluster B personality disorders in a population-based sample of Norwegian twins: A multivariate study. *Psychological Medicine*, *38*(11), 1617–1625.

Torgersen, Svenn, Onstad, S., Skre, I., Edvardsen, J., & et al. (1993). "True" schizotypal personality disorder: A study of co-twins and relatives of schizophrenic probands. *The American Journal of Psychiatry*, *150*(11), 1661–1667.

Trull, T. J. (2001). Structural relations between borderline personality disorder features and putative etiological correlates. *Journal of Abnormal Psychology*, *110*(3), 471–481.

Trull, T. J., & Widiger, T. A. (2003). Personality disorders. In G. Stricker, T. A. Widiger, & I. B. Weiner (Eds.), *Handbook of psychology: Clinical psychology, Vol. 8.* (pp. 149–172). Hoboken, NJ: JJohn Wiley & Sons Inc. Retrieved from http://ezproxy.shsu.edu/login?url=http://search.ebscohost.com/login.aspx?direct= true&db=psyh&AN=2003-04685-006&site=ehost-live&scope=site

Turkat, I., & Maisto, S. A. (1985). Personality disorders: Application of the experimental method to the formulation and modification of personality disorders. In D. H. Barlow (Ed.), *Clinical handbook of psychological disorders: A step-by-step treatment manual* (pp. 502–570). New York: Guilford Press.

Twenge, J.M., & Campbell, W.K. (2009) *The narcissism epidemic: Living in the age of entitlement.* New York: Free Press.

Tyrer, P., & Bateman, A. W. (2004).Drug treatments for personality disorder. *Advances in Psychiatric Treatment, 10,* 389–398.

Tyrer, P., Mitchard, S., Methuen, C., & Ranger, M. (2003). Treatment-rejecting and treatment-seeking personality disorders: Type R and Type S. *Journal Of Personality Disorders, 17*(3), 263–267. doi:10.1521/ pedi.17.3.263.22152

UK Department of Health, Hospital Episode Statistics (2010). The Health and Social Care Information Centre.

Veith, I. (1977). Four thousand years of hysteria. In M. Horowitz (Ed.), *Hysterical Personality* (pp. 7–23). New York: Jason Aronson.

Verona, E., Sprague, J., & Sadeh, N. (2012). Inhibitory control and negative emotional processing in psychopathy and antisocial personality disorder. *Journal of Abnormal Psychology, 121*(2), 498–510.

Wagner, E. E., & Wagner, C. F. (1981). *The Interpretation of Projective Test Data.* Springfield, IL: Charles Thomas.

Walker, C., Thomas, J., & Allen, T. S. (2003). Treating impulsivity, irritability, and aggression of antisocial personality disorder with quetiapine. *International Journal of Offender Therapy and Comparative Criminology, 47*(5), 556–567.

Walker, E. F., Baum, K. M., & Diforio, D. (1998). Developmental changes in the behavioral expression of vulnerability for schizophrenia. *Origins and development of schizophrenia: Advances in experimental psychopathology* (pp. 469–491). Washington, DC: American Psychological Association.

Walker, E. F., Grimes, K. E., Davis, D. M., & Smith, A. J. (1993). Childhood precursors of schizophrenia: Facial expressions of emotion. *The American Journal of Psychiatry, 150*(11), 1654–1660.

Walker, R. (1992). Substance abuse and B-cluster disorders: II. Treatment recommendations. *Journal of Psychoactive Drugs, 24*(3), 233–241.

Walsh, A., & Wu, H.-H. (2008). Differentiating antisocial personality disorder, psychopathy, and sociopathy: Evolutionary, genetic, neurological, and sociological considerations. *Criminal Justice Studies: A Critical Journal of Crime, Law & Society, 21*(2), 135–152.

Weaver, T. L., & Clum, G. A. (1993). Early family environments and traumatic experiences associated with borderline personality disorder. *Journal of Consulting and Clinical Psychology, 61*(6), 1068–1075.

Webb, C. T., & Levinson, D. F. (1993). Schizotypal and paranoid personality disorder in the relatives of patients with schizophrenia and affective disorders: A review. *Schizophrenia Research, 11*(1), 81–92. doi:10.1016/0920- 9964(93)90041-G

Weber, C. A., Meloy, J. R., & Gacono, C. B. (1992). A Rorschach study of attachment and anxiety in inpatient conduct-disordered and dysthymic adolescents. *Journal of Personality Assessment, 58*(1), 16. doi:Article

West, M., Rose, S., & Sheldon-Keller, A. (1994). Assessment of patterns of insecure attachment in adults and application to dependent and schizoid personality disorders. *Journal of Personality Disorders, 8*(3), 249–256. doi:10.1521/pedi.1994.8.3.249

Widiger, T. A., & Trull, T. J. (1998). Performance characteristics of the DSM-III-R personality disorder criteria sets. In Thomas A. Widiger (Ed.), *DSM-IV sourcebook* (Vol. 4, pp. 357–363). Washington, DC: American Psychiatric Association.

Widiger, T. A., & Weissman, M. M. (1991). Epidemiology of borderline personality disorder. *Hospital & Community Psychiatry, 42*(10), 1015–1021.

Widiger, Thomas A. (1995). Deletion of self-defeating and sadistic personality disorders. In W. J. Livesley (Ed.), *The DSM-IV personality disorders.*, Diagnosis and treatment of mental disorders (pp. 359–373). New York: Guilford Press. Retrieved from http://ezproxy.shsu.edu/login?url=http://search.ebscohost.com/login.aspx?direct=true&db=psyh&AN=1995-98726-017&site=ehost-live&scope=site

Widiger, Thomas A. (1998). Sex biases in the diagnosis of personality disorders. *Journal of Personality Disorders, 12*(2), 95–118.

Widiger, Thomas A. (2006). Psychopathy and DSM-IV Psychopathology. In C. J. Patrick (Ed.), *Handbook of psychopathy.* (pp. 156–171). New York: Guilford Press. Retrieved from http://ezproxy.shsu.edu/login?url=http://search.ebscohost.com/login.aspx?direct=true&db=psyh&AN=2006-01001-008&site=ehost-live&scope=site

Widiger, Thomas A., & Bornstein, R. F. (2001). Histrionics, dependent, and narcissistic personality disorders. In P. B. Sutker & H. E. Adams (Eds.), *Comprehensive handbook of psychopathology (3rd ed.).* (pp. 509–531). New York: Kluwer Academic/Plenum Publishers. Retrieved from http://ezproxy.shsu.edu/login?url=http://search.ebscohost.com/login.aspx?direct=true&db=psyh&AN=2001-01406-018&site=ehost-live&scope=site

Widiger, Thomas A., Frances, A., Spitzer, R. L., & Williams, J. B. (1988). The DSM-III-R personality disorders: An overview. *The American Journal of Psychiatry, 145*(7), 786–795.

Widiger, Thomas A., & Rogers, J. H. (1989). Prevalence and comorbidity of personality disorders. *Psychiatric Annals, 19*(3), 132–136.

Widiger, Thomas A., & Trull, T. J. (1987). Behavioral indicators, hypothetical constructs, and personality disorders. *Journal of Personality Disorders, 1*(1), 82–87.

Williams, J. M. G., Watts, F. N., MacLeod, C., & Mathews, A. (1997). *Cognitive psychology and emotional disorders.* Chichester, UK: John Wiley & Sons.

Wilde, O. (1890). *The picture of dorian gray.* New York: Signet Classic.

Wink, P. (1991). Two faces of narcissism. *Journal of Personality and Social Psychology, 61*(4), 590–597.

Wolff, S., & McGuire, R. J. (1995). Schizoid personality in girls: a follow-up study—what are the links with Asperger's syndrome? *Journal of Child Psychology and Psychiatry, and Allied Disciplines, 36*(5), 793–817.

World Health Organization. (1993). *The ICD-10 Classification of Mental and Behavioural Disorders: Diagnostic Criteria for Research.* Geneva: WHO.

Wright, N., & Owen, S. (2001). Feminist conceptualizations of women's madness: a review of the literature. *Journal Of Advanced Nursing, 36*(1), 143–150.

Yalom, I. D., & Leszcz, M. (2005). *The theory and practice of group psychotherapy (5th ed.).* New York: Basic Books.

Yen, S., Shea, M. T., Battle, C. L., Johnson, D. M., Zlotnick, C., Dolan-Sewell, R., Skodol, A. E., et al. (2002). Traumatic exposure and posttraumatic stress disorder in borderline, schizotypal, avoidant, and obsessive-compulsive personality disorders: findings from the collaborative longitudinal personality disorders study. *The Journal Of Nervous And Mental Disease, 190*(8), 510–518.

Yontef, G. (2001). Psychotherapy of schizoid process. *Transactional Analysis Journal, 31*(1), 7–23.

Young, J., & Klosko, J. (2005). Schema therapy. In J. M. Oldham, A. E. Skodol, D. S. Bender (Eds.), *The American Psychiatric Publishing textbook of personality disorders* (pp. 289–306). Arlington, VA: American Psychiatric Publishing, Inc.

Zanarini, M. C., Horwood, J., Waylen, A., & Wolke, D. (2004). *The UK verison of the childhood interview for DSM-IV borderline personality disorder (UK-CI-BPD).* Bristol, England: University of Bristol, Department of Community Medicine Unit of Perinatal and Pediatric Epidemiology.

Zanarini, Mary C, Yong, L., Frankenburg, F. R., Hennen, J., Reich, D. B., Marino, M. F., & Vujanovic, A. A. (2002). Severity of reported childhood sexual abuse and its relationship to severity of borderline psychopathology and psychosocial impairment among borderline inpatients. *The Journal Of Nervous And Mental Disease, 190*(6), 381–387.

Zanarini, Mary C., Frankenburg, F. R., Chauncey, D. L., & Gunderson, J. G. (1987). The Diagnostic Interview for personality disorders: Interrater and test-retest reliability. *Comprehensive Psychiatry, 28*(6), 467–480. doi:10.1016/0010-440X(87)90012-5

Zanarini, Mary C., Frankenburg, F. R., Dubo, E. D., Sickel, A. E., Trikha, A., Levin, A., & Reynolds, V. (1998). Axis II comorbidity of borderline personality disorder. *Comprehensive Psychiatry, 39*(5), 296–302.

Zanarini, Mary C., Frankenburg, F. R., Yong, L., Raviola, G., Reich, D. B., Hennen, J., Hudson, J. I., et al. (2004). Borderline Psychopathology in the First-degree Relatives of Borderline and Axis II Comparison Probands. *Journal of Personality Disorders, 18*(5), 449–447.

Zanarini, Mary C., & Gunderson, J. G. (1997). Differential diagnosis of antisocial and borderline personality disorders. In D. M. Stoff, J. Breiling, & J. D. Maser (Eds.), *Handbook of antisocial behavior*. (pp. 83–91). Hoboken, NJ: John Wiley & Sons. Retrieved from: http://ezproxy.shsu.edu/login?url=http://search.ebscohost.com/login.aspx?direct=true&db=psyh&AN=1997-36421-008&site=ehost-live&scope=site

Zanarini, Mary C., Gunderson, J. G., Marino, M. F., & Schwartz, E. O. (1988). DSM-III disorders in the families of borderline outpatients. *Journal of Personality Disorders, 2*(4), 292–302.

Zanarini, Mary C., Horwood, J., Wolke, D., Waylen, A., Fitzmaurice, G., & Grant, B. F. (2011). Prevalence of DSM-IV borderline personality disorder in two community samples: 6,300 English 11-year-olds and 34,653 American adults. *Journal of Personality Disorders, 25*(5), 607–619.

Zimmerman, M., Rothschild, L., & Chelminski, I.(2005). The prevalence of DSM-IV personality disorders in psychiatric outpatients. *The American Journal of Psychiatry, 162*, 1911–1918. doi:10.1176/appi.ajp.162.10.1911

Zlotnick, C., Rothschild, L., & Zimmerman, M. (2002). The role of gender in the clinical presentation of patients with borderline personality disorder. *Journal of Personality Disorders, 16*(3), 277–282.

Zuroff, D. C. (1994). Depressive personality styles and the five-factor model of personality. *Journal of Personality Assessment, 63*(3), 453.

Index